Writing Research Critically

This is not a standard guide to writing a dissertation, thesis, project report, journal article or book. Rather, this book will help researchers who are dissatisfied with the typical recipe approaches to standardised forms of writing-up and want to explore how academic writing can be used to greater effect.

Writing Research Critically shows that writing up is not just about 'presenting findings' as if the facts speak for themselves. As the authors show, there are certain vital skills that any writer needs to develop within their academic writing, such as the ability to:

- develop critical understanding and a personal academic voice
- question assumptions and the status quo
- frame the background and transgress the frame
- read between the lines when reviewing the literature
- strengthen interpretations and construct persuasive arguments
- challenge and develop theory and explanations
- develop ideas that create possibilities for realistic action.

Packed with examples from a range of writing projects (papers, dissertations, theses, reports, journal articles and books), this book provides a practical and refreshing way to approach and present research. Through case studies, the authors offer a step by step guide from the early stages of planning a writing project, whether an undergraduate paper or a professional publication, to the polishing processes that make the difference between a merely descriptive account to an argument that intends to be critical and persuasive.

Written in a clear accessible style, this book will inspire a wide range of researchers from undergraduates to postgraduates, early career researchers and experienced professionals working across a wide range of fields, and demonstrate how research can have more impact in the real world.

John Schostak is a Professor at the Education and Social Research Institute, Manchester Metropolitan University, UK.

Jill Schostak is an independent researcher, U.

D1422237

Writing Research Critically

Developing the power to make a difference

John Schostak and Jill Schostak

Routledge
Taylor & Francis Group

LONDON AND NEW YORK

First published 2013
by Routledge
2 Park Square, Milton Park, Abingdon, Oxon OX14 4RN

Simultaneously published in the USA and Canada
by Routledge
711 Third Avenue, New York, NY 10017

*Routledge is an imprint of the Taylor & Francis Group, an informa
business*

British Library Cataloguing in Publication Data
A catalogue record for this book is available from the British
Library

Library of Congress Cataloging in Publication Data
Schostak, Jill.
Writing research critically : developing the power to make a
difference / Jill Schostak and John Schostak.
p. cm.
1. Academic writing. 2. Research--Methodology. I. Schostak, John
F. II. Title.
LB2369.S37 2013
808.02--dc23
2012024148

ISBN: 978-0-415-59874-3 (hbk)
ISBN: 978-0-415-59875-0 (pbk)
ISBN: 978-0-203-07719-1 (ebk)

Typeset in Galliard
by Fakenham Prepress Solutions, Fakenham, Norfolk NR21 8NN

MIX
Paper from
responsible sources
FSC www.fsc.org   FSC® C004839

Printed and bound in Great Britain by
TJ International Ltd, Padstow, Cornwall

Contents

Introduction

So what today is frightening?

There is much. And in their writing people either address it directly, indirectly or ignore it as if it were not there. The absence of the political, the frightening, is compounded by the view that research writing is to be 'neutral', as a laying out of 'facts' and the 'objective' expression of findings undertaken according to well-defined procedures for the collection and processing of data. Yet no research is ever undertaken without a motive.

At the back of those motives is not just the curiosity of the scientist adopting a stance of 'neutrality' but a curiosity in-mixed with the whole range of emotions of everyday life that in every way subverts the neutrality, the objectivity. When scientists were pursuing the physics of the atom, lured by the excitement of discovery and the beauty of their mathematics, they did not have in mind its use at Nagasaki and Hiroshima. Not at first. But after World War II Einstein, having warned Roosevelt of the fear that the Germans were close to making an atomic bomb, reflected that:

> 'Had I known that the Germans would not succeed in producing an atomic bomb,' he told Newsweek, 'I never would have lifted a finger.' He pointed out, correctly, that he had never actually worked on the bomb project. And he claimed to a Japanese publication, 'My participation in the production of the atom bomb consisted in a single act: I signed a letter to President Roosevelt.'
>
> (Isaackson 2008)

When writing, what we sign up to matters. As a pacifist, what Einstein signed up to was something that he and many millions of others would live to regret. And as the man in charge of the first atomic test on July 16, 1945, Ken Bainbridge, put it: 'Now we're all sons of bitches.'

The world of today is no less – perhaps more – frightening than that of Einstein's time. Being engaged in research, however modest that involvement may be, we implicitly if not explicitly sign up to beliefs, values, attitudes and consequences that at first escape our awareness. Keeping science independent of politics has had important consequences for knowledge. The history of science has its examples of vested interests denying the findings of science and threatening scientists with imprisonment or death. Whether it is Galileo convicted of heresy for writing that the earth moved around the sun or Spinoza employing a pseudonym and writing anonymously about society to avoid personal attacks, inscribing the new has brought the wrath of traditionalists, even to the point of imprisonment and threats of death. Writing matters because it is foundational to the ways people see and manage the world.

The emergence of a scientific attitude challenged fundamental beliefs. Indeed, the scientific attitude became synonymous with being value free, or 'objective'. Here, objectivity would be defined in terms of the application of logical principles and procedures in the description, analysis, interpretation, validation and explanation of what can be observed. In this way a logical grid could be inscribed across the world, in order to describe and manage it systematically without recourse to subjectively held beliefs and values. It became the 'normal' science, as Kuhn (1970) called it, of modernity. The social sciences were drawn to the success of the physical sciences and developed their own approach to a values-free sociology, psychology, economics and politics. Such approaches were applied in business to produce the 'scientific' management of Taylor (1911) and its later incarnations as new managerialism or the modernisation of workforces and labour markets. In short, the scientific method was writing its 'little letters', as the psychoanalyst Lacan called the formulae of scientific theories and the use of statistical methods, into the organisation and management of the physical and social worlds of people's everyday lives.

Yet to understand the social and psychological worlds of people's lives, many argued that their subjective meanings could not be ignored. In short, the little letters of science and their methods of observation could not capture all that could be said and known about human life. It involves another kind of writing, a writing that begins its maps from the subjective accounts of people and draws upon the ways in which language in its fullest sense operates. It explores how values and beliefs operate upon the world and how in turn the little letters of science and the letters signed in fear, anxiety or love impact upon people's lives. What is most frightening is when we underestimate the power of the letter.

What is this book about?

This book is about the conflicts between the alternative forms of writing and their impacts upon people. If the normal sciences demand a writing that is devoid of feeling, values and subjective intent in the pursuit and application of 'objective' knowledge to people's lives, then to analyse, interpret, understand and theorise the impacts of this 'objective writing' requires a different approach to reading and to writing.

The overall aim is to counter the processes of simplification fundamental to the forms of normal science that Kuhn (1970) called a puzzle-solving activity. It involves what Derrida and others have called a double writing. Where the formulaic writings of logic seek unambiguous definition, a double-writing exploits the multiple meanings of ordinary languages as they are used by people in their daily lives. It is in the multiple meanings that more is said than can be defined and represented by logical, mathematical or statistical formulae. This book then is about the ways in which this fuller writing can be developed that more adequately represents the experiences, the needs, interests and demands of people in their everyday lives.

So how do we get started?

The strategy involves an un-writing of the normal pattern of writing up research. In brief, and crudely, the 'normal' pattern is when:

The introduction describes what the writing will be about, providing its focus and rationale. A background to the subject area will typically be provided that locates the writing in a history of progress leading to the chosen focus. This will give insights into the reasons for the writing and the 'gaps' in the overall picture of 'knowledge' that are to be filled in. How this is done is like a puzzle to be solved. To show in detail how this puzzle will be solved, its aims and objectives will be as precisely defined as possible. The organisation of the text – the sections, the chapters – will be provided and in so doing a summary of the argument presented.

The review of the literature typically has the following purposes: to identify the previous attempts at solving the puzzle, to identify the gaps in the literature – that is the issues, themes, problems that have been overlooked, not recognised before or simply dismissed as irrelevant. It will seek to identify the strengths and weaknesses of previous attempts or approaches. The features of arguments will be discussed and criticised if necessary. The methodologies employed will be described, discussed and critiqued if weaknesses, contradictions or lapses in reasoning are identified.

The methodology chosen to solve the puzzle or fill in the gaps will be formally described. If the methodology is well known and largely considered unproblematic it may simply be named. If the methodology is novel then it would be justified. Its job is to provide a warrant for the knowledge that is to be claimed. It will describe how objectivity, validity, reliability and generalisations are to be assured. The more the formal languages of logic, maths and statistics are employed, the stronger the arguments for the development of theories. However, all depends upon the very stringent assumptions and procedures of the formal languages being observed. As pointed out by

Cohen as long ago as 1944, the advances in science have been founded on the ability to purify substances so much that they can be manipulated with high degrees of precision under experimental conditions. However, this has not been the case in the social and psychological sciences. Human beings, no matter how similar they seem, in no way approach the artificially produced levels of purity of metals, acids and so on. Hence, statistical procedures in the social sciences have very limited success by comparison.

The methods are justified by and follow from the methodology. These will involve the methods of categorising data (whether refined liquids or unrefinable human beings!), collecting data, analysing the data and formulating interpretations, explanations and theories.

The ethics of the research will also be discussed in relation to the methods employed, particularly if these involve human subjects, the use of animals and impact on environments. The principles and procedures involved in gaining consent and minimising risks through ensuring confidentiality and anonymity will be detailed.

The findings will be described, analysed and summarised. These in turn will be **discussed and evaluated** in order to provide **conclusions** as to the extent to which aims and objectives have been met and new knowledge presented. In the conclusions there may be recommendations for 'next steps' or for policy.

Un-writing involves re-exploring each of these steps, de-constructing the assumptions upon which their logics are constructed. It is the companion to those forms of radical research (Schostak and Schostak 2008) that seek to make a difference by a radical democratisation of people's voices in the construction of research. How those alternative voices are revealed, included or excluded requires a counter argument. The sources used for the development and discussion of this counter argument include those that are most easily available through the news media and the internet generally as well as data and text drawn from a large-scale study.

What's the counter argument?

Each chapter takes a theme or themes that can be read against the normal paradigm for writing research. The implicit or explicit agenda of any form of writing is to embed particular ways of seeing and accounting for what is seen. Chapter 1, then, begins the process by exploring patterns of attention and inattention. These patterns are critical in determining objects as 'objects of consciousness'. Just as the objects of consciousness can be represented and manipulated so consciousness itself can be shaped in terms of what is seen or not seen. These ways of seeing and not seeing are embedded culturally at global and local levels of experience. The sources for discussion for this are in the texts routinely produced by news media and in the ways they can be read in relation to the key philosophical, political and social science texts underlying competing notions of 'science' and 'method'. A radical writing then opens up the frameworks of analysis employed by texts and discourses in order to identify a different range of agendas that are inclusive of people's experiences and voices in order to prepare for a different way of knowing.

Chapter 2 circles back over the issues raised in Chapter 1 to explore what is at stake for individuals, groups and communities in framing agendas that exclude or privilege certain voices over others. The stakes, it is argued, are always political and are framed by a struggle between what is private and what is public. In particular the stakes may be organised in terms of friends and enemies, hosts and strangers. The findings of science, it is argued, can be worked into strategies for the management of ways of seeing and then into the 'manufacture of consent' (Lippmann 1927). The machineries – or dispositifs, in the terminology to be developed here, drawing on Agamben (2009) – involved materially and symbolically frame ways of seeing, behaving and 'consenting' to action. These dispositifs inscribe people as a 'public' to be manipulated. What is at stake, therefore, is the very freedom of individuals to act in their own interests rather than those manufactured or imposed by others. The question then is how to disturb these frames and then generate an alternative notion of the public. The issues are explored by the very visible emergence of a 'public' during the beginnings of the Arab Spring of 2011.

Chapter 3 begins the work of identifying critical points of view. It does so by exploring the literature as a multiplicity of voices. The task is then to challenge the orthodoxies through which debate is managed or, indeed, eradicated under the dominance of those orthodoxies. The examples of Descartes' method in contrast to that of Spinoza are discussed for their implications in permitting or preventing voices to enter into debate. The difference in method can be employed to underpin differences in the conception of a 'public'. With the Cartesian split between the mind and body a particular 'story' can be told in terms of the management of the body by the mind. However, in its Spinozan formulation there is a democracy of powers as between mind and body. The one has no privileged position over the other. Similarly, in the body politic, science can be employed by governments (as 'mind') to master the political 'body', that is, the mass, the 'public'. The distinctions provide different ways of 'reading' a text in order to critique it. One text relates to another in a multiplicity of ways – it is intertextual. In order to read a given text, it is important to discover the other texts that provide, as it were, its source code. As argued in the chapter, drawing on Riffaterre and Althusser, a text may be read for its contradictions, its gaps, in order to discover its 'hypogram' or hidden text. By discovering the range of voices implicit in the production of a text a critical public begins to emerge. A critical public announces, or calls forth, a plurality of voices and of powers that can be read between the lines. This has implications for analysis and the mapping of different 'realities' that is the topic of exploration of Chapter 4.

An individual perceives and experiences the world mentally and physically through the sense organs as 'data', which is subjected to a sense-making activity – an embodied analysis – that, paradoxically, both cuts up the world and yet seamlessly constructs the real in terms of relationships to oneself and to others. Chapter 4 then explores these intersubjective relationships as they are expressed in texts and in discourses. Each has its own analytics of categorising and naming that is formed through an operationalising framework determined by the criteria to be found in a given agenda. These all function together to manage the plurality of relationships through an overarching logic which we call the dispositif of everyday power. The critical public is thus a 'textual public' inscribed by language and textualised by the texts and discourses of others grounded in a proclivity toward story-ing, underpinned by embodied experiences of engaging one's powers with others in a public work toward some end: a collective work of constant writing into being, not a simple given of observational analysis.

Representation, it is argued, has the effect of creating the 'visible'. What strategies of critique should come into play before the 'reality' that is constituted by a given representation, say 'x', is brought into public decision-making processes? Chapter 5 argues that in a Cartesian framework, since each sign, symbol or signifier replaces the real-in-itself with the real-of-representation, the thing-in-itself is 'murdered'. What is too often privileged is the representational map and not the reality of which it tries to be a map. Similarly, for the notion of the 'public', as a representation of views, the underlying powers of realising views as demands to be taken into account in debate and decision making are regarded as inexistent, as a 'phantom'. The Spinozan mode of being offers another way of creating the public as a space of forces such that people take their place in the public space of decision-making, In developing the argument for an effective public the chapter explores how a public is either constructed as an inscribed surface to be manipulated by elites, or the power to voice returns in the form of an effective public. It does this by exploring the embodied powers of people to form associations as a real basis for voicing concerns, debating and making decisions. It is in the contests between voices that a 'truth' may be realised or 'revealed'.

Chapter 6 argues that given multiple viewpoints, there is no single meaning or 'truth' that attaches to a given representation. This is explored through the concept of the child. In particular it focuses on the use made of the 'child' in a speech by Obama given in the context of fundraising at the start of his presidential campaign for re-election. What is politically exploited is the 'shiftiness' inherent in the process of interpretation such that any representation becomes 'unstuck'. The shiftiness of interpretations is essential to the real-politic of state power. The trouble with interpretation is that – like opinions – everyone has one. For this reason the range of interpretations is to be explored in term of the voices included and excluded by a given text. If there is a 'truth' to emerge, it is in this range as the foundation for debate rather than in the real politic that suppresses, represses, erases voices.

Chapter 7 explores the development of a writing project in relation to the multiplicities of possible interpretations. It is argued that such a project counters those forms of explanation that seek to hold dominion over the construction and use of 'evidence'. Rather it explores the struggles of protagonists who represent sides and in representing sides in a war of words lose their reality in becoming 'semblants'. The struggle for the writing project is to create the conditions under which differences can be brought into play that can undermine any one explanation in a curricular process of public reflection on experience in the course of contesting theories and explanations, that is to say, putting them at risk.

Chapter 8 explores the strategies involved in persuasion where one explanation or theory is supported when others are denigrated. It argues that rhetoric is more than just ornament since it provides an underlying structuring of the thought processes where data is transformed into evidence and particulars are drawn under more general categories. Through such a process, the strategies of rhetoric paint pictures in the head, as Lippmann called them. The chapter explores how these pictures are inscribed in people and their environments so that they inhabit, as it were, virtual terrains. The question then is how the pictures may be de-constructed as a first step to making a real difference to people's lives.

Chapter 9 explores how radical writing exploits the margins between categories, the shiftiness of interpretations, the gaps, the ambiguities to deconstruct and build counter arguments where each new voice drawn into a debate creates a new way of seeing and thus a new terrain enabling new forms of action. In this way the possibilities for critique are developed. It is in critique that Lefort's notion of the empty space of power that is left when the tyrant falls can be created as essential to the emergence of an effective public. It is argued that the forms of the master, whether as tyrants or as corporate power, is sustained by their mastery of symbolic fields and the consent of the masses. It involves what may be called a psychoanalytics which takes into account how a multitude is formed and how as speaking subjects people live in the world and are of the world. To maintain that world involves the creation of boundaries that set limits and guard against the 'excess' that comes from thinking critically.

The question of the new, of making a difference, is made in Chapter 10. How does a thinking subject make a difference? How is a community thought? How can a community be re-written? Each of these questions involves a re-mapping of the pictures in the mind, a re-framing of the spaces through which territories are imagined as stages for action. It is argued that space has been divided between a private and public and that the space for public debate and action has been crowded out by the private domains of elites who command the dispositifs through which ways of seeing, believing and acting are formed and fashioned whether through the manufacture of consent or through the subtle and the explicit use of force.

Chapter 11 argues that if all social realities are a stitch-up (in the sense of being inscribed as pictures in the mind by the dispositifs or machineries of Power), how are they dis-assembled? How are they to be dis-organised as a precursor to change? Rather than the routine processes of recipe-based action or the 'normal writing' of 'normal science', thinking disturbs the taken-for-granted and thus generates the conditions for the emergence of a public sphere for the expression of demands, interests, creative ways of seeing, acting and being in the world. It is essential for new beginnings. It may arise in the privacy of a consciousness and yet as earlier argued such consciousness is always already directed towards others and thus has its grounds in relations to others and otherness. Thus there is a need for writing otherwise and for the dignity of thinking with its openness to the other and otherness.

Chapter 12 takes the arguments to the limits, beyond the limits as a precondition for realising the conditions to make a real difference in the lives of people. To do so involves, it is argued, a game of limits where there is a sneakiness at the edges that enables new legitimacies to emerge. This allows mapping and territory to be co-created by people acting as effective agents who can re-imagine and re-occupy the place of power not to dominate but to engage freely and equally in debate as a basis for decision making and action.

In the end, there are no recipes to create public lives in mutual respect – only gestures towards writing.

Chapter 1

Agenda Setting – and the violence of writing

There is a now-famous experiment in perception. It involves a small group of people who pass a ball to each other. Some are dressed in black t-shirts and others in white. The audience is asked to count the number of times the ball is passed to those in white. Those who do the task assiduously get the right answer. However, they are then also asked if they noticed the gorilla that entered on to the scene of play. About half, it is said, do not notice. If they did notice, then they did not perceive the curtains changed colour, nor that a player dressed in black left the scene (Chabris and Simons 1999; www.theinvisiblegorilla.com/gorilla_experiment.html). The play of attention creates a perceptual surface upon which certain things appear as foreground to be noticed and others as background. As in the 'gestalt' experiments of Kohler, incomplete circles are still seen as complete circles – the 'mind's eye' as it were closes the gap to create the circle. This perceptual surface mentally constructed is without cracks and gaps. It is seamless. Yet there is much that is not noticed. When it comes to writing up research, just looking and recording is not enough. There are, in effect, multiple surfaces. This is often interpreted as there being surface readings and 'depth' readings, where the 'truth' or 'what is really going on' happens below the surface. We do not accept this reading but rather want to suggest that it matters how we put multiple readings together, not to see a 'depth' but to see multiply, alternatively, even subversively. In the gorilla experiment, there was a hidden agenda. In one sense, it could be argued that this was the 'truth' of the experiment. In another, that 'truth' has to be set alongside many others: the 'truth' of the ethics of doing such an experiment; the 'truth' of the discourse of science enabling the exploitation of people, positioning them into the 'dupes' versus the 'smart'; the 'truths' of the interpretations made by each person who sees, experiences and evaluates his or her identity and the identities of 'others' in relation to the experiment. The idea of the agenda being explored here is then that it emerges multiply through multiple readings. What is important is how the multiplicities of readings are put together and the effects that they individually and collectively produce on people.

This chapter takes what might be thought of as a 'big picture' approach to the agenda. This 'big picture' is the surface to be written upon. Any agenda, no matter how local or specific, will be conditioned and influenced by what the 'big picture' determines as 'real'-without-question. If any differences to the lives of people and the organisations that affect their lives are to be made, the 'big picture' must be opened up to reveal what is repressed, what is kept silent, what is accused of being nonsense.

Writing the Surface

A surface is in one sense invisible. Perceptually, it is what enables everything to be seen as a whole, as reality. There are no gaps in this perceptual real. However, each body that is seen is also a surface that raises the possibility of something beneath that surface. Beneath that surface there are only ever other surfaces, each posing a further 'depth', or 'behind', or 'underneath'. Whether it is the agenda of science to exhaust the possibility of there being yet-undiscovered surfaces through which the fabric of reality is woven as one text or it is the agenda to discover a reality beneath an illusory surface already begins to establish competing agendas, and through that competition arouses a politics of knowledge, of reality. Perhaps there is more to a surface than meets the eye.

The dominant descriptive and practical model for the modern sciences, since Descartes, has been the geometry of the visual where statements are defined unambiguously in ways that can be measured, sequenced logically and operationalised in order to be tested empirically. The key language constructed for this has been mathematics. In *The Crisis of the European Sciences* Husserl (1970) described what he called the mathematisation of the world. Its power in mastering the physical world has been impressive. It has done so by what we would call a closing strategy, that is, by seeking the ideal of detailed descriptions of observable phenomena that can be checked and re-checked by others without ambiguity, thus contributing to a sense of objectivity, a sense of closure. Each observable object once unambiguously defined can be classified into increasingly comprehensive taxonomies that in turn 'represent' the observable 'reality'. Indeed, rather than just representing a reality, it may be so accepted that it comes to be indistinguishable from it and so be that reality in such a way that analytics and the real seep into each other. So much so, that the mathematics employed to describe relationships between the taxonomically described objects may be spoken of as the 'deep' reality, the ultimate reality of everything. Once there is a clear taxonomic vocabulary then detailed observations can be made about relationships between one thing and another. There is an analytic framing enabling questions to be posed: if x varies will y vary because of it? Or, x has happened, what are the specific conditions that produced that event? By setting up experimental situations where everything is constant except for the specified objects (or variables) to be varied, any changes or outcomes due to the manipulations of particular objects can be identified. Hence, important statements like 'a change in x causes y'. The problem then is to transfer the practices that lead to particular desired results in the laboratory to the real world where there are so many more variables that can intervene and thus upset the results. If the essential (or necessary) structures underlying relationships between the taxonomically defined objects of the world can be described, then increasingly powerful explanations can be developed. Indeed, it may well be possible, as in theoretical physics, to predict the existence of objects simply because they are necessary to the coherence of a theory that has the potential to unify a whole field of study. Confirmation may take many years. But when it does happen, the power and prestige of science is enhanced further.

On the agenda, then, modelled after the physical sciences was the potential to engineer society in the way that the landscape, the transport systems, the factories could be engineered. On the one hand, the search was for social facts as solid as the facts of physics, chemistry, biology, medicine and engineering; on the other was the desire to develop theory as robust as the sciences of the physical world. However, to explain the social world and the mental life of people, the observation of 'facts' of behaviours in the way that Comte or Durkheim advocated, was not sufficient for those like Weber or Dilthy who saw alongside the observable, the meaningful, the subjective, and indeed with Freud the 'hidden' drives, the emotional and the irrational.

In the march towards industrialisation, towards giving the vote to ever more of the wider public there was the implicit if not fully explicit question of whose agendas are to be included and how they are to be engaged with in political, economic and social life. If science was uncovering the 'truth', the 'reality' of the world, then it could for example be argued that scientific reason would provide the best guide to creating a human world that fitted the reality discovered by reason. For Kant (1784) in his article 'What is Enlightenment?' it was to be the free use of reason publicly in all matters that would underpin freedom. He wrote his essay to explain what is required to achieve this ambition:

> Enlightenment is man's emergence from his self-imposed immaturity. Immaturity is the inability to use one's understanding without guidance from another. This immaturity is self-imposed when its cause lies not in lack of understanding, but in lack of resolve and courage to use it without guidance from another.
>
> (Kant 1784)

This is not about imposing one's will upon the world about and upon others. Rather if the use of reason is to be in public, then it is about the courage to create the organisations necessary for the public to use reason freely in all matters. Kant gave his answer at a time when the power of reason was being discovered and developed across a range of academic and practical disciplines. As such it provides a textual surface that can be read alongside other textual surfaces both to explore the use of Kant's writings as well to employ them in contemporary contexts to reflect again and again on the question: what sort of public would have to be created for the free use of reason by all?

It seems to us that in order to use reason at all, it has to go through a public, that is, a space where people can freely voice their arguments in ways that are open to rational scrutiny. The public then is a particular kind of 'surface' created through multiple voices engaged in the free use of reason to express their agendas. It is a surface upon which people can write their agendas as a method of gaining public assent. Without such assent freely gained in public, the accomplishment of an agenda would be at the expense of the freedom of others and thus would be invalid. Generalisation of a validly agreed agenda could then only be achieved through its public examination. Underlying the development of this sense of the public is a principle articulated through a term coined by Balibar (1994): *égaliberté*. In English this might be translated as equaliberty, meaning that freedom and equality are co-extensive. Similarly, in many ways freedom and money today are co-extensive – a point made by Simmel (2004). Hence those who have more money have more freedom at the expense of those who have less, or indeed no, money. Thus, if one person has the greater resource or strength to express his or her freedom regardless of the objections of another, then the freedom of that other is taken away. As a principle for building democratic public spaces that then impact on society, it is powerful. As a practice, of course, it has to contend with contemporary social, economic and political inequalities. In particular, it has to contend with how neo-liberal economic practices 'sell' democracy to the people it needs as consumers and citizens. The key contested surface then becomes the people, in particular, their bodies and their ways of thinking and speaking through which collective forms of social interaction and organisation are created and maintained.

Inscribing the people

The effects of power are in a very real sense written upon people. Essential to the adoption of one political form over another is the organisation and exercise of power. This power may be organised either consensually, where each person contributes his or her powers of thought and action to a common undertaking, or it can be organised through the threat of violence. For Hobbes (1651) the warring natures of people have to be subdued by a Leviathan whose violence or threat of violence is seen to be overwhelming. Underlying the stability of nation states is the threat of violence to subdue threats both to their populations and externally to neighbouring states. This is as true to modern 'democracies' as to monarchies and tyrannies. Through violence and the threat of violence, however nuanced or crudely expressed within a given political form, fear can be inscribed upon the bodies and minds of people whether as scars or as mental traumas that repeat their nightmarish effects time after time. Fear is written in and readable from the submissive postures and the servility of behaviour and the deference of the voice of those defeated by the violence of the strong. But what of those who

have grown used to the conditions under which power is enforced by violence
or the threat of violence?

> It is true that in the beginning men submit under constraint and by force;
> but those who come after them obey without regret and perform willingly
> what their predecessors had done because they had to. This is why men
> born under the yoke and then nourished and reared in slavery are content,
> without further effort, to live in their native circumstance, unaware of any
> other state or right, and considering as quite natural the condition into
> which they are born. There is, however, no heir so spendthrift or indifferent
> that he does not sometimes scan the account books of his father in order
> to see if he is enjoying all the privileges of his legacy or whether, perchance,
> his rights and those of his predecessor have not been encroached upon.
> Nevertheless it is clear enough that the powerful influence of custom is in
> no respect more compelling than in this, namely, habituation to subjection.
> (Boétie c.1552: 55)

Boétie wrote a call to freedom that analysed, according to the knowledge of his
time, the reasons for the subjugation of the many by the few. His basic solution
was for people simply to stop obeying. Since the people were millions and the
powerful elites surrounding the tyrant were hundreds best, there would be
nothing they could do – their power would simply fall away. The idea of civil
disobedience as a practice of protest is still powerful today, as is the practice of
what Boétie called voluntary servitude composed of habits of mind, discourse
and behaviour. The idea of democracy can be read alongside these discourses
of voluntary servitude and of civil disobedience as its antidote. If democracy
is a discourse and practice of political freedoms, it necessarily subverts all
organisations dependent on the subjection and servitude of people. However,
contemporary discourses of freedom and democracy have no existence outside
of the historical conditions through which their current meanings are lived and
contested.

Nietzsche argued that underlying the contemporary meanings of such
universals as freedom was the violence of the elites over the masses. It is through
the exercise of violence that one meaning dominates over, represses or erases
another. To understand the present configurations of meanings involves an
historical excavation, an uncovering of the organised powers of elites who seek
dominance. Perhaps even, in Nietzschian terms, it is a tracing to the source,
the original pure meaning of terms like democracy that have been historically
perverted, corrupted. In this sense the terms freedom and democracy can be
historically re-viewed, their validation deriving from a stripping away of the ways
in which they have been bent to the purposes of the powerful over time. The
generalisation of their meanings over a given population is then accomplished
through the application of force and their truth recognised and avowed by those
who are subjugated.

A Marxist reading of such sources of power over people draws attention to the prevailing material relations of production and also to the kinds of psychological accommodations people make when they exercise or are subjected to the demands of the powerful. The contemporary form of capitalism is neo-liberalism, which in brief:

> describes the idea that people are encouraged to see themselves as if they are autonomous, rational, risk-managing subjects, responsible for their own destinies and called 'to render one's life knowable and meaningful through a narrative of free choice and autonomy – however constrained one might actually be' (Gill, 2006, p.260; see also Kelly, 2006). From this position, the social context in which a person lives is reduced to their immediate interpersonal relations, and any personal, social or health problems, and their attendant solutions, are located within the individual. Neo-liberalism allows people to make sense of themselves in individualistic and psychological terms, understanding their consumption practices as freely chosen markers of their identity (Cronin, 2003). Neo-liberal rhetoric of individual choice and responsibility now dominates much of post-industrial sense making about what it means to be a good person. Such changes have been identified as powerful new forms of governance (Rose, 1989). For example, being asked to work excessive and low paid hours may not be considered exploitation but accounted for in terms of a worker's psychological characteristic of being a helpful person (Walkerdine, 2002). Thus, young people are developing their sense of self in a context in which wider discourses in society encourage them to understand themselves through psychological and individual discourses, rather than those that are communal or sociological.
>
> (Riley 2008)

In this account there is a complex discursive weaving of ideas and practices, psychological and social mechanisms, with forms of social, political and legal organisation to govern and construct the world about us. The relations of production and the forms of consumption are critical to how people are being subjected, indeed, subjugated to the dominant organisation of power. Riley's focus is the impact of neo-liberalism on young people's identities, subjectivities, activities and youth cultures. These impacts can be seen in the forms of dress, the use of technologies in dance cultures. Additionally, the

> relationship between the body and identity may be particularly important for young people, given that in comparison to adults, young people tend to have less control over other aspects of their lives. Young people may employ a range of body modification techniques, from dieting and weight training to cosmetic surgery or body art.
>
> (Riley 2008)

As a physical surface, the skin is a space of mediation between a 'self' and the world (again, whether real or imagined). It is the

> site of encounter between enfleshed self and society. The skin is where the self involutes into the world and the world into the self. Skin is a marked surface inscribed with texts of race, gender, sexuality, class and age before it is marked by ink. These corporeal expressions exist beyond the choice of the individual to define them. They are inscriptions created by historical and social consensus, while tattoos are usually formed through individual or small peer group consensus. Race and gender place the body within a hierarchical system before the subject can reflect on her or his capacity to represent the relationship of race and gender to self.
>
> (MacCormack 2006: 59)

In psychoanalytic terms, the impacts of social, economic and political forms of organisation appear like a symptom on the body, whether the physical body, or the social, political, economic, cultural bodies of collective life. At the extreme, Slevin (2008) traces the origins of contemporary cosmetic surgery to the First World War. He describes the Cartesian split between mind and body that enabled surgeons to develop reconstructive strategies for the appalling scale of bodily and mental injuries that occurred. The disfigurements were the signs of the collision between armaments and bodies, the marks of the impact of munitions as 'other' on the body, marks that could be read as the atrocity of war, placing it outside of social and productive normality. Surgery was then a process of rewriting and 'unwriting' the marks of the 'other' 'in the medical attempt to re-engineer the socially productive body' (Slevin 2008: 58). The skin, real or metaphoric, is the surface of inscription.

To take it further, Dejours (1998) in his study of the impacts on the minds and bodies of workers of contemporary managerial practices under neoliberal conditions draws upon Arendt's 'banality of evil' in his psychological analysis of how people come to tolerate the intolerable. In his study of work in France he writes that the Mitterrand period (1981–95) was characterised by:

> the implementation of new methods of management and of directing enter-prises which were expressed as the progressive questioning of the right to work and social benefits (Supiot, 1993). These new methods are accom-panied not only by lay-offs, but a brutality in working relations generating a lot of suffering. Certainly, it is denounced. But the denunciation remains completely without political consequences because without any concomitant collective mobilisation. On the contrary, this denunciation seems compatible with a growing tolerance of injustice.
>
> (Dejours 1998: 24; translation by JFS)

In another book (2003), Dejours writes more explicitly of the impacts of the intensification of working practices and in particular the assessment of performance against measurable criteria that is characteristic of contemporary management practices. Work, in his view, has been split between the official job descriptions and demands that can be measured and the realities of work that cannot. It is this split that is the cause of considerable suffering. The aspects of work that are described in measurable terms do not fit with what is actually required to do the job. People's working lives are inscribed and circumscribed by the demands of management. More generally, the very material practices through which the economic and political machineries are organised are the tools inscribing the minds and bodies of people. It evokes what Judge Schreber called the 'writing down system'. Schreber's father was a famous educationalist in nineteenth-century Germany whose writings influenced many within and outside of his country. He decided to bring up his children using his methods of strict rational control. One of the techniques was to write down on a board the times when a child did something that was not approved (as a more modern example see Rogers 1990). This was in the context of extreme techniques of control that dictated how the children sat, when they could go to the toilet, when they could eat, what they looked at. Not surprisingly, one of the sons – Judge Schreber – had bouts of mental illness and another committed suicide. Although little is known of the daughters, they were considered somewhat strange (see Schatzman 1973). Schreber wrote his memoires of his mental illness detailing the effects real or imagined on his body and his mind. These were subsequently analysed by Freud as a basis for his emergent theories of paranoia. At the extreme, when there is a maladjusted relation between a system of thinking and the physical realities of people, it reveals its effects in the flesh, mind and behaviour.

The instruments of writing down are everywhere in the economic, political, educational and cultural machineries through which power is exercised. It matters, therefore, how those machineries are organised. In Maladjusted Schooling, Schostak (1983) argued that schools were maladjusted to the needs and interests of young people and teachers. Their very organisation split people from addressing the issues that affected their lives and diverted their attention to the requirements for social order in the interests of economic, political and social elites. More generally, across the major forms of social organisation through which everyday life is managed, whether it is the split operated by religions as between spirit and body or by rationalists between mind and body, it is the mind that is called upon to control the body under some regime of power, whether this is considered to be of divine or human 'origins'. Such a split inscribed on the body is in a material, organic sense fatal, that is, it organises the fate of people as a lifetime of managing the split. Organisations are maladjusted to the extent that they are designed to reinforce and manage such splits rather than transform conditions for mutual benefit. The effects of the splits are both 'seen' and managed through language. They are seen in the ways in which they emerge as puns, slips of the tongue, and in the tattered remains of dreams in the waking consciousness. They are seen in 'involuntary ticks' or the obsessional cuttings, markings or modifications of the body that signify something is repressed or is not able to be said otherwise. These may be called 'abnormal' and treated as 'maladjusted' to social norms by the members of the very organisations that through the practices prescribed by managers and other specialists needed by the organisations routinely create them. The social construction of the 'normal' is very often hard to see.

What we are calling inscriptions on the body whether this is the individual body or the social body of a mass of people, the French sociologist Mauss (1973) writing in 1934 called body techniques. He had noticed differences in swimming techniques between one generation and another, differences in marching techniques between the British and the French and eventually:

> A kind of revelation came to me in hospital. I was ill in New York. I wondered where previously I had seen girls walking as my nurses walked. I had the time to think about it. At last I realised that it was at the cinema. Returning to France, I noticed how common this gait was, especially in Paris; the girls were French and they too were walking in this way. In fact, American walking fashions had begun to arrive over here, thanks to the cinema. This was an idea I could generalise. The positions of the arms and hands while walking form a social idiosyncrasy, they are not simply a product of some purely individual, almost completely psychical arrangements and mechanisms. For example: I think I can also recognise a girl who has been raised in a convent. In general she will walk with her fists closed. And I can still remember my third-form teacher shouting at me: 'Idiot! why do you walk around the whole time with your hands flapping wide open?' Thus there exists an education in walking, too.
>
> (Mauss 1973: 72)

However, this is more than just fashion or just a form of education. It is through the multiplicities of discourses, discourses for every aspect of life, for every place, time and context, that people may be choreographed by the way in which power is socially and culturally organised, even in the most minute details. The body techniques become ingrained, in Mauss's view 'educating' gender, national and racial differences (see Mauss 1973: 86). Thus, Mauss focused on the impact of social organisation on the body; indeed, the domination of conscious 'pre-prepared movements' over 'emotion and unconsciousness' creating such embedded habits that, in one of Mauss's examples, when French spades were given to British soldiers they could not use them; and in another example, when French buglers led the march, the British soldiers could not march in rhythm to the music. To explain this, Mauss pointed to the role of education, both in its formal sense (as schooling) and in its more pervasive sense of social learning through imitation, through being inducted into the rituals, ways of acting and any 'constant adaptation to a physical, mechanical or chemical aim (e.g., when we drink) is pursued in a series of assembled actions, and assembled for the individual not by himself alone but by all his education, by the whole society to which he belongs, in the place he occupies in it' (Mauss 1973: 76). Such themes described by Mauss were picked up and developed most notably by Bourdieu (1977) in his concept of habitus.

Rather than habitus, education organised as a system of schools and as a complex of discourses and practices can be better conceived as a dispositif (Agamben 2007, 2009). Agamben developed this Foucauldian term to include the totality of language resources, discourses, institutions, organisational procedures and mechanisms – in short, everything created through human action and interaction that in a multiplicity of ways determines, indeed overdetermines, ways of thinking and behaving. It is in a direct sense 'banal', a term employed by Arendt (1963) in her account of Eichmann. How, she asked, could such a man who did not look or act like a monster have committed such crimes against humanity in the concentration camp? In order for the camp to function it would take the combined small, bureaucratic, disciplined actions of many. At the back of such acts is the sense of duty, the sense of national and organisational pride, the sense of attention to detail and a job well done – all characteristics considered quite 'normal' and valued by managers and professionals in every organisation. Indeed, it is the role of nationalism in relation to 'people' or 'multitude' or whatever other word may be used to signify the totality of living human beings without implying any further split into identities that draw distinctions between members of one grouping or social, political, cultural category and another. For example, Billig (1995) introduces his concept of banal nationalism intentionally associating it with Arendt's concept of the banality of evil in the context of Western states that are always able to mobilise forces 'without lengthy campaigns of political preparation' (p.7) because populations have been prepared through the '(s)mall words' that 'offer constant, but barely conscious, reminders of the homeland, making "our" national identity unforgettable' (p. 93). With every 'small word' the idea of 'the people' – potentially meaning all the people in the world – is conflated with the idea of nation in terms of an 'us' as distinct from 'them'. The sense of 'us' is moulded through the discourses of belonging, of national character and daily reinforced through national sports teams, national anthems, national news items and, of course, the sight of the national flag. There are 'uncounted millions of flags that mark the homeland of the United States' which 'do not demand immediate, obedient attention. On their flagpoles by the street and stitched on to the uniforms of public officials, they are unwaved, unsaluted and unnoticed' (Billig 1995: 40). They are, in short, banal. This connection with Arendt's 'banality of evil' creates the effect of an 'intertextual generalisation'. That is, one text in evoking another text makes a relationship that goes beyond a single case or use and thus gathers under one category a wider range of particulars or instances that may not have previously been associated with each other.

Whether consciously or not, the mind and body are subject to a complex range of influences whether directly or indirectly. The effects are inscribed on the body and mind and expressed consciously or through slips of the tongue or neurotic ticks and obsessional behaviours or through dreams and visions. If such power to influence and bring about effects could be more consciously harnessed, then might it be possible to engineer society more precisely?

Engineering the People

As an early pioneer in the emergent public relations industry, Edward Bernays, the nephew of Freud, saw in his uncle's theories a means by which to shape the public according to the agendas of politicians and business leaders. In his view:

> Ours must be a leadership democracy administered by the intelligent minority who know how to regiment and guide the masses.
>
> (Bernays 1928: 127)

This intelligent minority formed what Bernays called the 'invisible government'.

> The conscious and intelligent manipulation of the organised habits and opinions of the masses is an important element in democratic society. Those who manipulate this unseen mechanism of society constitute an invisible government which is the true ruling power of our country.
>
> (Bernays 1928: 27)

Bernays has come to be known as the 'father of spin' (Tye 1998) whose contemporary impact was explored in a series of documentaries by the BBC (BBC 2002). His strategy of engineering the consent of the masses (Bernays 1947) was exemplified in campaigns that ranged from 'selling' Roosevelt's New Deal following the Great Depression to persuading women to smoke cigarettes in public. For the cigarette campaign he sought the advice of Brill, a psychoanalyst:

> Back in the 1920s, Bernays reasoned that if cigarettes were a symbol of male phallic empowerment/sexual power, then they could also be a way for women to challenge that power. A smoking woman was laying down the gauntlet to conservative, sexist social mores and in effect, taking the penis into her own hands. Or as Brill had said 'They would have their own penises.'
>
> It was a shift in selling by way of the intellect, to persuasion via unconscious desire. This was about what you buy making you 'feel good', rather than about what you may need and it's an idea that still drives the wheels of consumerism today, perhaps even more persuasively than ever.
>
> (Jane Bovary, Cigarettes and the Seduction of Women:
> http://hubpages.com/hub/Cigarettes-and-Suffragettes)

President Hoover quickly recognised the power of the new industry in 1928 when he praised an audience composed of members of the emerging public relations elite:

You have taken over the job of creating desire and have transformed people
into constantly moving happiness machines, machines which have become
the key to economic progress.

(reported in *The Century of the Self*, BBC 2002)

Paul Mazur of Lehman Brothers, who had worked with Bernays, said

We must shift America from a needs to a desires culture. People must be
trained to desire, to want things, even before the old have been entirely
consumed.

(Gore 2007: 94)

This process of engineering or manufacturing consent (Lippmann 1922) was
more generally explored by Herman and Chomsky (c.1988) in their analysis of
the impact of the media on public life.

The public, then, was to be re-written to meet the agendas of the political
and business elites. Available to the emergent public relations industries to do
this were the new mass media technologies that could reach mass audiences. In
short, if economics and politics were to be aligned, then the public were to be
'trained' by the public relations industry. What the public relations professionals
could and still can draw upon to accomplish this was a particular machinery or,
more accurately, architectures of machineries, by means of which

the harmless citizen of postindustrial democracies readily does everything
that he is asked to, inasmuch as he leaves his everyday gestures and his
health, his amusements and his occupations, his diet and his desires, to be
commanded and controlled in the smallest detail by apparatuses.

(Agamben 2009: 22–3)

By apparatuses, recall that Agamben refers to everything – language, discourses,
values, organisations, transport systems, communications systems, weaponry,
anything – that can be placed into a relationship to address an urgent problem
or crisis. Thus, in particular, it consists in all the resources that those in power
can readily draw upon to further their interests or to address particular economic,
political, social concerns that threaten their interests. In particular, the neoliberal
architecture is progressively created by the bringing or knotting together of
financial organisations, political organisations and legal frameworks, as well as the
policing of property, strikes and protests and, externally, the use of the military to
defend and provide access to resources. Such an architecture creates a particular
connected structure out of pieces that could be organised alternatively. Like
any architecture it has to be constantly maintained. That work is undertaken
through instructional talk and prescribed action that continually maintains the
sense of there being a system that is unchallengeable since it is itself the reality.
This reality is inscribed on people in all the experiences of their lives. As Mauss

put it, 'the triple consideration of the body, the mind and the social environment must go together' (Mauss 1979: 31). A critical writing that has as its object disentangling the complex of relationships and impacts may be conceived to counter the agendas formulated by neo-liberalism. It is in critically analysing this complex that the manifest and covert agendas of neo-liberalism appear as a text continually inscribed on people. It is a job developed in each of the following chapters of this book.

Finally writing the agenda as a demand

The agenda can be written as a set of demands that have to be taken into account if a decision is to be made and action undertaken. These demands differ according to different viewpoints. These viewpoints arise as splits that are drawn across a 'mass', a 'multitude', thus generating factions, classes, communities of interest and demand. Each protagonist may flag allegiances in a struggle to control an agenda. However, those 'flags' may be consciously or unconsciously inscribed. The tattoo is an easily visualised inscription, the body technique is less 'seeable' yet is fundamental to what makes people 'readable' as British, as female, as working class, as middle aged, who have agendas appropriate to their allegiance. And as each additional specification marks and positions the individual, then the individual becomes more tightly bound to his or her locale. Reading the signs of that locale as 'mine', 'my world' and its people as 'us' then divides an unaligned mass into a recognisable *dramatis personae* whose everyday routines and biographical details are variants of 'my story', 'our story' in relation to which each individual negotiates his or her place and inscribes his or her story-line as his or her 'unique' trajectory.

There is a real sense in which, because we are producers of inscriptions and of texts, we live within these texts, our demands are shaped by these texts. We constantly re-write them in innumerable variations in the production of our identities and our worlds as we make demands in everyday life. From the texts that we live and that live within us, motivating us, tripping us up, positioning us in relation to others, we can begin to identify the agendas that shape us as we shape them. These agendas are like matrices extending over our lives, our worlds providing the co-ordinates through which our actions are oriented and organised. It is only when the very matrices are disrupted that alternative agendas may be glimpsed, like the symptoms of some slowly developing disease, or the buried contents of some traumatic act. To understand a demand requires excavating the texts that shape it and that give it a force that is more than the conscious will can bear.

In a sense, agenda setting is a violence that cuts the whole into parts, that simplifies the complex, that reduces the ambitious into something 'realistic'; in another sense, it is what re-defines the realistic in order to produce counter-vailing agendas. The discovery of the work of these agendas is a work of research and education. It is a work of noticing what passes unnoticed, or is dismissed as meaningless, or repressed as inappropriate and noting these as signs of something else that desires to be said, to be seen to be felt. The signs of this something else are what we are calling here, the symptom of the text. At their most dramatic they challenge the legitimacy of the social, economic and political architecture(s) through which our demands are either made real or are repressed. At their most individual, they seem chaotic, self-destructive; or they appear as what makes the individual different, unique. In each case, they are demanding.

A writing agenda can be sharpened by the critical observation of these seven demands that compose and de-compose the agenda of this book: the demand of the universal, the demand of the split, the demand of alliances, the demand of the symbol, the demand of difference, the demand of free debate and the demand of legitimacy. Each of these has already been pre-figured in explorations in this chapter. Each is implicit to each. There is no hierarchy or specific sequence that they must follow. To write, however, involves an exploration of all in an act of re-creation where inscriptions perceived from a multiplicity of viewpoints are re-framed according to an agenda of free and equal openness to public debate about the conditions, purposes and meanings of people's lives and how these may be imagined, organised, re-organised and transformed through people's actions. How the demands of an agenda can work to produce a countervailing force can be seen in the demand of the universal expressed in a video posted on facebook[1] on January 18, 2011 by Asmaa Mahfou calling for people to meet at Tahrir Square on January 25, 2011. They did. It was the Day of Rage[2] that ignited another fire through which the Arab Spring became a symbol and a practice of freedom. She had said:

> Four Egyptians have set themselves on fire, to protest humiliation and hunger and poverty and degradation they had to live with for 30 years. Four Egyptians have set themselves on fire, thinking maybe we can have a revolution like Tunisia, maybe we can have freedom, justice, honour, and human dignity. Today, one of these four has died, and I saw people commenting and saying: 'May God forgive him, he committed a sin, and killed himself for nothing.' People! Have some shame! I posted that I, a girl, am going down to Tahrir Square and I will stand alone and I'll hold up a banner, perhaps people will show some honour. I even wrote my number, so maybe people will come down with me. No one came except three guys! Three guys and three armoured cars of riot police! And tens of hired thugs, and officers, came to terrorise us. They shoved us roughly away from the people. But as soon as we were alone with them, they started to talk to us. They said: 'Enough, these guys who burned themselves were psychopaths!'

1 See http://www.youtube.com/watch?v=SgjIgMdsEuk&feature=player_embedded
2 See http://www.youtube.com/watch?v=S8aXWT3fPyY

Of course, on all the media, whoever dies in protest is a psychopath. If they were psychopaths, why did they burn themselves at the Parliament building?

I'm making this video to give you one simple message. We want to go down to Tahrir Square on January 25th. If we still have honour, and want to live in dignity on this land we have to go down on January 25th. We'll go down and demand our rights, our fundamental human rights. I won't even talk about any political rights. We just want our human rights and nothing else.

Here is a demand for 'human rights', the call for a public space to voice the demand, the identification of a particular place for its concrete expression, the reasons for public mobilisation and finally the physical gathering of a 'public' to legitimise and express the force of the demand through the presence of numbers. Together they map out some possible elements of an agenda to be written anew across 'the people'.

The new demands expressed under the banner of the universal punched holes in what had seemed without fissures and gaps in what had been the prevailing social, economic and political order. The deaths could be read in the context of literal readings of a particular religious text, or discourses of 'normal' behaviour; that is, they could be read and criticised either as 'sin' or as 'psychopathic' behaviour. Under the universal call of human rights, a new reading could be proposed, one that unleashed the silenced and repressed demands for 'rights' through which the wrongs experienced by people could be addressed. This is a process of generating new readings rather like Althusser and Balibar's (1970: 9) 'symptomatic reading' of a given text which 'divulges the undivulged event in the text it reads, and in the same movement relates it to a different text, present as a necessary absence in the first'. They argue that:

> All that a simple literal reading sees in the arguments is the continuity of the text. A 'symptomatic' reading is necessary to make these lacunae perceptible, and to identify behind the spoken words the discourse of the silence, which, emerging in the verbal discourse, induces these blanks in it, blanks which are failures in its rigour, or the outer limits of its effort: its absence, once these limits are reached, but in a space which it has opened.
>
> (Althusser and Balibar 1970: 86)

What is being heard in such readings are previously silenced discourses, or discourses that could only be heard elsewhere that bring to the fore in a newly opened space, a new agenda. The 'simple literal reading' has a similarity with the taken for granted beliefs, values and opinions of 'common sense' discourses of 'what everyone knows', the routines and the 'by the book' practices by which people justify and reproduce their everyday lives. The counter discourses can only be heard in a new space, a space that is co-extensive with an emergent public able to hear, respond and act through those alternative discourses. This creates the conditions for a division in the body-politic and thus the creation of distinct agendas that imply distinct forms of the public. There then becomes a contest for legitimacy.

Asmaa Mahfou in her video called for people to come down to Tahrir Square. It was a call for strength in numbers, for the creation of alliances under the most encompassing universal: human rights, not just partisan political rights. When the people did come down to Tahrir Square week after week, despite the intimidation, the arrests and the killings, the Square became a symbol of courage, of protest and of the people proclaiming their rights. As a symbol, it was employed to stimulate protests across several other countries in the Arab world; and in Spain there were echoes in Madrid, in Greece in Syntagma Square and even in London in Trafalgar Square. In English, Tahrir can be translated as 'Liberation'. There is in this symbol a power to call, to demand and to unite. Much was made in Egypt that although it was sparked by the youth of the country, it drew people of all ages, male and female, working class and middle class, people of all occupations and of all faiths and none. Its power was that it was non-partisan, that it was of the people.

When the Western commentators and leaders assessed the emergent situation in Egypt and elsewhere they initially looked in vain for leaders. Without leaders, who could they talk to? Without leaders, how could an agenda of concerns be taken seriously on the world stage? When Mubarak finally fell, and when the celebrations were over, what was left in place was the military and all the other apparatuses used by the old regime to construct their agendas, their demands on the people. Protestors returned to Tahrir Square to 'save' their revolution. Political voices began to emerge as differences in demands were articulated. A space had opened up, but it was not yet a space where demands could be effectively debated, negotiated, decided upon and legitimately brought into action through the institutions of power.

Essentially, as we use the term, an agenda is a collective performance setting the key demands and issues for what is to be placed for public scrutiny, discussion, decision and action. The conditions under which it is done is the frame that determines what is at stake in having a public agenda. Writing the agenda is a process that emerges through engagement with questions and issues of concern relating to a specific focus for action. How that action is to be framed is the critical next step for its success.

Gestures towards writing

What is a writer to do? As stated in the introduction, there are no recipes to be proposed by this book. Rather, there are gestures. How an agenda will impact on the structure of the text, whether assignment, report, article or book, depends on the identification of splits and the demands that follow from being positioned socially, culturally, politically by a split. As a first gesture, then, a mapping can be made of the patterns of attention and inattention revealed in the analysis of data

– whether say from interviews, observations or media reports – in terms of the 'sides', the taxonomies and the contents of what can be seen or not seen. In the expression of demands and the organisation of responses to those demands the signs of legitimacies, malaise and their symptoms can be read. What are the prior texts implicit in a given call, a demand or rationale for a response to a demand? It is here where the founding processes of thinking, desiring, demanding under-lying what is to count as 'legitimate' may be discovered. And in the actions to shape or impose these legitimacies may be found the machineries for the construction of assent, consent and dissension. The agenda of concerns from each side compose then the matrix through which the writing will be framed.

Chapter 2

Framing the Background – transgressing the frame

What impels people to write? And in writing, how does research take on its sense of necessity, its demand to know? The answers, if any can be found for certain, are both personal and cultural. By cultural we refer to everything that is the product of human artifice; and the personal is how in facing the uncertainties of our finite lives we construct and present our biographies. At its broadest, the background is the totality of the cultural histories that impinge upon, inscribe and shape the personal. At its most individual, it is how the background is articulated as a project. Whether it is acknowledged or not, the agendas that shape each individual project are already conditioned by decisions made over the centuries, the millennia that have established the geo-political and economic territories that have through war and commerce carved the earth into the lands and properties of peoples, faiths, kingdoms, nations, states, corporations, wealth elites and the portions that remain for the 'governed'. What was common and open has become private and closed. The political and economic agenda that emerged during the industrialisation of the UK from the eighteenth century spread globally in the twentieth century until by the beginning of the twenty-first century the power of States had been compromised by the power of global finance. People had been dispossessed of their access to the common land, as in the enclosures that took place in England, where 'Between 1750 and 1850, parliament passed about 4,000 individual enclosures acts, each transferring a single piece of land out of common ownership and into the ownership of farmers and landowners' (Lazenby 2012), or the land races of the American West that dispossessed the native Americans, or the clearing of the Amazonian jungles. With the global dominance of the neo-liberal turn in capitalism people are similarly being dispossessed of public services, public ownership and indeed in response to the 2008 financial crisis their own incomes and private assets as a result of 'austerity' measures. The call to write as a redress for present injuries – or indeed, to maintain the conditions for the continuance of injuries – demands a continual framing and counter framing of backgrounds upon which what is foregrounded is constructed.

The historical background is continually in movement. Something of its traces can be historically picked out and seen as critical, decisive markers of change one way rather than another that shape the opportunities presented, the choices available at a given time and place for people to make a difference in their lives. The overarching problematic of the relation between what is possessed in common with what is privately possessed impacts on what is open to public discussion and what is closed for private decision. How to manage the relation between the private and the public has been central to democratic debates. Perhaps the key, even mythic, image is of the public meetings of the Ancient Greek democratic city state of Athens. Not all the inhabitants of the city state had the right to take part in the democratic meetings – women, children and slaves were excluded. But the ideal was that all valid voices could engage in the public debate. Such an ideal, it is argued, is not possible in nation states of millions. In the period leading to the French Revolution and American War of Independence there were debates about how best to construct forms of representation, where the few would represent the many. The move to representative forms of government impacts on the meaning of the 'public'. It is this impact that is critical for the framing of projects and the writing of research. It is what frames the stakes involved.

Framing the stakes

The stakes are always political whether or not the political nature is visible. In a sense, the political is the 'third' party in the room, whether seen or unseen. In the case of the Tahrir Square protests, the political effects made visible the relations between Mubarak, his government, the police, the military, neighbouring Arab states and the West. What was being placed on the agenda was the transformation of Middle Eastern and North African states through calls for democracy, the relationship between the West and the Arab dictatorships as well as the possibility for a renewal of the role of the public in democratic governance on a global scale. There is here a dynamic that moves from a few individuals making claims about immediate concrete circumstances through to abstract universals that take their meaning from the experiences of increasing numbers of people. Adopting a modernist or a Hegelian view, this movement might be seen in terms of historical progress and inevitable movement towards the end of history (Fukuyama 1992). People are in a sense the content of a universal as 'humanity' having 'human rights', and in wanting 'freedom', 'equality', 'democracy'. They are also the 'material surface' where the terms are either inscribed or erased. If such terms are not written on the people as their core political agenda, then they have no effective meaning, that is, there is no material basis for their existence in human discourse. The issue is about seeing what is at stake:

> It seems to me that we are living through a long revolution, which our best descriptions only in part interpret. It is a genuine revolution, transforming

men and institutions; continually extended and deepened by the actions of millions, continually and variously opposed by explicit reaction and by the pressure of habitual forms and ideas. Yet it is a difficult revolution to define, and its uneven action is taking place over so long a period that it is almost impossible not to get lost in its exceptionally complicated process.

(Williams 1965: 10)

This is a revolution not quite seen, not quite nameable, but there is an impression that it is 'genuine'. If it can be read at all, it can only be with another text in mind. But what text?

In a book on the philosophy of mathematics, Tragesser (1977) employed a useful term. It was in the context of mathematical puzzles that seemed unsolvable over decades, even centuries, yet mathematicians felt there was a solution. Rather than an apprehension of the total solution, there would be an incomplete understanding that it could be found, a 'prehension' of its solvability. Similarly with the 'revolution'. Researchers and political commentators talk of great changes impacting on global, national and local institutions. These are not arbitrary intuitions since they are based upon events taking place. However, the precise definition of what counts as an 'event' and its interpretation alongside other 'events' are very much open to dispute. There are many ways in which what is experienced can be storied as an event and narrativised as a sequence of events. For Hegel there was an historical trajectory where all the opposing views would be synthesised into a final absolute state of affairs that would in effect be the 'end of history', that is, the end to the need for a struggle between competing ideas since the perfect state had been achieved. Marx saw this in materialist terms leading to the perfect society of communism. At the fall of the Soviet Union, Fukuyama (1992) declared that the end of history had been achieved – liberal Western market democracy had won. Huntington (1993, 1996) however, pointed to what he called the 'clash of civilisations', where 'The great divisions among humankind and the dominating source of conflict will be cultural' and not primarily ideological or economic (Huntington 1993: 22). What such conceptions of the organising splits through which history is to be articulated overlook are the actors as 'ordinary people' composed of the multitude of individual human beings populating the earth, not as representatives of a 'faith', a 'culture', an 'economic class' or a subject or citizen of a state. What is at stake in writing is the overlooked perspective, absent from the articulations of histories written by the powerful. It is there that the revolution resides, not as a finalised or finalisable vision but as the voice to be heard.

Absenting the voice

For individuals facing the impersonal machineries of governance, whether central or local government, the militaries, the police or the vast industrial complexes, financial corporations, retail chains and public sector services that dominate everyday living and thought of making a change, getting one's voice heard is daunting. Each person is just a small voice in amongst millions. Everyone is framed by the sheer weight of numbers and the complexity of social, political and economic organisation. It is this sheer complexity that for the ordinary citizen appears as a 'swarming confusion of problems' (Lippmann 1927: 24) and led Lippmann to argue that the idea of a public involved fully in political and economic decision-making is fantasy. Ordinary people have enough to do simply living their lives: earning money, looking after children, having some fun when they can. They do not have the time, he argued, to be informed about all the pressing problems faced by governments as they wrestle with economic or political matters. Rather than bringing the voice of people to bear upon the problems, their voices are to be absented and replaced in the arenas of decision-making. Only those who are expert enough and have the time to devote to political questions will know enough to be able to contribute to decision-making. The remainder, the vast majority, will in some way need to be persuaded or compelled to accept the decisions made by the few that it is in their best interests. Thus, Lippmann made the distinction between the decision-makers and the rest, who merely have 'opinions'.

Opinions, rightly, matter. It is essential that a sufficient proportion of the voting public is persuaded of a course of action otherwise civil unrest might occur. There is then a critical distinction to be made between those who have the knowledge and the power to decide and act and those who only have an opinion. Lippmann's argument is thus that the vast majority of people cannot be expected to engage fully in democratic decision-making. Their role is that of being bearers of opinions about things that are essentially external to their immediate day-to-day tasks of making a life for themselves. For Lippmann, a vote is 'a way of saying: I am lined up with these men, on this side. I enlist with them. I will follow. I will buy. I will boycott. I will strike. I applaud. I jeer. The force I can exert is placed here, not there' (Lippmann 1927: 56–7). Moreover,

> The public does not select the candidate, write the platform, outline the policy any more than it builds the automobile or acts the play. It aligns itself for or against somebody who has offered himself, has made a promise, has produced a play, is selling an automobile. The action of a group as a group is the mobilisation of the force it possesses.
>
> (Lippmann 1927: 57)

Since there are always competing interests, Lippmann (1927) reads the vote as a substitute for fighting (p. 59), and thus an election is 'sublimated warfare' (p. 60) where people align themselves 'for or against a proposal' (p. 61), hence 'by their occasional mobilisations as a majority, people support or oppose the individuals who actually govern' (p. 62). For these reasons he considers the public to be but a phantom, a useful phantom for manipulation by the real decision-makers.

It is this kind of theory regarding the 'public' and what it is capable of that enables the public relations approach to identifying publics and swaying them, or in Lippmann's terms 'manufacturing consent' for the purposes of those who actually govern. Those who govern Bernays (1928) called the 'invisible government' – that is, the broad elite who actually govern, rather than those who are its representatives and are elected by a voting public to govern. It is why Badiou (2008) advised not voting in the French presidential election of 2007, since regardless of name and regardless of 'left' or 'right' there was no choice, since all were neoliberal politicians and the vote would simply elect the management team for a neoliberal government. In short, there was no real choice, hence no real need to vote. Similarly, for many, not just in America, Obama was a symbol of hope for real change that seemed realised when he was inaugurated president January 20, 2009.

For decades politics had been framed by a logic of friend and enemy expressed under Reagan (1983 www.nationalcenter.org/ReaganEvilEmpire1983.html) as the Soviet Union being 'the Evil Empire'. The same logic was employed after 9/11 when Bush (2002 www.washingtonpost.com/wp-srv/onpolitics/transcripts/sou012902.htm) declared a 'war on terror', naming Middle Eastern nations he considered to be supporting terrorism as the Axis of Evil. Obama seemed to represent the possibility of a reconciliation, a new beginning. All the more so, it seemed, in the context of the worst recession since the 1930s. However, as time progressed, for many the disappointments grew (Janson 2009; Mearsheimer 2011; Moor 2011; Roberts and Schostak 2012). For Klein (2009), Obama played his campaign like selling a brand: he 'really is a super brand on line with many of the companies that I discuss in *No Logo*'. There was a gap between the image that Obama portrayed in his presidential campaign and the reality of the policies of his presidency,, as pointed out by Rosenberg (2011). However, it is unsurprising that once in 'power' that power cannot be exercised without the already established mechanisms and organisations of power. There is no governmental blank slate.

Mechanisms of framing

To run for high political office requires substantial backing. This is not surprising. Nor is it surprising that that backing is organised to reproduce and maintain the prevailing order of power. To do this requires the dispositifs discussed in the previous chapter. For Agamben (2009) contemporary capitalism produces these dispositifs, that is, the assemblages of practices, discourses, knowledge, resources and organisations that constitute the machineries of power. In developing this idea, he proposed two large classes of beings:

> Living beings (or substances), and on the other, apparatuses in which living beings are incessantly captured: On the one side, then to return to the terminology of the theologians, lies the ontology of creatures, and on the

other side, the oikonomia of apparatuses that seek to govern and guide them towards the good.

(Agamben 2009: 13)

The Greek term *oikonomia* – or economy – signified the management of the household, that is, more broadly, the government of the affairs of people. This partitioning of the world is what simplifies it for governmental purposes. It is, economically and politically speaking, the fundamental framing creating the conditions for inscribing people as those who are or are to become the subjects of administration – 'every apparatus implies a process of subjectification, without which it cannot function as an apparatus of governance, but is rather reduced to a mere exercise of violence' (p. 19). The specific form(s) of this administration depends on the agendas in play and which of these are dominant and which can threaten that dominance. A dispositif in the way that Agamben develops the term comes into play as the connections between discourses, tools, organisations – indeed, anything – that can be activated to meet a given problem or aim. Finally, in the contemporary age:

> What defines the apparatuses that we have to deal with in the current phase of capitalism is that they no longer act as much through the production of a subject, as through the processes of what can be called desubjectification. A desubjectifying moment is certainly implicit in every process of subjectification. As we have seen, the penitential self is constituted only through its own negation. But what we are now witnessing is that processes of subjectification and pro-cesses of desubjectification seem to become reciprocally indifferent, and so they do not give rise to the recomposition of a new subject, except in larval or, as it were, spectral form. In the nontruth of the subject, its own truth is no longer at stake. He who lets himself be captured by the 'cellular telephone' apparatus – whatever the intensity of the desire that has driven him – cannot acquire a new subjectivity, but only a number through which he can, eventually, be controlled. The spectator who spends his evenings in front of the television set only gets, in exchange for his desubjectification, the frustrated mask of the couch potato, or his inclusion in the calculation of viewer-ship ratings.

(Agamben 2009: 20–21)

The individual is increasingly inscribed in terms of 'addresses', not so much the fixed address of home and landline, but the mobile numbers that move with the individual whether phone, computer, credit cards, social security number and passport. These are the numbers that begin to define the identity; the more they cross-correlate, the more the individual is a prisoner or hostage of the apparatuses that inscribe him or her. In 1961, in his last speech as president, Eisenhower named the emergent dispositif of the time the industrial military complex:

This conjunction of an immense military establishment and a large arms industry is new in the American experience. The total influence – economic, political, even spiritual – is felt in every city, every State house, every office of the Federal government. We recognize the imperative need for this development. Yet we must not fail to comprehend its grave implications. Our toil, resources and livelihood are all involved; so is the very structure of our society.

In the councils of government, we must guard against the acquisition of unwarranted influence, whether sought or unsought, by the militaryindustrial complex. The potential for the disastrous rise of misplaced power exists and will persist.

(Eisenhower 1961)

Eisenhower thus warned that 'public policy could itself become the captive of a scientifictechnological elite'. Over the decades, since the rise of neoliberal market ideologies and their capture of the politics of the developed nations of the West, the military industrial complex has further complexly intertwined with finance, educational institutions, pharmaceuticals and the media in ways that that over-determine the lives of people and thus comprise the pervasive background 'frameworks' of Western neoliberal market democracies. When governments change, they remain fundamentally in place, run by the same elites as before.

Disturbing frames

Since a given framework creates the conditions for a particular strategy of attention, to undo it needs a countervailing strategy of observation. For that, attention itself has to be variously disturbed, suspended, disabled. In order to free his mind from the frameworks of the day, Descartes philosophically doubted all that his senses perceived, all the traditional knowledge transmitted through his schooling until, he argued, there was a remainder that he could not doubt: that is, his act of doubting or thinking. Husserl developed this approach of suspending the taken-for-granted assumptions of the reality and validity of what is perceived, known and believed that in turn was developed into sociological approaches to the study of everyday life by Schutz (1976). In this approach, it was by adopting the attitude of the stranger (Schutz 1964) that the 'naturalistic' belief in the realities of everyday life could be challenged. The strategy was to render the familiar unfamiliar. Or more actively, for Garfinkel (1967), it was to cause trouble, so that people would have to make clear the impact of the trouble on the orderly surface structure of their lives. In this way, the tacit understandings, processes and structures of everyday life could be manifested. For example, acting like a social scientist, questioning everything during an ordinary social meeting, a dinner date, would soon become problematic. A simple opening statement is 'Hello, how are you?'" To respond by further asking, 'What do you mean? Do you mean how am I in my health, my work, my finances …?'

unless there had been a prior set of events, a background making such specific questioning relevant and expected, would seem bizarre, when a usual response would be 'Fine, thank you, and how are you?' The response to Garfinkel causing such trouble was typically anger. There was an affective dimension to the typical practices, routines and understandings of everyday life. Breaking the normal pattern would cause eruptions of anger, or feelings of fear and anxiety. Combining such philosophical and sociological approaches with psychological and psychoanalytic practices such as stream of consciousness, free association and dream analysis, it can be argued that the 'unconscious' and 'repressed' motivations and meanings of discourses and practices become open to analysis. What each of these approaches has in common is to manifest what normally passes unseen or unspoken and yet has effects on people and their everyday activities. These effects may be experienced as 'inexplicable' eruptions, breakdowns that in each case are signs of something 'outside', 'elsewhere', or excluded. Indeed, it is the view from the marginalised, the deviant, that has often provided insights into what counts as 'normal' behaviour. What this signifies is an essential split at the heart of consciousness that drives attention one way or another. It is the split that enables or disables articulations between what is seen and what cannot be seen in the ways that attention is organised to create a seamless 'reality'. It is the operation of the split to articulate one 'reality' while repressing another that underlies our conception of the 'frame'.

The operation of the split could be seen in various ways and to different effects when the financial system fell into crisis in 2008, when Wikileaks placed into public thousands of leaked cables in autumn 2010, when the people of Tunisia set alight the 'Arab Spring' in 2011, or in the protests against 'austerity measures' demanded to reduce sovereign debts, and could further be seen when the 'hacking scandal' of Murdoch's *News of the World* finally aroused 'public outrage' in the UK in July 2011. In each case, there was the question of 'legitimacy' that could only be resolved by reference to a 'public'. The public, as it were, emerged from the taken-for-granted background as a key structure of the state. But this 'public' was manifested in very different ways, took on different meanings and was used for quite different purposes in the different contexts.

Crowds in the streets can be managed by police and trouble labelled as 'mindless' violence perpetrated by thugs, criminals, subversives. But a public, in the sense employed here, can be neither policed nor ignored, since it is the very foundation of the legitimacy of the police. Politics and the law derive their authority from a people organised as a public. Lippmann's (1927) 'phantom public' is not a public in the sense intended here, but maintains the fantasy of a public in order to provide legitimacy for the decisions of the elites who act on its behalf. The ever-present danger for elites is that an effective public emerges instead of a phantom public. The public is both an essential part of society, essentially unstable in the sense that it is always open to the question of its own legitimacy and essentially excluded from the apparatus of state governance. It may be shocked into consciousness of itself as a public by the awareness of atrocities and scandals. It is the ever-present possibility that people withdraw their assent, and as Boétie wrote in his pamphlet in c.1552, when the people stop obeying the tyrants, the tyrants fall, as in Tunisia and Egypt. However, as in Egypt, protest is not enough if the fundamental machineries of the state remain to suppress an effective public. Similarly, when it was alleged that *News of the World* reporters had illegally hacked into the mobile phones of the murdered school girl Milly Dowler, those of the relatives of dead British soldiers and those of the victims of the 9/11 attacks, 'public opinion' turned, News International share prices fell, Murdoch closed the *News of the World* and Rebekah Brooks, his Chief Executive of News International, eventually resigned. What was revealed in the scandal was the extent of the relationships between the police and reporters and the close relationships between senior politicians, Rupert Murdoch, his son James, Rebekah Brooks and other senior News International employees. However, this was a scandal played through the media with reference to an outraged 'public'. Although the 'public' continued buying News International publications and watching its television channels, suddenly UK politicians lost their fear of the power of the Murdoch empire, symbolised by the notorious headline in the *Sun* tabloid newspaper following the 1992 election, stating 'It's The Sun Wot Won It' (Saturday April 11, 1992). Nevertheless, this was not a transformative moment bringing down the dispositifs of power. On the wider scene, the overall dominance of corporate power over politics, as evidenced in the aftermath of the financial crisis of 2008, had been left largely unchanged by this or any other scandal. Indeed, the success of the dispositifs implementing neoliberal market strategies has been seen by Harvey as a progressive process of accumulation by dispossessing the public while enriching the private, governing elites. For Harvey (2006), then, 'accumulation by dispossession is about plundering, robbing other people of their rights'. Disturbing this process is typically framed as a demand for change, which if not heard is positioned as protest, struggle or, indeed, as revolution. It could be seen in the voices of the Arab Spring, or in the outraged public responding to injustice and scandal and in the challenges posed by Wikileaks. Such events have at least identified the potential for a countervailing public. Is it possible that an emergent public can be provided with its own countervailing dispositif? This is the field of action where what is at stake is framing the narrative of the disturbing event itself defining what can or cannot be told, what can or cannot be seen.

Keeping invisible the narrative framing

Story-ing – as wilful and intentional activity – frames our lived experiences into a narrative that has a past, a present and a future, and it is itself composed of many stories branching out into networks of intricate relationships with other stories and story-ings. In other words, story-ing constructs both time and space into chunks – it frames them – in ways that make sense to ourselves and to others. The management of story-ing is thus critical to political and economic governance.

Such stories are very personal, very individual and universal. In every story each of us recognizes a sense of the universal, a sense of the fatal and of finitude. The story begins as a personal and mysterious beginning: we are born – or, in Arendt's terms, we enter a world of appearances from a nowhere. It has a middle: we live as a child, an adolescent, an adult and we age – or, in Arendt's terms, we develop and grow, unfolding into a standstill of 'bloom and epiphany as it were' (Arendt 1978: 22), and then enter 'a downward movement and disintegration'. The story ends as finally we die – or, as Arendt puts it, we completely disappear from this world of appearances into a nowhere.

Each individual becomes the actor/agent of, and in, his or her story, and this story embraces and intermeshes with the stories of others, and with the story-ings of others, thus creating a potential for the plurality of voices and agencies that together may compose a public. As actor and agent the individual casts – frames – his or her self within a personalised story as hero, friend, spectator, witness, supporter, foe, victim, revolutionary, adventurer, explorer and so on, and this identity will contain elements of many of these surfaces. Whatever the frame within the fragment of the story under the spotlight at any point in time, it will be subject to dynamic change from moment to moment and from space to space as that story unfolds and interlinks with others. In casting oneself as a hero, for example, the individual searches out ways and means to think as a hero would, act as if she or he were a hero, look for particular opportunities to engage within the moment and space of an event seeming[ly] as a hero, thereby achieving the Arendtian it-seems-to-me appearance-as-hero. Seeming the part demands engaging in ways of thinking, doing and saying with oneself and with others through some medium of communication that possesses a grammar and a syntax: language, sign language, established repertoires of moves, of gestures, of body language, of mime, of ballet and so on. As speaking beings, we are born into a world of language, and thus conditioned by language as we learn to speak it, live in and of it.

It is this power of the story that public relations professionals employ to provide a unifying 'picture in the head', as Lippmann (1922) called it, that enables individuals to cope with the world and its vast territories, its social, cultural, economic and political complexities and the millions of people who compose nations. For him,

> at the level of social life, what is called the adjustment of man to his environment takes place through the medium of fictions.
>
> By fictions I do not mean lies. I mean a representation of the environment which is in lesser or greater degree made by man himself. The range of fiction extends all the way from complete hallucination to the scientists' perfectly self conscious use of a schematic model, or his decision that for his particular problem accuracy beyond a certain number of decimal points is not important. A work of fiction may have almost any degree of fidelity, and so long as the degree of fidelity can be taken into

account, fiction is not misleading. In fact, human culture is very largely the selection, the rearrangement, the tracing of patterns upon, and the stylizing of, what William James called 'the random irradiations and resettlements of our ideas'.[1] The alternative to the use of fictions is direct exposure to the ebb and flow of sensation. That is not a real alternative, for however refreshing it is to see at times with a perfectly innocent eye, innocence itself is not wisdom, though a source and corrective of wisdom. For the real environment is altogether too big, too complex, and too fleeting for direct acquaintance. We are not equipped to deal with so much subtlety, so much variety, so many permutations and combinations. And although we have to act in that environment, we have to reconstruct it on a simpler model before we can manage with it. To traverse the world men must have maps of the world.

(Lippmann 1922: 10–11)

If the public relations task of governance is to render invisible the workings of governance in the interests of the elites by engineering or manufacturing consent, as both Bernays and Lippmann would have it, the counter writing task is then to make visible those machineries, strategies and processes that are employed to manufacture and manipulate pictures in the head. Dispositifs are the machineries producing the framing practices of hierarchical governance through which people can be inscribed into such key framing structures as leader–led, hero–coward, master–servant, friend–enemy, stranger–host by composing and influencing the patterns of attention and inattention, desire and revulsion, security and fear in the formation of the 'public' whose images of the world, whose distinctions between 'real' and 'fiction' and whose definitions of right and wrong can be manipulated within the prescribed frames. The story that is told matters. It structures identities, relationships, behaviours, actions, outcomes by structuring what is to be perceived, accountable and re-countable. The desire of elites is to control the dispositifs through which governance is organised as a means to drive their domination of the public down into each individual's very inner life of perceptual and psychic organisation. Each individual is the 'surface' to be inscribed by machineries that write down, name, address, ascribe to sides, allocate rank and prescribe and distribute rewards and punishments. The power of this process is in keeping it invisible and maintaining the fiction of a 'public' that in some way controls its leaders and its fate by being able to change leaders.

Towards visibility

The ceaseless construction of pictures in the mind to serve the interests of an 'invisible government' betrays the ever-present possibility of its de-composition,

1 Footnote given by Lippmann, p. 10: James, *Principles of Psychology*, Vol. II, p. 638

re-composition and thus countervailing view. Any story is differently experienced according to one's prescribed address within it. Narratives of struggle against unfair reward or punishment can be inscribed as sub-plots to a prevailing narrative of 'justice'. How perceived rights are recognised, ignored or abused become a focus around which experience may be framed to story systematic injustice and thus render it visible. As news items, as means of making a living, it is the livelihood of investigative journalists and the proprietors of news outlets to tell the story. More generally, as researchers and as writers, countervailing stories can be told that place people as active composers of their story and thus active in producing alternative *dramatis personae*. Becoming self-visible in the process of story-ing one's fate involves being active in re-casting the *dramatis personae* and re-framing the taxonomic net of namings and their framing of the visible, the invisible, the meaningful and the meaningless.

Framing in the re-story-ing of particulars (whether people or their objects of consciousness) is like casting a fishing net – at the same time as constructing the net – to catch meaning or something else, something that surprises, shocks, rips apart. The net is a meshwork that is part string or rope – of a material nature – and part holes – a no-thing – woven into as a networked lattice. Without the two there is no net. Ordinarily it is simpler to make the material, the visible and tangible part of the whole that appears within the frame for discussion. But making the no-thing visible (by virtue of the boundaries of the rope that provide a sense of 'hole') but not tangible as is the framework of ropes and strings, changes the perspective for discussion towards structures that 'dictate[s] what that object comes to be – by what is allowed to get away' (Diprose and Ferrell 1991: viii). The act of framing has power, such as the power to place into the picture x but not y, the power to ignore, dismiss and ultimately exclude – all of which is to say, the power to create seamless perceptual worlds. The use of the fishing net metaphor is apt because it embodies the fuzziness of language, which itself does not simply describe what is.

> It is rather that the strings of meaning produce the holes in the material world in such a way that what is represented is as much a product of the unsaid as of the said.
>
> (Diprose and Ferrell 1991: viii)

Of course, the metaphorical analogy of the net used as a frame is powerful inasmuch as it sets going the illusion of a real out there, based upon already existing meanings or a finite set of interpretations that can be caught and hauled in.

Critical writing explores the conditions under which a catch and its 'hauling in' can be created, inscribed in the real as it reels in the inscribed as a 'public' that legitimises processes of decision-making. For Lippmann and Bernays the public is essentially composed from a herd (Ward 1924) or a crowd. It is in the management of the heard and the unheard that the public is moved one way or another in a matrix composing the real and the fictional. Crudely, there is 'a fictionality' of what society assumes to be real, and there is 'a reality of its fictions' (Weber 1987: 152). But this is not simply to question the very existence of 'truth' itself but to regard the style of truth in relation to fiction. Even if a text presents as atomistic, as unconnected fragments, it yearns for connection, for interconnection, for seamlessness. It yearns to be taken as an expression of, a claim about, an instance of, a representation of some truth about the world that is other than the discourse about it. Where it projects an agenda of coherence, of a 'surfacing' that is already, and always already, at work it invites subjects to engage in interpretation, elaboration and acceptance of its webs of meanings fashioning a sense of the 'real', of 'desire' and the demand to be listened to and taken into account. Where it projects care to conceal something below the surface, new possibilities for leakage and interpretation appear. It is through the text that the recognition of a life in common, if in opposition, is manifested as the symptom through which meaning finds its place in the lives of people as *theirs*. From each viewpoint it can be told, shared, discussed, disputed, denied. The text becomes a particular tying together of people's voices who can only signal their meanings, co-ordinate their actions, express their intentions, formulate their plans and know how they stand, whether together or against others, through the discourses they mutually create. Bound by how they talk and think about their selves, what they say to or about each other, and the objects of the world that they can perceive, imagine and think about. This discursive binding, a kind of rhetorical tying in knots, a weaving, a chainmailing, a struggle to unify or separate, to associate or disassemble creates the reality of a life in and amongst others. It is their style of living.

> Roughly speaking, 'style' simply consists of the individual manner in which the speaker or writer selects, then uniquely combines, words from an internalised lexicon. Aesthetic standards find their expression through this process of word selection and combination. Traditionally, however, especially in rhetoric since Quintillian, style has been more loosely defined as that manner in which an author or speaker communicates his ideas.
>
> (Frank 1999: 148)

Rather than simply a 'manner' of communication, style, as we are using it here, is not independent of meaning and of the life that lives it. Implicitly there is in the styling of some textual surface a stylus, an instrument – a dispositif composed of multiple instruments and machineries – through which marks are made to create an aesthetically organised signifying surface by which we mean a visible, audible, feelable sense of the 'real' that is experienced 'internally' as something 'objective', something independent of ('external' to) any subjective whims and fancies. It is a strategic space created through a play between individual embodied expression and general sense making sharable and utilisable by all speaking beings, thus fixing the experience of being an individual with being part of a greater whole. This sense of the whole of which an individual finds a place is what Rancière (2004) refers to as the aesthetics of politics, that skin like the paint on the surface of a canvas, the pixels of a computer screen that creates an image, the shaping of the marble that produces a form. In each case, the canvas is not the picture, nor is it its support; the pixels are not what is seen, nor the marble what is sensually experienced in the touch. In each case there is a strategic play between the absent (the landscape visualised in the painting, on the screen, the body imagined that is not the marble), the repressed (the material substance) and the present (the being there of the living subject that is always other than what can be named but cannot be represented as 'present' as 'distinct' without the naming). And finally there's the negative structuring that creates the conditions for the emergence of a meaningful content.

There is an essential uncontrollability of the dynamically emergent associations through which texts are produced and the densities they compose as rhythms, rhymes, puns, ironies, metaphors and all the tricks and technologies of rhetoric play havoc with the senses. If a public is to emerge from such intricate densities as a space capable of exploring its differences and disagreements (Rancière 1995) without resorting to violence (see Mouffe 1993, 2005), then countervailing dispositifs are required to suspend the workings of the machineries of elite power so that the multiplicities of voices can be drawn into a space of free debate, decision-making and action in the creation of new forms of social organisation framed to include and foreground rather than exclude and background their multiplicities of demands. The resource to do this is explored in the next chapter.

Gesturing towards writing

To write up radical research (Schostak and Schostak 2008), that is research that seeks to make a difference by the inclusion of voices, necessitates a reframing of perception to create new visibilities, audibilities, touchables and sensualities. It is to include the I of no account whose perspective has a different framing that brings into picture a different story, or a different meaning to the story. In handing the stylus to this other-I, a *dramatis personae* is re-formed and reframed. Its centre has shifted from the commanding-I to the subordinate- or excluded-I. Telling the story from that de-centred position changes everything.

The telling position of the story reframes research and action through its writing. An ethnography deliberately seeks out a range of perspectives in order to picture life from the multiple points of view of the people. Each view brings into association – or dissociation – the multiplicity of views. The instrument of writing can be deployed to erase, to privilege or to equalise the views either by hierarchising or equalising its signifying strokes. This framing gesture is critical in what is pictured and what is left 'outside' as an Other that cannot become represented within the frame. The writer makes decisions with every inscription of an 'in' or 'out' of the picture. If the research is a case study – a 'bounded instance', as many like to call it (Simons 1981), or an emergent complex of associations forming a 'part-whole' relation where all boundaries are fuzzy as others may conceive of it (cf. Ragin and Becker 1992; Schostak 2002) – then whether the case is imposed by design or is designed through the interaction of voices makes a critical difference to the meanings, the understandings, the explanations that can be conceived.

The case upon which action is built determines the actors, the members of the *dramatis personae* who are able to voice a demand for action and those who are the object of that action. It determines what questions can be asked, by who, how, to what effect and for whose purposes. If the case is already framed by the elites who control the machineries of power, then the action undertakes to reinforce that power, not de-construct. If difference is to be made, then it is in the interests of power; otherwise difference is to be written out. Action research carried out in the contexts of business organisations, schools, hospitals and other forms of corporate organisation is done so within the frame of policies, mission statements, performance criteria. What are the background texts that must be read alongside the mission statements in order to render visible what is being excluded? How is what is excluded to be incorporated and inscribed within the frame of action research? The outcome of the action may be evaluated from the point of view of the elites or of the full range of voices. That is a question for writing the final text. It is a question for the writer who now must decide.

Chapter 3

Reviewing the Literature for critical points of view – seeing/reading between the lines

The literature is a multiplicity of voices. With each voice agendas emerge. Each text is itself a framing of voices and their agendas, shaped to present a debate slanted towards a conclusion. Within that debate can often be detected the friends, the strangers, the guests, the hosts and the enemies that are entertained by the writer. So, there is a problem. It is that whilst acts of framing bring and impose order, those very processes of ordering and categorisation select and edit so that some things are chosen to be foregrounded, others to be background and yet others to be excluded. In the writing task, agenda setting and framing pin possibilities and options down to what is regarded as 'realistic', 'plausible', 'do-able', 'true'. However, there has to be a moment when the literature appears like the vertigo experienced over a sheer and endless drop. Engagement with the literature is the essential step in widening out, indeed seeing the limitless possibilities for open debate with a public extending over centuries, even millennia. Making a voice map of the public space of debate is a way of trying to locate what is at stake in adopting a given way of framing the world and its agendas. Getting a sense of the historical development of major debates, discovering the tributaries, the dead ends, the forgotten, the overlooked, is all a part of the gradual sense of knowing where you are, where you stand, in relation to others. In particular, who claims to know what and why? What kinds of arguments are being made, and why? What are the assumptions at the back of explanations and theories? What happens if the assumptions are challenged or changed?

From a review of the literature it is possible to sketch and fill out the details of the problematic, that is, the knot of problems, issues, concerns, interests that each of the voices in the literature have historically addressed. In determining how they address their chosen problems, the outlines of their methodologies can be formulated. Then it is a question of what is at stake expressed by each voice in the choices they make in exploring, examining and forming their conclusions using their chosen methodologies in relation to the problems they address. Which voices have they included in their own reviews of the debates, which have they excluded, and why? By asking such questions as these a literature review then can be designed specifically to increase the power of a given argument, set of findings, recommendations and conclusions that have implications for action.

Broadly, then the process of reviewing the literature provides the opportunity to focus on a particular author's strategies of pin-pointing, inclusion and exclusion by allowing the voices and perspectives of a range of others to be included. It is a mapping exercise to include all voices of the *dramatis personae* of the historical debates that have taken place, including those that have been excluded in the agenda setting and the framing strategies of given authors. The literature review looks for a range of supporting arguments coming from this diverse range of voices, in order to set them alongside countervailing positions, again from a range of stances, and all of the positions in between. The aim of reviewing the Literature for critical points of view is to strengthen one's project proposal, one's discussion section, one's methodology section and one's argument and it is achieved by throwing the net wide to ensure a good catch and making use of the haul in some appropriate manner. By taking the multiplicity of critical points of view into consideration the review sets a given research project, dissertation, assignment and publication within an increasingly inclusive public space where we are all political actors making a case and formulating what is at stake.

Formulating the public space of debate

A public space takes its substance, its vitality, its power from the density of debate. If a teacher wants only the words taught to be returned unchanged, unexamined, unchallenged, then there is no density of debate, only a univocity of transmission and retransmission. In short, there is no public space without the possibility of challenge. And if there is challenge, then there is the public scene of contest – a contest that, if it is to be inclusive, socially just and valid, is to be arranged through the formulation and performance of the methodologies for debate between free and equal voices. The question is, for each voice: what is to be understood?

The question itself demands an answer that is not a mere reproduction. It has within it the seeds of a challenge to the norm – that Barthesian *doxa* (1977), Rabaté's (2002) toolkit – the status quo by disturbing and unsettling it by its demand for understanding. The *doxa*, we might say, is the authorised body of 'what is known, believed, valued' that may be transmitted as a 'teaching', a course for an examination, a mission statement for an organisation, a policy for a government; the toolkit, a beloved expression of managerialist delivery systems, that collection of authorised techniques for the production of a text, a course of action; and the status quo is the frame within which all authorised agendas are set and evaluated.

Think again of Descartes' overturning of the authorised knowledge and methods for knowing of his time. It was a revolution. It may not have been unique in the full history of human thought, but it was decisive for European thought that has become known as 'Enlightenment thinking' or 'modernity'. Its decisiveness could not be said with any kind of certainty at the time of its thinking. It could have passed unnoticed. Its meaning, its value, its significance has been written into that moment in terms of 'what it has become' for us today. This future anterior that places an always-distancing past and future together within an always-moving present is essential to naming events, events that come to have a significance. The Cartesian moment set into train a method for those who were exploring the possibilities of the method for their own interests. Although a contemporary, and influenced by Descartes, Spinoza took a different critical decision regarding the relation between mind and body that has enabled countervailing discourses to proliferate. In tracking such proliferations of authorised and countervailing discourses that are knotted in public debate, it is not a matter of making exhaustive accounts without regard to a particular problem, issue, concern or interest motivating a given text. It is a question of how the critical decisions that had been made in constructing a particular attitude, practice, field of action and domain of study impact upon contemporary discourses and practices in our everyday lives.

If there is a split between mind and body, then the framing problematic concerns their proper relation and the influence between the one and the other. If there is no split then the issue of their 'proper' relation does not apply in the same way. For Spinoza neither mind nor body were reducible to each other, but neither were they separable. Thinking is as much a power of the body as is feeling and muscular strength. Rather than the mind dominating the body or the body dominating the mind, there was a 'democracy' of powers where each was to be thought of as equal to the other. The Cartesian split could easily fit the traditional theological split between mind and body that placed the source of corruption of the spirit in the body. With the Cartesian focus on the thinking being, the source of rationality, then reason could easily be promoted over the body. With reason as Reason, then modernity could be its object and become subjected, mastered according to its designs. There is a kind of useful – if only apparent – neutrality about reason: decisions could be justified according to the necessity of reason and the progress towards a rationally produced 'good' society.

Allied to empiricism, a rational science could be produced that concerned itself only with discovering knowledge based upon the observation of the 'facts'. This accrues its own orthodoxy that becomes its *doxa* – its common opinion, its taken-for-granted knowledge or approach to gaining knowledge – through which a canonical literature (an author-doxy) is constituted. Kuhn (1970) called the development of such orthodoxies based on canonical texts 'paradigms'. Effectively, they were 'ways of seeing' as much as of acting. Over time one paradigm prevails over another and constitutes 'normal science', a domain that has sufficiently delineated its objects of inquiry, accumulated its facts, constructed widely accepted theory and identified the 'gaps', the anomalies, the key questions yet to be answered. It constitutes, therefore, in Kuhn's terms, a 'puzzle-solving' frame. This 'normal science' typically splinters into ever specialised disciplines and sub-disciplines each maintaining the overarching puzzle-solving frame. The approach to a literature review under such a frame therefore involves tracing the texts that compose the disciplines, sub-disciplines and particular problems to be solved. The dominance of such a paradigmatic frame makes it very difficult if not impossible to 'see otherwise' and thus to allow a marginal or countervailing paradigm to be understood as anything but 'non-sense'.

In order to find the critical points of challenge, not to smooth them over, but to ruffle them, increase their amplitude and threaten the orthodoxies, an approach is required that traces the disagreements, identifies the founding problematic(s) and asks what was left out. It can start by a crude tracing of the historical line of a given theme, question, issue, problem or concern. What was in discussion at the time of the emergence of the line of research can provide insights into the points of contention, the politics that favoured one approach rather than another, and the beliefs that were being threatened. In his book on scientific revolutions Kuhn showed that, historically, rather than a paradigm succeeding because of the rational case for it, it was more because the adherents of the older paradigm died, leaving the younger adherents of the new paradigm to develop it. Feyerabend, adopting a similar view, argued that often scientific theories were adopted not rationally, but because they fitted the beliefs of its proponent. Kepler, for example, believed that the sun was the symbol of God, thus it made sense to him that the planets revolved around the sun, rather than the sun revolving around the earth. When Darwin's *Origin of the Species* was published in 1859, Harris (1968) argues, it was not so much that Darwin's discoveries influenced anthropology and the emergent social sciences and, particularly, the socio-economic idea of the survival of the fittest, but that the emergent social sciences influenced Darwin. Indeed, the phrase 'survival of the fittest' is not Darwin's, but was first used by Spencer, one of the founders of sociology, and was later picked up by Darwin. Freeman (1974) considered that Darwin had clearly begun to develop his notions of 'descent with modification' from the time of the final year of the voyage of the *Beagle* and that this 'well prepared mind' was enriched by the thinking of Malthus. Freeman saw no relation between Darwin's and Spencer's ideas as such. But, as Claeys (2000) argues,

> Darwin's discoveries occasioned no revolution in social theory, but instead involved remapping, with the assistance of a theory of the biological inheritance of character traits, a preexisting structure of ideas based largely, though not exclusively, upon a Malthusian and economic metaphor of the 'struggle for existence.'
>
> (Claeys 2000)

Spencer's idea of the 'survival of the fittest' has been entwined with Darwin's views on evolution and turned into a concept of social Darwinism that has been used to justify free market competition. Although the term 'social Darwinism' was rarely used between 1916 and 1943, the use of the term exploded largely through the influence of Hofstadter, even though he used the term to critique its employment! Many have argued that, indeed, there is little of Darwin in 'social Darwinism' (Leonard 2009). Rather, Hofstadter drew on both Spencer and Sumner in his linkage and criticism of social Darwinism with *laissez-faire* markets. What Leonard (2009) shows is the complex and confusing use made of Darwin, Spencer and Sumner by supporters of free market economies over more collectivist approaches to social, political and economic governance. Although 'social Darwinism' may have little to do with Darwin's own theories, it brings into play images of struggle, the fit surviving through combat, selfishness, greed. For social Darwinism's contemporary revival, Leyva (2009) refers to the popular 'ethnologies' of those such as Ardry (1961), Morris (1967) and Tiger and Fox (1971), who 'depicted humankind as naturally aggressive, selfish, racist, and sexist'. Leyva sees such views resurfacing in neo-liberal economics and goes on to describe in particular the impact on the American policy of 'No Child Left Behind' (NCLB) developed by the Bush administration and passed into law in 2002. The upshot of this policy, it is argued, is to create the conditions for school failure in order then to argue for the introduction of schools becoming for-profit organisations left to compete in the marketplace (Huberman 2003; Trammel 2005). The 'good' schools will survive as the 'bad' schools fail. It is the free market economy applied to education, initially early childhood education. However:

> This initiative opens the way for substantial higher educational reforms, through privatization to occur not only in the world, but also in the United States, a signatory of the WTO agreements.
>
> (Torres 2008: http://newpol.org/node/283)

Stuart Hall (1980) used the term authoritarian popularism, and it is useful to explore not only how at the time Thatcher, as Prime Minister, was able to gain popular support for her attacks on working-class movements and social protections and benefits, but also to explore how, in the years of 'new Labour', attacks on personal liberties (Russell 2006) were sustained and paved the way for the Coalition Government under a conservative Prime Minster. Thus David Cameron could pick up the threads of an agenda leading to the privatisation of the National Health Service, the introduction of 'free schools' and academies to increase market competition and at the same time make substantial cuts to social and community services under the theme of the 'Big Society'. These agendas that are central to a neoliberal project of transforming nation states into capitalist-friendly markets are being systematically inscribed into all areas of public life. In many ways, it does not matter what particular political party is in power, or what particular slogan – whether the 'modernisation' of New Labour or the 'Big Society' of Cameron is used. It all amounts to the strategy of 'there is no alternative' that Thatcher employed during her years of office. Apple (2003: 4) describes how in America:

The objectives in education are the same as those which guide its economic and social welfare goals. They include the dramatic expansion of that eloquent fiction, the free market; the drastic reduction of government responsibility for social needs; the reinforcement of intensely competitive structures of mobility both inside and outside the school; the lowering of people's expectations for economic security; the 'disciplining' of culture and the body; and the popularization of what is clearly a form of Social Darwinist thinking, as the popularity only a few years ago of The Bell Curve with its claim that people of color, poor people, and women are genetically deficient so obviously and distressingly indicates.

The 'wider set of ideological commitments' described by Apple are played out across institutions in the public and private sectors constructing what may be called a hegemonic dominance through which elites are able to maintain their influence and control over key political, economic and cultural discourses and machineries of power. These discourses play a double game. They both invite and exclude; they confer validity and render invalid. At the level of a state, for example, nationality broadly confers a valid right to a voice, thus excluding foreigners and problematising immigrants. There are conceptual, theoretical and actual territorial borders to take into account in the legitimating discourses that either maintain or subvert such border making. Attempting to map the complexities involves trying to identify what has been absented in the texts constructed to support given view points. To do this, Chantler (2007: 141) picks up on a term in the literature proposed by Walter (2004):

> Within policy and academic writing on both domestic violence and citizenship or refugee studies, there are gaps at the intersections of 'race' and gender. Citizenship is closely bound with notions of 'home', belonging and security, and therefore who is perceived as being entitled to be part of 'home'. William Walters uses the analytic domopolitics (2004, p. 241) which 'at its heart is a fateful conjunction of home, land and security'. Walters acknowledges that different countries have different understandings of homeland, but most draw on common themes of home and family, home as a place of safety and refuge, thus creating a notion of insiders, of 'us', whilst simultaneously constructing the unwelcome outsider: 'Hence domopolitics embodies a tactic which juxtaposes the "warm words" (Connolly, 1995 p. 142) of community, trust, and citizenship, with the danger words of a chaotic outside – illegals, traffickers, terrorists: a game which configures things as "Us vs. Them".'

> (Walter 2004: 241)

By denigrating the 'undesirable', providing the targets for resentment and 'justifiable' anger, the implicit 'desired' is promoted as the 'ideal', the 'birthright', the 'legitimate'. The desired is 'us' as the denigrated is 'them'. This double voice creates the conditions for a phantomised public that feeds back the opinions articulated in the popular news media as 'our' opinions. Once in place it renders all other discourses 'unserious' and inaudible as meaningful. They are rendered 'mindless'. The term 'domopolitics' creates a re-focusing to render connections visible that narratively produces an 'us' separated from a 'them'. It is a step towards reformulating a space of debate enabling silenced, demonised and vulnerable voices to be brought on stage where demands can be heard. There is a twofold task in creating re-focusing tactics and strategies to enable a greater range of voices. The one is to show how phenomena are composed and aligned under 'sides'; the second is to re-align in ways that erode the antagonisms that silence, denigrate and dismiss voices.

A review of the literature, then, begins with what may be called a stripped-down public where voices are excluded if, for example, they are found to demand more than the elites are willing to give. It identifies what counts as an effective 'public' that is, let's say, a public composed only of the decision-making business elites who through their corporate interests control entire industries. The kinds of texts that proliferate each drive the concepts, the practices, the forms of organisation into every field of action: academic, professional, political, economic, cultural, news media, public relations, everyday discourses. Leading members from each field of action provide a *dramatis personae* representing voices in a public presentation of the 'real'. Their multiple texts reinforce each other to give the semblance of an evidentially based picture in the head. How can it be challenged?

It cannot be challenged unless there is a public that includes alternative views that has access to the machineries of governance in politics, the legislature, the military in all its internal and external forms and the market place. Adopting a neo-liberal extreme, the stripped-down public is a world fictionally characterised by Ayn Rand's *Atlas Shrugged*, a world wherein the public is minimal and equated with 'socialism', 'welfare', 'dependency'. As such, the public is the burden carried by the great capitalists, each one a Rand-style Atlas. In Rand's circle was the former Federal Reserve Chairman Alan Greenspan. He commented in his autobiography about the real influence the book and the philosophy of Ayn Rand had on him. Rubin in *The New York Times* (September 15, 2007) saw it as 'one of the most influential business books ever written'. This influence on the economic policy adopted in relation to the contemporary financial crises were explored in an article by Shlaes in *Bloomberg Businessweek* (2011) by inserting a recent paper by Greenspan alongside extracts from *Atlas Shrugged*. As such Rand's book provides a potent narrative of American market capitalists whose talent and work are described as literally shouldering the world. When Obama became President, at the height of the financial crisis, sales of this book, first published in 1957 rocketed (*The Economist*, February 26, 2009 http://www.economist. com/ node/ 13185404). Rand developed essentially a 'utopia of greed', a view of the market dominated by corporate wealth and the giants of capitalism unfettered by 'society' – a view that entwined with Margaret Thatcher's famous interview where she gave her opinion that public help for people had gone too far, saying: '"I have a problem, I will go and get a grant to cope with it!" "I am homeless, the Government must house me!" and so they are casting their problems on society, and who is society? There is no such thing!' (Thatcher, 1987: Interview for *Women's Own*: http://www.margaretthatcher.org/document/106689).

Rather than a neo-liberal focus on the profit motive, self-interest, or, in Rand's terms, greed, for Thatcher in her interview there is a smaller focus – not so much the Atlas as the small but self-sufficient individual and the family for which he or she is responsible. This has a more neo-conservative flavour of 'traditional' values that focus on self-responsibility, working hard to achieve, family and being a good neighbour. It evokes a sense of the 'good' poor and the 'bad' poor'. Such a return to conservative values are typically seen as an antidote to the excesses of neo-liberal unregulated or 'free' markets driven by profit, self-interest and, indeed, greed in Rand's sense. The line between self-interest being good and being bad is always problematic in the relation between the neo-liberalism that propels markets and the neo-conservativism that is called upon in the management of relationships between people, governments and elites. Implicit in Thatcher's interview is not so much that there is no society, but that helping others depends on first helping yourself. The wealth would then 'trickle down' to the poor. Unfortunately, the experience of 'trickle down' has rather been 'flood up'. Over the period from 1980–2011 there has been a reversal of trends in terms of the gap between the poor and the rich. Indeed, an article by Stigliz, the Nobel prize-winning economist, points out that in America:

> The upper 1 percent of Americans are now taking in nearly a quarter of the nation's income every year. In terms of wealth rather than income, the top 1 percent control 40 percent. Their lot in life has improved considerably.
>
> (Stiglitz 2011)

A similar story is told in the UK, where a report by the Trades Union Congress (TUC) showed that the rich–poor gap was widening and had been doing so since the middle 1970s:

> The report found a 'sharp divide' in earnings growth between different professions, with medical practitioners enjoying a 153% pay rise since the late 1970s and over 100% for judges, barristers and solicitors.
>   The wages of bakers fell by 1% in the same period, by 5% for forklift truck drivers and 3% for packers and bottlers, the TUC said.
>
> (*The Guardian*, June 6, 2011)

More generally, worldwide, 'Social injustice is killing people on a grand scale' (2008 WHO report). Such views seem to provide a counter voice. They gesture to alternative literatures that test out claims and find them lacking, contradictory or having injurious consequences.

The discourses and the practices that 'write' this injustice throughout the world, it has been variously argued, are attributable to the economic, political, legal and law enforcement machinery shaped by free market philosophies that underpin freedom without equality and draw upon 'social Darwinian' views of the survival of the fittest. The literature supporting this 'voice' is now extensive (see, for example, Harvey; Norton; Klein). The issue is the extent to which there is a real space of debate between competing views. To what extent do the countervailing discourses circulating in the economic, political and philosophical literatures inscribe themselves in the talk that is then produced in the day-to-day lives and practices of people? This will be taken up more fully in the following chapters. However, a first draft of what is at stake in the move from the identification of competing literatures to the formation of a real space for public debate can be illustrated by the political and media responses to the UK riots in August 2011. Following a meeting of the emergency committee, known as Cobra, to plan strategy, David Cameron said:

> It is all too clear that we have a big problem with gangs in our country. Continued violence is simply not acceptable and it will be stopped. We will not put up with this in our country. We will not allow a culture of fear to exist on our streets ...
>
> But there are pockets of our society that are not just broken but are frankly sick. When we see children as young as 12 and 13 looting and laughing, when we see the disgusting sight of an injured young man with people pretending to help him while they are robbing him, it is clear that there are things that are badly wrong in our society. For me the root cause of this mindless selfishness is the same thing that I have spoken about for years. It is a complete lack of responsibility in parts of our society, people allowed to feel that the world owes them something, that their rights outweigh their responsibilities and that their actions do not have consequences. Well, they do have consequences.
>
> (Cameron, extract of speech August 10, 2011)

The debates necessary to map and review the underlying conditions that increase the likelihood of violence are curtailed by such a political response and by the media responses that sought to close down alternative explanations. The BBC (The Competing Arguments used to Explain the Riots, 2011 http://www.bbc.co.uk/news/magazine-14483149), for example, provided a summary of some of the different views put forward as explanations of the riots. Not all of these were seriously in the political frame as a basis for decision-making. Thus the analysis of the riots was already prefigured – or framed – in the voices that were in the political decision-making roles. Each voice that has a political decision-making role can claim its history, its evidence and its theoretical and methodological resources. But the histories of the gangs are long and little has changed to improve the alternative prospects of the young people drawn into gangs over the decades (e.g. Thrasher; Patrick; Pearson; Schostak 1983, 2012). To open up the chances for real change in their families, their neighbourhoods, their communities requires an opening to the range of perspectives, theories and understandings that can be brought to bear in the space of public debate where decisions are made.

The political responses to the riots cannot be heard without echoes of Thatcher's *Women's Own* interview and its resonance with the range of neo-liberal and neo-conservative discourses dominating the machineries of markets, policing and contemporary economic and political policy making. Such texts overlay each other, not necessarily consistently, but weaving together discourses, texts and practices required for the operation of these machineries. This overlaying of texts where one text draws upon, echoes, reinforces or elaborates another is often referred to as 'intertextuality'. In effect, intertextuality de-thrones the status of a given author or speaker as the sole reference point of authority for the meaning of a text or discourse. That is, for a given text there are other texts, elsewhere, that are required for a fuller – or in some views 'truer' – reading or interpretation. Riffaterre called the hidden text a hypogram (1978). Balibar and Althusser looked for this other text inspired by a Freudian reading of symptoms. Each is looking in a sense for the single true code to unlock a particular repressed, hidden or displaced meaning. It was Kristeva (1984) who coined the more expansive term 'intertextuality' to refer to a profusion of potentially interrelating texts. Even where one text negates another, the juxtaposition of texts – whether on the surface of debate or hidden – conditions the possibilities for debate and interpretation. The role of intertextuality and how it is managed to produce decision- and action-shaping discourses will be developed further in the following chapters. However, for the purposes here, a review of the literature is never enough. The review can set out the range of competing voices, the research and evidence upon which their views are based, the theoretical frameworks and the philosophical principles. But it is the power to be heard that counts. A blog comment by an NBC reporter, Nick Fletcher, nicely illustrates the management of what is seen and what it takes to be heard:

> LONDON – As political and social protests grip the Middle East, are growing in Europe and a riot exploded in north London this weekend, here's a sad truth, expressed by a Londoner when asked by a television reporter: Is rioting the correct way to express your discontent?
>
> 'Yes,' said the young man. 'You wouldn't be talking to me now if we didn't riot, would you?'
>
> The TV reporter from Britain's ITV had no response. So the young man pressed his advantage. 'Two months ago we marched to Scotland Yard, more than 2,000 of us, all blacks, and it was peaceful and calm and you know what? Not a word in the press. Last night a bit of rioting and looting and look around you.'
>
> (Nick Fletcher, Blog undated; http://worldblog.msnbc.msn.com/_ news / 2011/08/07/7292281-the-sad-truth-behind-london-riot#. Tj83Lj9oMJR.twitter)

The riots opened a space for 'seeing', but what is seen depends upon the contextual discourses used to 'read' and the courses of action adopted depend on who has access to the machineries of decision-making and to the execution of action.

In the mass news media, the political fora, the organisations of State governance, the corporate-dominated markets, the voices arguing for alternative narratives for the production of the good life are effectively crowded out of the available expert forums and institutions through which resources are allocated. Rioting may be seen as a short-lived and symbolic process of re-distributing economic resources, or it may be seen as 'mindless violence'. It may be seen as the eruption of simmering anger against daily injustice or as a breakdown in traditional moral values. Each view can be brought into debate. What are the literatures that go with each view? What are their arguments, their methodologies of 'proof', or at least of providing supporting evidence? The development of shared knowledge about the world proceeds co-extensively with the production of a vital public space where disagreements are the focus of debate and voices are heard and taken into account. It is the quality of the public space more than the quality of the individual researcher's beliefs that is critical to the quality of the knowledge that is shared. That quality depends on the extent to which voices are included, heard and taken into account. Voices may be discounted as 'not serious'. Rail (2011) points to the American media managing dissenting voices by calling them 'not serious'. In particular, he instanced the Green political activist Ralph Nader not being allowed to participate in televised presidential debates because he was not important enough, albeit drawing 'enough liberal votes away from Al Gore to cost him the state of Florida' (Rail 2011). It seems, then, that if the public is to become more than Lippmann's 'phantom public' shaped by the PR industry, reproducing its discourses as if they were its own, all voices must be treated as 'serious'. Rather than the limited range of real dissent in public debate, the public becomes composed not with a uniform thread stretching without break from first to last stitch, but through a criss-crossing of voices that challenge, seduce, threaten and compromise producing tangles perhaps more often than the occasional smooth surface. The narrative of progress would have it that these tangles can be undone and replaced by rigorously tested and accredited knowledge. However, rather than a narrative of progress, there may be narratives to be drawn into debates where disagreements are welcomed as evidence of a thriving democracy and of cultural diversity and creative productivity (Rancière 1999). It is this latter possibility that enables the development of a critical rather than a phantom public.

Underwriting the public and the critical others

If the public is to exist effectively as a sphere of debate and decision-making that takes into account all voices underwritten by the literatures that have been historically produced in mutually critical debates, then what is the politics required to underpin its possibility and its realisation in practice?

Rancière (2005) distinguishes between two forms of the political – le politique and la politique. The first is the politics of administration, a settled politics of everyday policy making and policy applying normality. The second arises in the disagreements, the challenges, the eruptions in the normal where, at least for a moment, a space is created where everything could change. This provides two ways in which a public can be underwritten. Something of the potential and the dilemma can be illustrated by the Humanities Curriculum Project (HCP), a project directed by Lawrence Stenhouse that had considerable influence in the late 1960s and 1970s in the UK (Stenhouse 1975; Rudduck 1983). The point of interest is the construction of the public space for debate between the students who were principally reluctant and disaffected with schools. All voices were to be valued and subject to rational debate based upon evidence. Teachers were placed in the position of being the 'neutral chair', ensuring the rules of debate, ensuring all who wanted to speak could speak and present their views but never providing their own judgements as to the merits of one view over another. Debate and evidence were critical. However, as one experienced HCP teacher put it, 'What about the little fascist at the back of the class?' This was our friend and colleague Bev Labbett, who thought long and hard about the key principles that should underlie learning together. He called it 'sensitive neglect' (1988). For him, the challenge point for HCP was whether or not to allow the fascist voice. To allow it was offensive. Not to allow it broke the principles governing the public space of debate.

The political question is who is 'in' and who is 'out'? For Carl Schmitt (1996) and Leo Strauss (1988), both influential in the development of the neo-conservative political philosophies that have underwritten the domestic and foreign policies of Western liberal market democracies (Norton, Klein), the political begins with identifying 'friends' and 'enemies'. In the context of neo-liberal arguments concerning socialism and 'Big Government' being the enemy of free markets (Hayek 1944; Friedman 1962; Rand 1957, 1992), the battle lines are drawn as to what constitutes the 'good society'. The challenge point to this reduction to 'either/or' politics is 'All', that is, what Badiou (2005) would call the One-many. There is then a counter philosophical literature that can be historically traced and called upon where a new beginning for thinking the public can be founded.

It is a literature that challenges the split produced by Cartesian methodology between thinking and the passions of the body, between the mind and the physical world that echoed the spirit–flesh split of Christianity amongst other religions, as well as the traditional male–female split in many of the world's dominant cultures aligning the male with Reason and the Female with Feeling and in many cases with sinfulness or corruptibility. Spinozan thought has adopted an approach that sees the mind and body together, not reducible to each other, but co-equal. Being human means having the power of thinking just as much as the power of feeling, of creating a mental world of expression and representation just as much as acting in a world of others. It is echoed in the domain of Merleau-Ponty's political which *is* grounded upon 'the consequence of our being embodied actors within an intercorporeal milieu' (Coole 2008: 90). For Merleau-Ponty there is a 'non-Cartesian process whereby meaning and matter are irreducibly entwined' leading to the embodiment of political actors and to the inevitability that 'the ineluctable presence of the non-rational must be considered' (Coole 2008: 89). Giving primacy to perception and arguing that reason in action is inseparable from the corporeal provenance allows him to dismiss 'the kind of dualist presuppositions that underpin rationalist regimes', to decry the 'violent and inefficacious politics that relies on subject–object opposition, and that alternates between idealist and objectivist approaches to collective life' and to offer a challenge 'in the name of the lifeworld where co-existence appears and intersubjectivity is forged' (Coole 2008; 89–90).

The public as an intersubjective space is also in this Spinozan-like view a space of powers. It is the dynamic arrangement of powers, how they are associated with each other in social organisations to accomplish goals. Rather than machineries that impose upon people, shaping their powers in the interests of a few, people are free to underwrite their own frameworks, agendas, forms of organisation and courses of action in public spaces of debate. However, such a space is repressed in relation to the dominant formations of public space, the spaces of crowds, herds, organised labour and the disciplining of children to accept obedience as a norm. These are the everyday spaces that 'everybody sees', 'everybody knows', everybody takes as 'normal', 'real', 'the way it is'. Each depends on the other not to challenge, subvert or introduce the radically different. The normal has its texts and its discourses to underwrite the sense of predictability through which the 'real' is sustained. For example, after the early weeks of protest of the Arab Spring people longed for a return to 'normality', that is, the normality of trading, home life, work and having a social life. It is a 'normality' underwritten by power-as-usual. After the ninth day of protest Al Jazeera reported calls from the Egyptian army for protestors to 'return to normal life' with military spokesman Ismail Etman saying:

> The army forces are calling on you ... You began by going out to express your demands and you are the ones capable of restoring normal life.
>
> I call on the conscious youth of Egypt, honest men of Egypt, we should look forward to future, think of our country, Egypt. Your message has been heard, demands understood, and we are working day and night to secure our homeland for your interest, the honourable people of Egypt.
> (Al Jazeera February 2, 2011; http://english.aljazeera.net/news/middl eeast/2011/02/20112210516616914.html)

Although in Egypt the army was held in high regard by the people, the protests continued. This popular status enjoyed by the army was used by the protestors chanting that the people and the army were hand in hand (see for example Naiman 2011), a strategy that continued after the fall of Mubarak as the protestors attempted to save their revolution (see for example Al Jazeera August 13, 2011a). For them, a 'normal life' without rights, without the hopes for freedoms for which many sacrificed their lives, was unthinkable. However, the military presented a resistant reality that could oppose as well as support. As an organisation and disciplining of the powers of people-as-soldiers, the ability of leaders to control the army can be ultimately challenged by an appeal by 'protesters-as-people' to the soldiers as 'people'. There is a sense of 'sameness' underwriting the social differences as between 'soldiers' and 'protestors' just as within the protestors occupying Tahrir Square there were people of different faiths, occupations, social classes and generations. This 'sameness', this essential equality, was necessary to underwrite the demands for freedom, for democracy.

As a key theme in the production of the public – whether as a phantom public or as an effective public – 'normality' cannot be understood without exploring the ways textuality is organised through the various forms in which people's powers to underwrite their social worlds dynamically interact. The key words, key themes and issues and the framing discourses and texts of 'normality' that emerged from the agendas of people, military and government, form the lines of exploration that can be taken whilst searching and sorting the historical literatures that are produced in public debates. The possible lines of enquiry and exploration vary widely. They can be the straightforwardly linear as in disciplinary and sub-disciplinary academic debate. Or they may spin off tangentially, playing with meanings, crossing disciplinary boundaries, dissolving boundaries, then returning to and re-framing starting points with new views, creating new nets to be cast across the scenes of debate(s) in attempts to fix and represent something of the

> pell-mell ensemble of bodies and minds, promiscuity of visages, words, actions, with, between them all, that cohesion which cannot be denied them since they are all differences, extreme divergences of one same something.
>
> (Merleau-Ponty 1968: 84)

It is this play of irreducible differences, this multiplicity, that underlies the textuality of the 'same' human world. It is this textuality that can be mapped for the literatures defining particular historically composed issues, problems, themes. There is a textuality to be reviewed for challenge points. These challenge points build the capacity for an analysis that is inclusive of voices in debate.

Gestures towards writing

If ethnography writes the people as an expression of the collective powers to think, imagine, feel, act and produce, then it opens the way for constituting the people as a public. The arrangements through which the powers of people are organised determine the extent to which the public is effective or phantom. It is a *dramatis personae* of powers, their organisation and their effectiveness on behalf of all or some of the people.

A case study set up to explore the intersubjective relations between people as they organise in some endeavour in the context of the broader ethnographic description maps out the *dramatis personae* and their actions towards each other, their use of resources, their practices, their forms of organisation and the boundaries they establish or break. What then are the literatures that are explicitly or implicitly drawn upon to justify or attack their actions, their forms of organisation and the kinds of relations and identities they establish, value, denigrate, silence or deny? There are prior histories of texts and discourses about text through which key ideas, visions, philosophies of political, economic and social organisation impact on everyday behaviour. Which are included and which excluded?

A space for public debate, decision-making and action is vital for any form of action research. An ethnography may be undertaken that shows how a people organises or inhibits organisation to create a practice, an organisation and spaces for debate. Action research then focuses on the possibilities for action being undertaken to meet stated objectives. Writing reviews the literatures to identify how the possibilities for action is either enabled or inhibited. Action within a radical research design (Schostak and Schostak 2008) seeks to democratise debate, decision-making and action in all forms of social organisation. It thus sets in motion an evaluation of action in relation to the principles of democratic inclusion in the creation of a public space as essential to all forms of social organisation. Radical writing draws then upon the literatures of democratic philosophy, theory and practice in relation to the competing or agonistically opposed literatures and the observed practices of ethnographies, case studies, action research and radical research weaving the literature alongside the discourses and representations of everyday life to underwrite the creation of an effective public.

Chapter 4

Analysis and the deconstruction of realities – working/synthesising data

What is the purpose of analysis? Analysis, on the one hand, is a process of clarifying the meanings, the nature, the functions of the key 'phenomena' or 'objects' of study. On the other, it involves a process of breaking down what was complex into something that is considered 'simpler', more 'primordial' or 'essential'. Analytic categories are thus the result of decisions made about how to cut up the world – or worlds – to make it amenable for science as a structure of knowledge. It is through such 'cutting up' that data emerges as something that can be perceived (mentally/physically) and made to count as having its place in the 'real'. As Kuhn (1970) and others have pointed out, what counts as data having a reality for theoretical and practical purposes under one paradigm may simply vanish or be reduced to nonsense, fiction or fantasy under another. Thus if it can be argued that key ways of categorising what counts as data are not as clear as believed, then whole structures of theory and 'knowledge' that depend on those categorisations are at stake. In short, what has been taken as 'real' may be threatened.

Whatever the real is, it is experienced as 'there', or rather 'there and here', and there are no gaps through which a hand may poke to see what is behind 'it'. Eyes open and it is there. Eyes closed and the sensation of 'it' is all about inseparable from but distinguishable from an 'in here'. It is as if there is an all-surrounding, all-pervasive screen upon which sensations unceasingly flicker producing the sense of the 'real', the something that is always there and within which 'I am'. Without memory there is not much sense.

Freud wrote of 'screen memories' which involved traces and overlays in the conscious and unconscious systems of the mental apparatus. The metaphor begins with the 'mystic writing pad'. This was a recent invention at the time that Freud saw as a way of expressing the relation between the system for the conscious perception of the world and the system that in effect 'stored' the impressions made by the senses. There were two 'systems' or "parts' to the apparatus: the first, the transparent celluloid sheet, which overlaid the second, a brown wax.

The transparent sheet itself was in two detachable layers, with the lower layer being in contact with the slab of wax. With a stylus marks could be made on the upper surface which then left impressions on the wax. To erase or 'destroy' what had been written the double sheet covering the wax was raised. The two-layered system covering the wax thus had an upper surface upon which marks could be made without leaving any permanent trace, but acting as a protective layer, and a lower, more fragile layer that actually received the marks. Those marks could be seen only as long as the two surfaces remained in undisturbed contact with the wax block below. Lifted away from the block the traces would vanish. However,

> it is easy to discover that the permanent trace of what was written is retained upon the wax slab itself and is legible in suitable lights. Thus the Pad provides not only a receptive surface that can be used over and over again, like a slate, but also permanent traces of what has been written, like an ordinary paper pad: it solves the problem of combining the two functions by dividing them between two separate but interrelated component parts or systems.
>
> (Freud 1925: 211).

It thus provided a model for thinking about and also communicating Freud's ideas concerning the relation between the systems that deal with the immediate sense impressions and the systems that record these more permanently.

> We need not be disturbed by the fact that in the Mystic Pad no use is made of the permanent traces of the notes that have been received; it is enough that they are present. There must come a point at which the analogy between an auxiliary apparatus of this kind and the organ which is its prototype will cease to apply. It is true, too, that, once the writing has 'been erased, the Mystic Pad cannot "reproduce" it from within; it would be a mystic pad indeed if, like our memory, it could accomplish that. None the less, I do not think it is too far-fetched to compare the celluloid and waxed paper cover with the system Pcpt.-Cs. and its protective shield, the wax slab with the unconscious behind them, and the appearance and disappearance of the writing with the flickering-up and passing-away of consciousness in the process of perception.
>
> (Freud 1925: 211)

At the level of Freud's perception-consciousness (Pcpt.-Cs.) system, there are simply the impacts of external stimuli. James (1890: 462), writing of the newborn baby, postulated that initial experiences of the world about would be 'one great blooming, buzzing confusion'. What then creates the conditions for sense, order, coherence?

There are, of course, many theories. There are those that look for innate faculties or say a genetic code that necessarily processes the stimuli to bring order. Others see the order arising externally and imprinting upon a '*tabula rasa*', a clean slate, or interaction with external conditions shaping behaviour through a process of reward and punishment. Or it may be some combination of all. For Arendt, it is the appearance to consciousness that is significant:

> The world men are born into contains many things, natural and artificial, living and dead, transient and sempiternal, all of which have in common that they appear and hence are meant to be seen, heard, touched, tasted and smelled, to be perceived by sentient creatures endowed with the appropriate sense organs. Nothing could appear, the word 'appearance' would make no sense if recipients of appearances did not exist – living creatures able to acknowledge, recognize and react to – in flight or desire, approval or disapproval, blame or praise – what is not merely there but appears to them and is meant for their perception. In this world which we enter, appearing from a nowhere, and from which we disappear into a nowhere, Being and Appearing coincide.
>
> (Arendt 1978: 19)

Acknowledging, recognising and reacting are essential for the creation of a living, shared, intersubjective world. These are processes by which people attend to something that appears in common to each. According to Arendt, then, we live in a world of appearances where we appear to others and others appear to us, and whilst, in some senses, we can appear to ourselves this 'would never suffice to guarantee reality' (Arendt 1978: 19–20). Acknowledging presupposes that something has been marked out, recognising it means that it has been noticed and marked before and can be again. And reacting to the something that has been marked out accords it an objectivity, a being there or here in a way that can be touched, handled, approached or avoided – it assumes in each case an embodiment of some sort that through the actions and reactions, mutual recognitions and acknowledgements of what is seen, heard, felt generates a sense of the real. In short, a world of appearances calls for spectators, and therefore:

> nothing that is, insofar as it appears, exists in the singular; everything that is is meant to be perceived by somebody. Not Man, but men inhabit this planet. Plurality is the law of the earth.
>
> (Arendt 1978: 19)

Already in this text there is something odd, something that jars and is out of date. It is the language category 'man' as an unproblematic general category for lumping together all human beings regardless of gender. Already, the text itself has called out a reaction. The contemporary audience as a category has emerged, say, from about the late 1960s or from the 1970s as a consequence of the increasing influence of feminist criticisms and critiques of male-oriented discourses through which the everyday is framed to accord greater power to male agendas. Even the term 'world' itself is etymologically derived from ver (man) and ald (age) meaning 'man age', that is, the age of man as distinct from the age of nature before the emergence of people. In recognising ourselves and our own distinctiveness we recognise the other as the non-living and its many forms. Our categories by which we identify ourselves in relation to others and to the other as 'not us' as Arendt points out make sense only if there is a plurality that cannot be reduced to One alone. It is through the plurality that the multiple recognitions, acknowledgements and reactions create and re-create a world. And in this play of recognitions, acknowledgements and reactions language does not simply mediate – it creates, produces and reproduces as sensory experiences are formulated into the key categories through which the world and its parts are named and organised into relationships.

Every discourse has what we call its analytics, its system of categories together with the codes by which distinctions are made between a 'this' and a 'that', thus forming entities that can be deposited into classes and sub-classes until some singular entity is recognised as being 'unique', 'individual' and is nameable as such in relation to other unique, individual, singular beings that together compose the 'plurality', the 'multitude', or indeed the people rather than People. Analytic categories are produced because they are useful to someone for some reason in relation to managing their 'world', that is their intersubjective relations to others and the physical world that is 'other to people' but is humanised through being named. Finally, in order to manage everyday life, every analytics has its own operationalising framework that a given agenda calls into play. This logic of relationships as between discourse, analytics, framing and agenda is what we refer to as the dispositif of everyday power. It will be developed further in the following chapters. However, since they are interrelated, each dimension of the dispositif will be implicated even if one term is privileged during discussion over the others.

Discourses and their analytics

A first crude distinction may be made between ordinary language analytics and those formal analytics that involves the languages of logic, mathematics and statistics. A helpful Wikipedia (2012) definition of what we mean by formal analytics is: 'Analytics is the application of computer technology, operational research, and statistics to solve problems in business and industry.' Analytics here has been framed by the agendas employing mathematical sciences in conjunction with market decision-making agendas. The definition, however, in itself, cannot be understood except as variously framed by a multitude of ordinary language analytics that find a use in some way for the formal analytics.

A key issue is that of naming a phenomenon. At times it is critical in terms of how to act. In the case of the UK riots in August 2011, after a quiet protest outside a police station concerning the lack of information in relation to the police shooting of Mark Duggan, rioting began:

> The BBC, for one, began last weekend by calling them 'protesters', presumably because the initial rioting in Tottenham on Saturday was, or

appeared to be, a protest at the lack of a satisfactory police response to questions about the death of Mark Duggan. It was a term the corporation continued to use for at least two further days, drawing a small storm of criticism from members of the public who took to Twitter to express their disapproval.

'Why do the press keep calling the rioters here protesters?' asked Linda Keen. 'They're not protesting about or for anything.'

Rob Steadman agreed: 'This has nothing to do with protest.'

In similar vein, Ed Gerstner demanded: 'Seriously, @BBCnews, stop calling these people protesters. They're criminals, or rioters. But not protesters.'

(John Henley, *The Guardian*, 10 August 2011)

Henley began his article recalling that 'One man's terrorist is another man's freedom fighter.' However, the question of whether these were protestors, or whether the riots were in anyway legitimate, was soon largely resolved throughout the mass media in favour of using a variety of terms like 'criminal', 'thug' and 'hooligan':

The tabloids, in any event, have had few linguistic qualms. 'Copycat cretins' was how Metro described the rioters on Wednesday. The Mirror opted for 'gangs of mindless yobs', the Daily Mail 'anarchists', and the Sun 'morons', 'thugs' and 'idiots'.

(John Henley, *The Guardian*, August 10, 2011)

Such terminology keys into a long-standing discourse and fear of mobs, crowds, hooligans and, as Brace called them, the 'dangerous classes' (see, for example, Brace 1872; Humphries 1981; Pearson 1983; Schostak 1983, 1986, 1993; Shelden 2001). It is in turn a discourse that leads to further discourses of retribution and of how in the longer term to manage them.

The two major political parties on the 'right' and the 'left' of the governing elites had to show unity in relation to the media's representation of the public mood and also to distinguish themselves from each other. Formulating his response around his chosen theme, 'the broken society', Cameron made a speech in which he said:

On schools, welfare, families, parenting, addiction, communities; on the cultural, legal, bureaucratic problems in our society, too, from the twisting and misrepresenting of human rights that has undermined personal responsibility, to the obsession with health and safety that has eroded people's willingness to act according to common sense – and consider whether our plans and programmes are big enough and bold enough to deliver the change that I feel this country now wants to see.

(Stratton 2011)

This is a speech that has hooks into the key discourses of his target – broadly, conservative, right-wing-leaning audiences – and is framed by neo-liberal economic philosophies and neo-conservative social and political philosophies that identify the cause of social problems generally with too much public expenditure creating a dependency culture as well as 'broken' core social values.

The alternative discourse by the Labour Party leader shifts the focus towards material conditions produced by economic policies:

> The Labour leader will also taunt the prime minister, saying that when Cameron was developing his analysis of 'broken Britain' in opposition he acknowledged that deprivation mattered as much as culture in explaining antisocial behaviour.
>
> Miliband will say: 'I don't understand why he has changed his mind. The world hasn't changed. Maybe it isn't his view of the world that has changed, but his view of what would make him popular that has changed. I am clear: both culture and deprivation matter. To explain is not to excuse. But to refuse to explain is to condemn to repeat.'
>
> (Stratton, 2011)

The question is, then, which one of these analytics will find legitimation from 'the public' to enable acceptance of the proposed policy solutions?

How these categories are arranged in order to create sense and formulate 'reasons' and processes of reasoning depend on how categories are formulated, the extent to which the boundaries between categories are durable and resistant to erosion and how reasons and reasoning come to be recognised, acknowledged and actionable. An analytics, then, is not given. It is a work of construction between multiple viewpoints. It is not the work of an individual subjectivity, but of a plurality of subjects engaged in constituting an intersubjective domain as the grounding condition for thinking, knowing, valuing, feeling and acting. The analytics itself is not a thing outside of intersubjectivity but establishes a relation to what appears to consciousness as an intersubjectively recognisable field of experience. This appearance is, as Arendt writes, what it seems to be since we are both subjects and objects inasmuch as we perceive and are perceived at the same time. Living creatures 'make their appearance' and in this appearance this '[s]eeming – the it-seems-to-me, dokei moi – is the mode' (Arendt 1978: 21). And 'Seeming corresponds to the fact that every appearance, its identity notwithstanding, is perceived by a plurality of spectators' (Arendt 1978: 21).

In this work of becoming public for a plurality of spectators, there are two aspects for Arendt: an 'appearingness' and 'a kind of disguise'. Another way of saying this, perhaps, is to refer to a phenomenology of appearances that are always, as a nudge towards Sartre, an appearance of something for someone in a ground or context of 'a plurality of spectators'. For Sartre there is this 'directedness' that is the hallmark of consciousness, what in Husserlian phenomenology is referred to as 'intentionality'. It is in directing attention towards a 'something' that a world of objects of consciousness is produced through their appearances. Whether it is a 'table' or a 'person' attention is directed towards, the manifold appearances of the 'same thing' as perspective is changed, as the senses from touch to sight, to smell to hearing are all employed to build up a picture of this 'something' that remains the 'same' throughout all the variations of perspective and sensual experience of it. It is such a multidimensional process of being directed to what appears that the subject's own patterns of thinking, feeling, seeing, being, acting are woven into the ground of intersubjectivity as a sense of increasing familiarity, of becoming and being at home. It is this 'home' or field of familiarity – or, as Bourdieu (1977) called it, 'habitus' – that is mapped out through the networks of intentionality (Schostak 2002: 79–80; 2010; Schostak and Schostak 2008: 88–90) that binds individual to individual and their physical environments into a shared, or sharable, picture of the 'real':

> If we consider the whole scale of human activities from the viewpoint of appearance, we find many degrees of manifestation. Neither labouring nor fabrication requires display of the activity itself; only action and speaking need a space of appearance – as well as people who see and hear – in order to be actualized at all.
>
> (Arendt 1978: 72)

In thinking of this whole scale of human activities, Arendt signals a connection to her tripartite division made in her book *The Human Condition* (1998) of human activities into labour, work (fabrication) and action. In labour people are merely involved in satisfying their biological needs, but in work they are fabricating a human world of things like tools and homes. Only in action, she argues, do people think about, debate and take decisions concerning what kind of politics they want in order to build the kind of society they want. In this view, then, there are three kinds of intentional relationship made to the world about. In her view, they are hierarchically ordered with labour at the bottom and action at the top. Drawing upon Arendt's work, Dejours (1998) argues that work involves the other two and that they are therefore not separate or really hierarchically ordered. Thus work also satisfies biological needs and incorporates activities that are 'merely' the labour directed to, say, 'searching', 'going and fetching', 'catching' and so on as the material required for work; that is, activities directed to making things like tools, furniture, building. And work requires the development of skills, the passing on of knowledge and the exchange of insight, ideas and plans. Work, then, demands not just the skills of fabrication, but attention has also to be directed towards how to arrange the work process itself, how to ensure that people's knowledge and ideas are voiced, heard and acted upon. These are the very acts involved in what Arendt calls 'action', the political level of human engagement. That is to say, in the work process itself, the political is already embryonically emerging. Indeed, work as an outwardly facing public activity can be said to be the foundation of the political. As such, it is the condition for the emergence and the intersubjective realisation of analytics.

Engaging with work and its analytics in this expanded sense, the life of the mind itself is 'sheer activity' (Arendt 1978: 72). The sole clue to its outward manifestation is, as Arendt says, absent-mindedness where during thought an individual appears to withdraw from the world of appearances and be 'bending back towards the self' (Arendt 1978: 22). There is then a critical relation between the internal and external. Whilst this is difficult to account for by virtue of its invisibility and its sheer non-appearance, it – as a time-out and of almost disappearing back on the self – does not negate our being in and of a world of appearances. Can invisible and soundless mental activities ever 'find an adequate home in the world' (Arendt 1978: 23)? The work of analytics is just this attempt to make a home. This theme will be taken up in the following chapters. Here it is noted that thoughts and 'home' are in a sense neither 'inside' nor 'outside'. Mental activity has the characteristic that Lacan called extimacy. This is a combination that for one set of purposes can be called 'intimate' and for another 'external' – hence combing the two: extimate. In particular, that most human of activities. 'language,' is experienced as utterly intimate within one's thoughts but also as external since it is the shared resource of people. Any category of language and its analytic unfolding is already both inner and outer, both intimately of oneself but with a history of use pre-dating, its particular use and open to use by others far remote in time and space from the individual. It is in this sense that the individual is inscribed by language and textualised by the texts, discourses and analytics of others. In short, the invisibility and non-appearance of mental activities is made to appear through the medium of language in public spaces fabricated textually, discursively, analytically. It was, in various ways and at various times, this recognition of the 'extimate' nature of language that brought about what has been termed the linguistic turn in the study of people and their culture and society.

Simple observation is insufficient. As Mead (1934) pointed out, observation of a person's action is not by itself enough to reveal what it means. Weber (Heydebrand 1994) saw that Durkheimian (1938) 'social facts' were not enough. It is what those facts 'mean' to a given people at a given time. Dilthy (1977), rather than taking geometry or the mathematical sciences as the model for the study of social forms, drew inspiration from history in order to explore what a proper method for the social sciences might be like. Indeed, as Arendt pointed out, no mental act – thinking, imagining, reflecting – is ever 'content with its object as it is given to it' (Arendt 1978: 73) but transcends it in 'an experiment of the self with itself' (Arendt 1978: 74). In that sense, an analytics is always discontent with itself in the realm of thinking as in the realm of inter-subjective debate and action. The objects of the material world do not have such volition nor miscontent with its nature. Public life, then, is better thought of as a collective work of constant writing of the analytics of people into being rather than a simple given of observational analysis. Thus, the analytics explored here is co-derived from and co-extensive with the experience of engaging one's powers with others in a public work towards some end. It is in that sense always an emergent and transcending framework, transcending in the sense of going beyond the given of observation. There is in this emergence and transcendence always a narrative dimension as the work in question is always to be accountable and recountable for collective, public organisation. Here, however, we will explore the analytics of the public through its dimension of being open to story-ing by individuals as a way of organising and making sense of 'appearing' and 'appearances' to self and others.

Analytics as a work of public story-ing

An analytics involves a public story-ing. It is a work of identity and identifying, of composing a representable reality that can be made accountable, recountable and actionable. However, although identities can be carefully chosen for particular purposes, they must be fit for purpose:

> Four years ago, I stood before you and told you my story – of the brief union between a young man from Kenya and a young woman from Kansas who weren't well-off or well-known, but shared a belief that in America, their son could achieve whatever he put his mind to.
>
> It is that promise that has always set this country apart – that through hard work and sacrifice, each of us can pursue our individual dreams but still come together as one American family, to ensure that the next generation can pursue their dreams as well.
>
> That's why I stand here tonight. Because for two hundred and thirty two years, at each moment when that promise was in jeopardy, ordinary men and women – students and soldiers, farmers and teachers, nurses and janitors – found the courage to keep it alive.
>
> We meet at one of those defining moments – a moment when our nation is at war, our economy is in turmoil, and the American promise has been threatened once more.
>
> (Obama, Democratic convention speech 28 September 2008,
> http://www.huffingtonpost.com/2008/08/28/barack-obama-
> democratic-c_n_122224.html)

Obama's speech in Denver is, of course, carefully crafted to fit prior story-ings. It is how identities are put together with events, reasons, values and actions that tell a story, making that story more than an accidental series. It is how the story is framed into sides inscribing relations of us and them that takes it beyond the personal to the political and it is the agenda that marks the telling of the story that makes it purposive and actionable. Whatever the frame for the fragment of the story under the spotlight at any point in time, both frame and story will be subject to dynamic change from moment to moment and from space to space as that story unfolds and interlinks with others to accomplish an agenda. In casting oneself as a hero, for example, the individual searches out ways and means to think as a hero would, act as if a hero, look for particular opportunities to engage within the moment and space of an event seeming[ly] as a hero, thereby achieving the Arendtian it-seems-to-me appearance-as-hero. The character adopted in the telling of the story is the guise that is presented, that appears and gives the semblance of the 'hero'. This is the semblant that stands in for hero and the speaking subject who is telling the story. Through the semblant the individual engages in ways of thinking, doing and saying internally with the self as subject of the speaking, as well as externally with others as audience or as co-producers. In short, we inhabit the stories we tell and that can be told and through them make a home. We become our 'semblants' in the telling of the story as others spin their own variation to take their place as semblants in the stories that they can tell in relation to the story they are hearing. The telling of the one story can be the hearing of a million as it weaves into the stories of others:

> It's a story that began here, in El Dorado, when a young man fell in love with a young woman who grew up down the road in Augusta. They came of age in the midst of the Depression, where he found odd jobs on small farms and oil rigs, always dodging the bank failures and foreclosures that were sweeping the nation.
>
> They married just after war broke out in Europe, and he enlisted in Patton's army after the bombing of Pearl Harbor. She gave birth to their daughter on the base at Fort Leavenworth, and worked on a bomber assembly line when he left for war.
>
> In a time of great uncertainty and anxiety, my grandparents held on to a simple dream – that they could raise my mother in a land of boundless opportunity; that their generation's struggle and sacrifice could give her the freedom to be what she wanted to be; to live how she wanted to live.
>
> I am standing here today because that dream was realized – because my grandfather got the chance to go to school on the GI Bill, buy a house through the Federal Housing Authority, and move his family west – all the way to Hawaii – where my mother would go to college and one day fall in love with a young student from Kenya.
>
> I am here because that dream made my parents' love possible, even then; because it meant that after my father left, when my mother struggled as a single parent, and even turned to food stamps for a time, she was still able to send my sister and me to the best schools in the country.
>
> And I'm here because years later, when I found my own love in a place far away called Chicago, she told me of a similar dream. Michelle grew up in a working-class family on the South Side during the 1960s. Her father had been diagnosed with multiple sclerosis at just thirty years old. And yet, every day of his life, even when he had to rely on a walker to get him there, Fraser Robinson went to work at the local water filtration plant while his

wife stayed home with the children. And on that single salary, he was able to send Michelle and her brother to Princeton.

Our family's story is one that spans miles and generations; races and realities. It's the story of farmers and soldiers; city workers and single moms. It takes place in small towns and good schools; in Kansas and Kenya; on the shores of Hawaii and the streets of Chicago. It's a varied and unlikely journey, but one that's held together by the same simple dream.

And that is why it's American.

(Obama 20008, 'Reclaiming the American Dream', (http://www. presidency.ucsb.edu/ws/index.php?pid=77030#axzz1VSVNsqkU)

The individual story is consciously being written into the history of a nation adopting the analytic categories, the rules of organising categories to be storied as intersubjectively and personally recognisable by audiences – and more than that, into its foundational myth: the American Dream. Such a myth, as used here, is not a fanciful story of beginnings for amusement only. It involves an analytics of time, place, Identity, identities, processes of identifying, facts, values Being and beings set into relation with framing discourses and motivating agendas. The dream says something about the nature of society and one's place within it. The American Dream is aspirational. When individuals write themselves into it, telling their stories as realisations of the dream, it works to create the public necessary for the reality of the dream itself. The Dream is a 'surface' when one such as Obama can write 'my grandparents held on to a simple dream – that they could raise my mother in a land of boundless opportunity' and 'I am standing here today because that dream was realized.' By playing mythical time alongside biographical time and the historical time of wars, struggles and sacrifices, Obama inserts his figure as the semblant that stands for the aspiration of all in all times and places across 'America'. America itself is the semblant of the future fulfilment of dreams. It is the Being that unifies all the individual beings who align their dreams with the Dream.

The semblant, then, is the analytic category of the actor that comes on to a stage to realise the 'seeming to be' of another category. When a film star plays the hero, all elements of the story can be categorised and arranged in relation to the hero. Propp (1968) analysed Russian folktales into what he thought were their five key structural elements, which could then be set into relation with thirty-one functions dealing with introducing, unfolding and ending the story and seven character types who defined the fields of action. Not all of these category types are always present in stories. However, the model Propp derived has been applied to novels, films and digital games. In the story that Obama is writing into the myth, many of the elements are incorporated. There is the dramatis personae of grandparents: Michelle and her parents, and Obama. There are the conjunctive elements of 'falling in love', enlisting in the army. Each person has the motivation of the dream. The grandparents are cast into a heroic position with America in the role of providing the necessary help as a land of boundless opportunity to the hero, getting the chance to go to school through the GI Bill, buying a house through the Federal Housing Agency. The war in Europe and in Japan implies the villains to be struggled against. The key helpers to the family alongside America as land of opportunity are the GI Bill, the food stamps, the Housing Agency – each suggesting the need for a little extra help in the form of public assistance even for 'heroes', that is, the small heroes of everyday struggles who through holding on to the dream made the country great. At one level, the sequence of events may be simply written as two people meeting, having a family, going to war, getting jobs, getting old, getting ill. But their son seeking to become president adds another level: the Dream of endless possibilities, of achieving, of building a free nation. In the story of the son succeeding, the son that stands before you as president, there is also a sub-textual agenda implicit in the examples of public assistance, and even a suggestion has been planted here in the diagnosis of multiple sclerosis for a need to reform medical care, an agenda that became significant in his presidency.

In effect such a model as Propp's acts as a formalised analytics by which to write a particular story into a multiplicity of stories, or to universalise a particular story and its 'hero'. Each story acts like a surface on to which to inscribe other stories and agendas. As an alternative to, or perhaps supplement to, Campbell (1968), drawing on a Jungian psychoanalytic framework explored what he saw as the archetypal structure and symbolic content of myths seeing these as universal. And there is something of that archetypal dimension in the Herculean struggle of the family, particularly the father crippled with multiple sclerosis still determined to work. Berne's transactional analysis provides yet another model for analysis in identifying the game-like structures that are played out between rescuer, persecutor and victim. The key characters may play different roles at different times. At one point the grandfather is a hero of the struggle, persecuted by hardship through the depression and the war, and is himself a rescuer of the nation as soldier, but also a victim of disease implicitly needing the act of rescuer. Obama himself is that rescuer for all. However, as the story of the presidency unfolds, the game continues as he becomes the persecutor of the freedom of the American people in the eyes of the Tea Party, who object to his approach to the financial crisis and to welfare, and the rescuer (through UN-based coalitions) of the people in Libya rising up against the dictator and the protector of American interests abroad. When at last Obama goes there will be another individual who will take the place of the Semblant, the representative of the American People, the American Dream. And the games will continue.

More detailed analysis may be made of textual strategies by focusing on, say, the analytics of the genealogies of key concepts, adopting the ordinary language strategies, say, of analytic philosophy, Marxism, symbolic interactionism, phenomenological description of appearances and their intentional analysis, critical realism, semiotic analysis, the processes of grounded theory, and the more politically critical strategies of gender critiques, antiracism, postcolonialism as approaches to doing radical research and all the other approaches that may be found across the disciplines of the social sciences and the humanities. All of these provide ways of thinking about an analytics that seems to be in play without being reduced to it or fully co-extensive with it.

For politicians and their speech writers an analytics becomes a powerful tool for spinning stories into the minds of a 'public'. As previously described, Lippmann (1922), as a pioneer in defining a 'public' for the public relations industry, saw creating pictures in the minds of people as an essential factor in engaging with and shaping public opinion.

> It is the insertion between man and his environment of a pseudo-environment. To that pseudo-environment his behavior is a response. But because it is behavior, the consequences, if they are acts, operate not in the pseudo-environment where the behavior is stimulated, but in the real environment where action eventuates. If the behavior is not a practical act, but what we call roughly thought and emotion, it may be a long time before there is any noticeable break in the texture of the fictitious world. But when the stimulus of the pseudo-fact results in action on things or other people, contradiction soon develops. Then comes the sensation of butting one's head against a stone wall, of learning by experience, and witnessing Herbert Spencer's tragedy of the murder of a Beautiful Theory by a Gang of Brutal Facts, the discomfort in short of a maladjustment. For certainly, at the level of social life, what is called the adjustment of man to his environment takes place through the medium of fictions.
>
> (Lippmann 1922: 10–11)

At the back of Lippmann's 'pseudo-environment' – which may nowadays be thought of as a 'virtual environment'– is the machinery of an analytics generating the possible pictures in the head that are employed as the map of reality through which people are able to co-ordinate their actions to some purpose(s). At its most general, an analytics brings together:

a)   the one and the universal. This can be read to include the one as a single individual, a single group, a single community, a single class, a single people, a single nation. As in the Obama speech, the single individual, the single family, the single nation is merged with the universal foundational myth: the American Dream, The Promised Land and all that this entails. As the 'world's leading democracy', the bearer of the Dream, America can project itself as being in the vanguard and thus as having a mission to spread democracy across the globe. It is generative of grand mythological narratives. Chosen People

b)   the one and the many. The single entity, however defined, takes its meaning from an aggregation of many individuals, and in turn the one becomes the representation of the many, speaking for the many. As one like you, I represent you, becoming the semblant of semblants. It produces either a discourse of leadership in order to 'get the message across' to the many or a discourse that insists on the one being faithful to the demands of the many. Although generative of grand narratives, they are not mythological as such, although may be combined with a mythological analytics. Rather, they are constructive of Power in the grand Totalitarian, Great Leader and Third Reich sense. The Great Leader is not a God, but may become one in the eyes of the people, who in turn become a People, whether a Master Race or a Great Nation or Classless Class as in a proletariat serving the One who is the Semblant of the many, the symbol and sole representative of its unity.

c) the many and the many. The many may be seen as a collection of individuals pursuing their self interests or as a collection of individuals pursuing mutual interests. In each case their individuality is defined by the collectivity. The many may be organised as a democracy in the fullest sense, where all individuals are involved in decision-making debate, or as a decision-making subset that decides on behalf of the others; and they may be organised as a perfect market where no one voice or demand outweighs any other so that through price discovery mechanisms resources are allocated optimally, or as an oligopolistic or indeed as a market engineered by monopolies where resources are organised and allocated according to the ability to manipulate prices. Under each case the democracy of the many, however operation-alised, may be fully identified with the prevailing mode of market allocation. In the neoliberal market philosophies and practices influenced by Hayek and Friedman the market is seen as equivalent to democracy. The analytics of democracy is reinforced by the analytics of the market. What is critical is the definition and practice of both democracy and the market that a given analytics enables or disables. Such analytics are generative of local narratives, of choice within and between the many, of territorialisation, transformation and re-territorialisation as the many form and reform into other configura-tions of the many. The many has no absolute fixed point, no centre, no One to command the totality. It is in that sense post-structural, albeit generative of structures as it continually deconstructs to re-form new configurations of the many. It is postmodern in that it rejects the Grand Narrative of the Modern but keeps the semblance of the modern in its technologies, its use of the sciences of the modern as well as transforming all cultures and tradi-tions into 'the many' that are on offer in the market.

d) the multitude with the public as its place of appearance, its critical space. As the totality of individuals composing the population globally that is, the multitude, of course a multitude can be recomposed into may sub-sets, as for example the many of a given nation state, a community, a faith. However, with a multitude there are neither grand narratives nor local narratives since these would compose the multitude into sub-sets living the narratives, being bound by the *dramatis personae* of the narratives. The multitude is the ground, as it were, for the composition of analytics that emerge through the play of people's powers as living beings to constitute a public and to generate the conditions for freedom with equality in the continuous creation of new forms of social organisation – this is a theme to be more fully developed in later chapters. The multitude is all individuals conscious of their constitutive powers. The 'Arab Spring', for example, has given hints of this awareness where people called both on their own people and also the people of the world as a multitude who together constitute the equalising concept of 'humanity'.

An analytics determines how representation is managed and the work of the public organised and produced. As such an analytics may, in Lippmann's terms be adjusted to the life and experience of the individual or maladjusted. In the sense of a felt adjustment or maladjustment each analytic may become a counter-vailing analytics to the others. It is the felt sense of adjustment or otherwise that creates the conditions for contests of representation, interpretation and theori-sation, the felt sense of layers and proliferating surfaces that can be attenuated, stretched and twisted without ever being 'cut' to create from itself new surfaces from its own destruction. Surfaces can be laminated and knotted to give the appearance of a unity, a togetherness, a synthesis that produce the effects of 'locality' and 'localness', nationality and 'People', friends and enemies, and the effects of 'globalisation'. An analytics creates a world that is both virtual and real in its effects. Indeed, the extent that effects are experienced, the virtual becomes in affect the real for an individual, a many, a One or a multitude. In the experience of multiple realities as one virtual reality clashes with another, the contests of the countervailing powers and their analytics generate by turns threat, anxieties, seductions, pre-figurative organisations, hope and its partial fulfilments and disappointments. These play out in the strategies for making claims about reality to be taken up in the following chapters.

Gestures towards writing

If ethnography involves the close living with others to gain insights into their perceptions, their meanings, their stories and their processes and practices of social organisation then this entails gaining insight into the analytics of their worlds as a basis for writing. They are accessed through language, the classifi-cations employed, the grammar through which meanings are expressed. This linguistic turn will be further developed in later chapters. Here it has focused on the narrative forms within which *dramatis personae* are set on stage as protago-nists in dramas. Alternatively, for Levi-Strauss (Leach 1965), it was for example seen in the underlying logics of the structure of kinship systems. For him, it was a search for the universal patterns of human thinking. For C. Wright Mills (1940) it involved a closer focus on situated action and the ways in which motives are verbalised, thus identifying vocabularies of motive. There is, in learning the ways worlds are talked about, a sense of learning a new language. There has to be a close attention to the details of talking, of making accounts, of representing realities and of signifying allegiance. The way a jacket is buttoned may signify to a gang member either friend or enemy (Patrick 1973). Ethnographic writing then seeks to represent the realities of a given way of seeing the world to enable outsiders to see that world by setting out its categories, its analytic practices to produce the lived meanings of public story-ings of selves and others.

To write a case is very much to understand how people construct and present their 'selves' in communities and how in the many organisations of their formal and informal relationships they shape the boundaries of their practices in common, make distinctions and co-ordinate their actions on the basis of a shared and lived sense of reality. The case, in this view, takes its sense, its 'reality' from its experienced connection or embeddedness in a wider world of living in which a 'people' is defined as possessing a perceptible and representable world in common. The case is to be recognisable to others in a world of cases. The case takes its sense, its possibility, its realisability from its recognition as sharing a logic, an analytics through which it can be produced and reproduced for a public.

Action research is not content with representation of the same, with understanding present workings. It desires, it negotiates, it promotes, it demands to inscribe change. If it seeks to improve the quality of action within a social context (Elliott 1991), then it must either work within or on the analytics through which the possibilities for actions are produced and reproduced. A radical move is made in action research by introducing into the public voices that have been excluded, voices that change the story. But these moves are to look ahead at the ways in which writing inscribes difference in the development of effective publics.

Chapter 5

Representation, revelation and repression of particulars and universals as a basis for making claims about 'reality'

So what is real? And how is it to be represented? This can be taken in three ways: it is a question of what is seen and how it is written down; it is then a question of how what is written down from observation is then employed in a body of writing that uses it as 'evidence' of something; then it is how, as evidence, it represents a 'reality' to be taken into account in decision-making.

First of all, some mark, letter, a word or symbol of some sort stands for a given meaning pointing to the thing (real or imagined) talked about. Similarly, in artistic terms a picture or a performance may be thought of as a copy of, or mimicking or giving the illusion of or being the semblant of some 'real' thing or event. In politics representation concerns how the voices of individuals and groups are to be taken into account in decision-making. One person may have the role of representing the voices of many. The key question in each case is whether the representation is somehow faithful to the 'original'; or whether, as Baudrillard (1994) might say, the representative (or copy) precedes the original; that is to say, without the framing or structuring brought about by the artificial, the real cannot be perceived or pointed out as 'clear' and 'distinct' from everything else. Representation, in this sense, has the effect of creating the 'visible', thus founding an aesthetics, an ethics and a politics of the real (Rancière 2004). More than that, it recalls a totalising apparatus of surfaces upon which all appears, as distinct from surfaces where all makes its impression, and as in Freud's Mystic Writing Pad all passes as attention shifts to make place for impressions of the new.

It is this shiftiness that is the challenge, a challenge addressed within the intersubjective space of the challenge. How can everything be pinned down? Representation or storytelling, as it were, lurks between and within the public and the private, constructing the bridges, the ties, the relational knots that compose the virtual landscapes that can be fought over for territory, for control and for exploitation. In separating the visible from the invisible, the nameable from the unnamed, the sayable from the unutterable, the audible from the inaudible, representation creates the conditions for what is to be counted as 'objective', 'valid', 'natural'. But in the shiftiness of our representations of the real there is a need, desire or demand for some certainty and we look to some other for recognition, for acknowledgement, for confirmation – '[w]hen our eyes touch' a question takes hold of me, as if it comes to me, of me, and that question [la question] arrives unannounced, uninvited, touching me before letting 'herself' be seen – almost as if a visitation were upon me (Derrida 2005: 1). Along with any representation of the real there is a question of whether the other recognises, acknowledges and responds to that representation. How do I appear before the other? What is being made of this appearance? If there is a 'touching' of the eyes and if these are the windows of the soul, then what is seen? Are these windows transparent or opaque surfaces? What is revealed or concealed and what is written on the surfaces opened or guarded by the eyes? And when there is speaking, how in touch is the hearing? And in holding hands, is this joining possible only because there is separation, a being out of touch?

Representations in and out of touch with the real

The shiftiness of representations is essential to language, the condition of shared meaning. A tree is not a tree but a mark or sound that is made to appear when pointing out a particular instance of 'tree' in a field. Tree is not tied to 'tree'. It is not the unique name of this unique 'tree' but shiftily moves when pointing out all sorts of other instances of 'tree' until some invariant set of characteristics of 'tree' mark it out as different from 'shrub', 'bush', 'hedge'. When two eyes meet in gaze with each other, there is the question of each other's being, existence as other, identity, 'real' face, and the question of what is being addressed. So this

> question could not happen to me except by being said as much as touched upon – by the other – belonging first to the other, come to me from the other who was already addressing it to the other.
>
> (Derrida 2005: 1–2)

In the address, there is both a direction and an arrival point. How do you know when you have arrived? It is this tree, not that tree, that I meant when I said 'Meet me at the tree.' It is in the nature of an address to have a fixing, not a shiftiness. In the meeting of eyes, the contact of surfaces, there is a felt resistance and in the resistance there is a basis for the 'traction' of meaning, a taking hold, a fixing in terms of 'this is what I meant, not that'.

Saussure revealed the shiftiness and the need for fixing in his exploration of signifieds and 'their' signifiers. Dominance was given to the signified, the content, the concept, the meaning to which the mark, the signifier, is bound to be used to announce, or denounce, the signified. He wrote the relation:

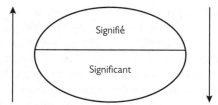

Figure 1a Saussure's concept of the sign

(Saussure 2005: 158)

where Signifié is the signified and Signifiant is the signifier. Between them the bar indicates that these are of two different orders of being, around them the ellipse denotes boundedness keeping them together with the arrows implying that the signified can indicate the signifier and vice versa. They are bounded counterparts. In any language, there is a pile, as it were, of possible substitutes for a given word or concept, but only one is meant in a given communication: tree, sapling, bush, hedge, plant. The possible words allow conceptual discriminations to be made according to context. Each word, as Saussure says, binds concept with acoustic image, but the value that each word takes is because it is part of system that allows discriminations to be made. For the relationship between the signifier and the signified, he gives the metaphor of cutting a piece of paper. As a cut is made, a new surface and its boundaries are created (Saussure 2005: 157). On one side might be written the word 'signifier' on the other is its 'signified'. If the paper is cut again, it is like attempting a finer discrimination in terms of the significance of the signifier–signified relationship. However, for the discrimination to hit its mark and bring about a signification requires more than just the signifier–signified relation itself. It requires, as below, a series where the value of each member is in question when set alongside each other and there are choices to be made. To try and point out a tree in the field by the word 'plant' is not as valuable as saying tree. More valuable still, if there are several trees of different varieties, is to name the variety of tree itself. The most valuable is the word that picks out the exact tree. It does this because it is set into relation with other words that although close in meaning are still not exact enough. In this sense, the value of a given sign depends on its relations with other signs in the series. In formal terms it is a system of differences where each term takes its value because it is different from all the others.

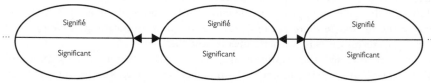

Figure 1b Saussure's concept of the value of signs

(Saussure 2005: 159)

There are then two axes involved in the construction of signification. There is the vertical relation of signifier and signified composing a solid binding to produce the 'sign'. There are then the horizontal relations of a series of neighbouring signs that are the result of making systematic differences to point out nuances between 'this' and 'that'. Each sign cuts up the perceived world of experience, in a sense replacing the real-in-itself with the real-of-representation. Magritte in 1929 jokingly highlighted that his painting of a pipe is not the pipe itself (*Ceci n'est pas une pipe*). For Hegel (1979: 221) 'The first act, by which Adam established his lordship over the animals, is this, that he gave them a name, i.e., he nullified them as beings on their own account.' For Lacan this essentially means that the symbol is the 'murder of the thing' (Lacan 1977: 104). Politically, this has interesting consequences.

Recalling Lippmann's (1927) phantom public, the system of political representation that it invokes under the name of the 'public' is essentially non-existent. In effect, the real of the public has been annulled, or in Lacan's terms 'murdered'. Like money, as a system of representation, its value consists in being a medium of exchange. There is, as in any economic crisis, the fear that a particular currency may fail to be redeemable by some real product or service. That is, it no longer serves as 'money'. In developing the notion of the value of a sign, or of forms of representation generally, Saussure made an explicit comparison of his formal system of the sign with money. This is picked up by Baudrillard (1994: 6) in his book on symbolic exchange:

> Saussure located two dimensions to the exchange of terms of the langue, which he assimilated to money. A given coin must be exchangeable against a real good of some value, while on the other hand it must be possible to relate it to all the other terms in the monetary system. More and more, Saussure reserves the term value for this second aspect of the system: every term can be related to every other, their relativity, internal to the system and constituted by binary oppositions. This definition is opposed to the other possible definition of value: the relation of every term to what it designates, of each signifier to its signified, like the relation of every coin with what it can be exchanged against. The first aspect corresponds to the structural dimension of language, the second to its functional dimension.

This distinction between the structural and functional dimensions of a representational system provides a way of thinking about the formal and the real. With the money system being essential to capitalist accumulation, the slippage of value from its connection with function makes money-as-value an end in itself. Perhaps this can most clearly be seen in what has been called 'high-frequency trading' on the stock markets, a process that is often seen by outsiders as 'mysterious' (Charles Duhigg, *New York Times*, 23 July 2009). It involves computers set up near the stock exchanges to cut transmission times and programmed to buy and sell again in milliseconds. Essentially, it is so fast that no actual money exchanges hands. Its effect is to push up or push down prices. It creates the illusion of demand and the illusion of there being liquidity in the system when in fact there is none other than the lightening-fast buy-and-sell instructions:

> 'We have a market that responds in milliseconds, but the humans monitoring respond in minutes, and unfortunately billions of dollars of damage can occur in the meantime,' said James Angel, a professor of finance at the McDonough School of Business at *Georgetown University*.
>
> (Nelson D. Schwartz and Louise Story, The New York Times 6 May 2010: http://www.nytimes.com/2010/05/07/business/economy/07trade.html)

Rather than a price discovery process, this is a market making process. Price discovery is supposed to identify the value (as price) of a good or service in terms of what people are willing to pay in balance with what firms are willing to make at that price. It is then able to allocate real goods and services optimally: say, a firm is willing to supply a thousand tons of wheat at x price and there are customers willing to pay that price for that quantity. The higher the price goes less people will want it, albeit the supplier would be willing to supply more at that price. Since there would be surplus that no one wants at the higher price, the price would have to fall and the firm would then deliver less wheat because there is no market for the wheat at that higher price. This process is price discovery creating a market at the speed of human decision-making. However, through high-frequency trading the illusion of a market can be made. Nina Mehta of Bloomberg (2011) reported that 'The stock market's fastest electronic firms boosted trading threefold during the rout that erased $2.2 trillion from U.S. equity values, stepping up strategies that profit from volatility, according to one of their biggest brokers.' It is neither real demand nor real supply that is involved in this volatility – it is a play created through digital blips standing for currency that stands for real goods and services. As Mehta put it: 'These systems are so fast they can outsmart or outrun other investors, humans and computers alike.' There is then a disconnect between the value and the reality of the market composed of people who demand and firms that supply. There is no functional relation between the two.

A further reality disconnect can be made between function and work. Functionality occurs in relation to an organisation or a system. In the organising strategy of division of labour, each individual performs a function that, when aggregated to others, completes a particular project, service or product. Adam Smith in his *Wealth of Nations* noted the great advantage that division of labour had over one person trying to do everything. By breaking up a complex job up into small steps and assigning each step to an individual, that individual learns to do his or her part of the job more skilfully as well as faster and faster. Hence more is produced and of a better quality in a given time. This functional framework for the organisation of work activities creates highly specialised skills for a part of the whole. When demand falls or is supplanted by some superior product (as in horse and carriages being replaced by motor cars) for a particular product, or changes in technology for some part of a product (as in introducing information technology), then individuals may find themselves with no function to fulfil. Now unemployed and searching for a new job, their skills are not necessarily appropriate for the new technologies, products and services. Or they may find the skills learnt for one product are also required for another. Whatever is the case, function has been separated from the real output or product made or delivered. This is itself aggravated by the disjunction between the functional activities undertaken and the owner of the product or service that results from them. The employee has nothing but his or her skills, if any. All created value is in the ownership of the employer. At some extreme future scenario, it is possible that all functions are carried out electronically, even the production of complex products through the development of 3D-printing technologies (Richmond, 2011) as an extension of the high-frequency trading model to all spheres of economic activity. In this future scenario the employee as value creator is not needed.

The modernisation of work has thus on the one hand functionalised the activities and skills of people and on the other rendered them as employees who have no ownership stake in the final product. This means that their activities as employees can be routinised and made increasingly programmable. As functionaries all having the same skill sets and performing the same activities, they are essentially indistinguishable one from another. They are thus always replaceable by individuals (or machineries) able to fulfil the same function more cheaply. Just as there is no ownership of the product, there is no security in employment only functionality. In unemployment, there is no other functionality than to apply for a job when it becomes available. When there are few or no jobs available, then pools of 'labour' are burdens, excess, residual matter. The analytical logic of the system values only the elements necessary to it. Rather like the statistical analytic of psychologist Thorndike (1904), something only exists if it can be quantified or otherwise measured as a term of value in the system. In order to be operational, this analytics excludes and reduces.

Work, in Dejours's (1998, 2003) analysis of it, is quite different from employment and from the imposed divisions of labour that exclude the individual participants in the organisation of work from mutual ownership of a collective enterprise. By placing the emergence of the political, Arendt's 'action', in the experience of people engaging together in the organisation of work Dejours establishes work in the real of people's powers to act, to create and to voice their views in co-operative co-production. Work in this full sense of the term is generative of the public as an active principle in contrast to the public as a ghost, or, at best, a mystic pad to receive the shaping influences of the public relations industry and the systems of training and schooling. What, in the context of work, does representation mean?

The Spinozan return of the real

Spinoza, in a sense, stands as the possibility of an alternative modernity (Mack, 2010). Rather than the modernity that thrives on the split between mind and body and the hierarchical principle of God over nature, mind over body, head over heart, the most talented leading the less and the untalented, Spinoza offers the possibility of a democracy of powers. For him it is not a question of a split but rather a co-equivalence of God and nature, so that:

> By the help of God, I mean the fixed and unchangeable order of nature or the chain of natural events: for I have said before and shown elsewhere that the universal laws of nature, according to which all things exist and are determined, are only another name for the eternal decrees of God, which always involve eternal truth and necessity.
>
> So that to say that everything happens according to natural laws, and to say that everything is ordained by the decree and ordinance of God, is the same thing. Now since the power in nature is identical with the power of God, by which alone all things happen and are determined, it follows that whatsoever man, as a part of nature, provides himself with to aid and preserve his existence, or whatsoever nature affords him without his help, is given to him solely by the Divine power, acting either through human nature or through external circumstance.
>
> (Spinoza 2004: 44–5)

This provides an analytic of powers rather than an analytic of Power employing reason as a mechanism of dominance. For Balibar (1998) Spinoza's analytic of powers unfolds as a free democracy of equals. It is a different way of seeing, of recognising and of responding. Rather than an 'x' on the ballot paper representing a 'voice' or a vote, for a semblant that takes the place of the voter, it is the voice itself that takes its place and speaks, makes its mark, inscribes and writes in the place of decision-making. The value of the vote is in the power of its use in the work of creating the public as a space of forces rather than the phantom space of Lippmann (1927). Rather than value being separated from function and from work, they are integral. In this sense, to be represented is to be in the place of decision-making, using one's voice and having it taken into account in the work to be undertaken.

This move to the real of the voice rather than its replacement by a semblant can be seen when Merleau-Ponty says 'I am my body' (Merleau-Ponty 1962: 150) and this body is not an objective body but a lived body (corps vécu) that is:

> irreducibly saturated with and supportive of my lived attitudes to the world, a body with a 'momentum of existence' (habitual projections of meaning) that exceeds any biomedical objectified 'body at this moment'.
>
> (Merleau-Ponty 1962: 82)

Rather than the phantom public, there is the embodied public, or rather, the public of embodied subjects voicing their experiences, views, insights, demands. Merleau-Ponty called this lived body an 'inborn complex', which according to Morris:

> has the sort of meaning at the crux of a Freudian complex. But in the body as inborn complex, meaning does not arise at a psychological level: it is born at an organic level that is pre-personal, which is thence modulated through one's bodily engagement with the intersubjective world, engendering a complex personal relation to the world.
>
> (Merleau-Ponty 1962: 82–5; Morris 2008: 114)

In the Freudian analytic a complex consists of a knotting or pattern of emotions, memories, perceptions, feelings, wishes that may appear symptomatically as body markings, twitches, gestures, dreams, slips of the tongue. This then provides some insight into the meaning Morris gives of the 'in born complex' of Merleau-Ponty. However, what if this insight is developed further through the linguistic turn of Lacan's return to Freud? Jacques-Alain Miller (2005) gives a Lacanian definition of the 'complex' as 'a prestructure'.

> That is what is lacking, the concept of structure. It is nevertheless that which he tries to define, in a tortuous way obviously. He tries to define it at the same time as a form, and as an activity. It is as a form that it is necessary in development, determining a dated reality, thus representing, by a fixed form, a certain reality of development – there, from the point of view of origins; and, on the other hand, as an activity, that is to say as prompting repetitions of behaviors, of lived emotions, as a certain number of experiences happen. He gives a definition of it that is not made up only of what is at stake as unconscious. 'It is this that complex defines, that it reproduces a certain reality of ambiance, and for two reasons. 1) Its form represents this reality in what is objectively distinct at a given stage of psychic development; this stage specifies its origins. 2) Its activity repeats in lived experience the reality thus fixed, each time that some experiences occur that would demand a superior objectification of this reality; these experiences specify the conditioning of the complex.'
>
> (Miller 2005)

The calling forth of a 'prestructure' is interesting in terms of being 'something' – some concept – being needed because a structure is missing in Miller's struggle with Lacan's textual struggle to define 'complex'. The concept makes possible the calling into being of an 'object', the 'prestructure'. It is a 'something' that consciousness is now directed towards. To represent is to make consciously visible as an object of consciousness. In Kuhn's (1970) account of scientific revolutions, the revolution is essentially a radical transformation in 'seeing'. What is not an object under one representational system is an object under another. Under one system scientists 'saw' 'phlogiston' as a basic objective phenomenon of physics; under the Daltonian system it was 'atoms'. The two systems of 'seeing' were incompatible. The phlogiston system was the 'dated' reality' inhibiting the development of a new 'reality. It is a part of the role of an analytics to focus on or determine the 'object' through a system of concepts that bring about an objectification – a making of objects – by concepts. It is the objectification performed by concepts that allows the 'real' to intervene, which presumably means that the real can either be better navigated, manipulated, transformed under the system of representation, or the real interrupts the framework of concepts through which it is subjected to a range of organisational strategies. It could be that the phlogiston way of seeing the world leads to a series of crises in terms of how reality is to be represented when what is experienced does not 'fit' the objectification called for by the concept. The 'superior' Daltonian system of objectification may resolve the crisis. However, there may be other co-existing systems of representation – say status systems that give prestige and wealth to those that hold the phlogiston theory who may then attempt to erase, repress or indeed criminalise the alternative way of seeing the world. Similarly, Miller argues that the stage of Lacan's prestructuralism moved towards a structuralism which in turn gave way to a post-structuralism. In more contemporary terms multiple ways of representing and objectifying the real through systems of representation can be seen to be at stake in the issue of whether a) climate change exists and b) if it does, it being the result of human activity. The science underlying climate change can be disputed, but for most scientists it is accepted that human activity is a critical factor. This conclusion is in conflict with corporate interests and corporate interests have considerable influence on politics and the popular mass media and can set about 'rubbishing' or vilifying those who hold to a theory of climate change a) happening and b) happening because of human activities. Similarly, in the teaching of children, in the UK during the 1960s and 1970s there was an increasing move towards child-centred teaching, discovery learning and progressive, even democratic forms of education. This was attacked in a campaign in the press as the source of school failures to 'discipline' and teach 'basic skills' during the early Thatcher government (cf. Schostak 1993) and increasingly replaced by more teacher-led, authoritarian forms of teaching with an emphasis on test scores and what became known as school effectiveness, or in Reynolds' terms high-reliability schools (cf. Hammersley 2007; Reynolds and Stringer 1996). It was not an educational discourse that prevailed, but the more prestigious discourses of 'traditional discipline', tests, performance management and fitness for market.

The interaction between the multiple systems of representation bearing on the issue of the reality of climate change and its causes or schools and their failures can be seen as an example of a complex articulating a clash of social, economic, political and physical powers or forces where what is at stake are alternative 'realities'. Each system or way of representing what is 'real' stands in place of the real, in the place of the real. Each proponent of a way of representing the real makes a claim about its developmental status in relation to the other proclaimed ways of representing a real. The complex, so articulated, is a functioning part of the analytics through which statements about an intervening 'real' can be made in relation to a progression or succession of realities, where one is seen as developmentally dated and another is seen as superior and thus that it ought to surpass and replace it. This analytic is thus explicitly aligned with Hegel's dialectic in the Phenomenology of Spirit where 'that which he names objectification' is 'developed in this succession of forms of objectification which follow one another by conflict and then are resolved through crisis'. The crisis demands a resolution.

Take the crisis in currencies that hit the Western economies as part of the aftermath of the 2008 financial crisis. A currency is a valid token of stored value if it is generally accepted in exchange for goods, services and other currencies. However, if there are doubts about a state being able to repay its debts, then investors will try to get out of the currency for some safer form of stored value, typically precious metals like gold and silver. As the value of the currency falls, so the value of the metal rises. This demand for gold or silver over currency is as a result of an 'intervention by the real' eventually posing a crisis for the currency, particularly those who still possess their 'wealth' in the form of the currency and find that the currency is becoming increasingly valueless, fearing that their wealth disappears along with the currency that is losing its status as 'money'. Handling a crisis, of course, does not necessarily mean it will be handled appropriately. The characteristic of a complex is that solutions once tried, are tried and tried again, as a complex prompts 'repetitions of behaviours'. Symptoms of some underlying cause, or rather, some discounted, or misrecognised cause occur like riots, increases in criminality and violence which in turn call forth the same solutions that have previously failed but may at least calm the situation for a period.

Ultimately, if there is to be a real rather than a symbolic solution, all representations of the real have to be reconciled with the real. In the economic example, goods and services are exchanged for currency as a token of stored wealth. In a firm, there is the currency paid in exchange for a particular product that it sells. The amount in currency received is written in the sales account which needs to match the amount that is received in the bank account and again cross check with the account of the actual item that had been dispatched to the customer. There are, in this brief example, several systems of representation. There is the system of accountancy set up and employed by the firm selling a product which, at certain points of exchange, has to be compatible with the system of representation run by the bank. There is the system employed by the customer, which again, at a certain point where the exchange has been made, has to agree with the systems employed by the firm and the bank. At stake in these systems is the real product and its value in currency that is being exchanged and recorded as being exchanged. There is also a system of 'fairness' at play. The good is exchanged at a certain price because both sides in some way consider it 'fair'. The bank costs for handling the accounts of the exchanges are paid because in some way they are 'fair' or at least argued in relation to some other system of representation as 'unavoidable' or 'necessary' in terms of safety, or in terms of facilitating the national and global monetary system. Of course, the reason why the elaborate and interconnecting systems of exchange are in place is because other systems of representation are organised around what is good and what is bad. There are moral discourses valuing property rights and abhorring theft and fraud. Each system of representation is directed towards the item that is being exchanged and determines how it is being represented at any given time. There is, in short, an overdetermination of the object represented, that is it is not just determined by one act of consciousness and one system of representation but by a multiplicity.

Overdetermination provides a means of keeping the 'real' at bay as one system is backed by another system of representation without the need of reference directly to some 'real'. Thus a system of exchange is supported by a system of legal representation guaranteeing property rights, which in turn may be backed up by moral systems of representation whether these are in turn religious or not concerning what is 'right' and 'wrong', which in turn may be backed by systems of 'fairness' and 'social justice'. This system of 'backing up' depends on one system being accorded the status of the real to justify a course of action at any given time. Thus it can be said that 'x' has to be done because in reality there is no other choice: as Prime Minister Thatcher famously said in relation to her economic strategies, 'there is no alternative'. It is a statement that continued to be made in response to the financial crisis of 2008 and its aftermath, where banks had to be saved by the tax payer because there was no alternative and cuts to welfare for the poorest and other 'austerity measures' had to be made because the debts incurred in saving the banks left no alternative. A key solution in the crisis involved the printing of currency. The more currency, the more 'liquidity' in the system, the more that people could borrow and hence the greater the volume of exchanges that could take place. However, this did not happen. The financial system used the increased liquidity to finance more speculation, restructure their debts and pay themselves bonuses. Little of the money 'trickled down' to the people who were the 'real' in terms of actually paying through their taxes to save the banks. In the European countries where protests and riots took place, it could readily be seen that the underlying backup was provided by the police and their use of force. In the Middle East, it could be seen the extent to which dictators were willing to go in using the police and the military to crush their people in the interests of maintaining the ruling structure of political order. The issue for any people under the governance of a given state is the extent to which they are willing to lose their civil liberties and their sense of freedom in the interests of maintaining social order and security.

Ultimately, any system of representation has to be backed up by something real, that is, its tokens and its symbolic value have to be 'cashed in' at some point. All currencies are essentially promises to pay. People have to have faith that this promise will be met. When confidence in a currency is diminished then people will search for some other system of representation. For many, this is 'gold'. Gold cannot be arbitrarily increased in supply. New deposits may be found, but any new source will not dramatically add to the quantity in the world. Hence, it becomes the preferred medium of exchange above currencies. Gold takes on the status of 'money' and stands in place of the real (that is representing the stored value of goods and services), in the place of the real. Bearing the mark of reality is the 'thing' around which all else takes its value, its subject positioning, its identity and its relation to others. However, now imagine an earth where no one works. Gold does not produce anything. Imagine an earth where nothing grows. Gold cannot be eaten. If anything is to have the mark of reality, it is work undertaken in relation to the vital resources of the planet that sustains life.

The representational work of the social

The work of the social begins in no other place than the embodied engagement each individual makes in relation to the other being faced. If two gaze into each other's eyes, are they touching? Are they striking or stroking each other? But are we talking about eyes or gazes? Do we not have to choose between looking and exchanging glances or meeting gazes and seeing, very simply seeing? And before even that, do we not have to choose between 'seeing rather than the visible' (Derrida, 2005: 2)? And yet 'precisely, when my gaze meets yours, I see both your gaze and your eyes, love in fascination – and your eyes are not only seeing but also visible' (Derrida; 2005: 3). There is a work of 'looking' here that involves the other beyond the anonymous and involves choices being made in terms of what is being seen and what this seeing represents in terms of the anonymous, the personal and the intimate. The look is ambiguous until responses are made, acknowledged and valued in some way. It might be a provocation – 'Are you looking at me?' – a provocation that is also a well-practised threat, as in the Robert de Niro character in the film *Taxi Driver* rehearsing in front of the mirror; looking at oneself looking back, playing a part, being a semblant for oneself, an actor, acting a part, being an other to oneself, as if it were real. In this cameo there are many boundaries, separating self and other, self as other. At one level, there is a demand to move from the sub-strata, as it were, from what Merleau-Ponty calls the anonymous life of the body and meet the gaze of the other in some particular way. It is not enough to just lock oneself away so that 'I can close my ears, lose my self in some pleasure or pain, and shut myself up in the anonymous life which subtends my personal one' (Merleau-Ponty 2003: 191). Also, over and above this anonymous life of the body there are multiple contexts projected and others implicit – as, say audience in the cinema, reader of a text representing the cameo – but that are not themselves the object of attention. Which of these is to be endowed with the 'mark of reality'? Which of these are to be assumed as the personal and which are the anonymous others of which social life is largely composed? And when does the anonymity of the roles, the types, the stereotypes, the classes and categories through which social life is organised become subverted by the intimate, the particular, the individual? Indeed, how violent within the anonymity of social life does one have to be to get a reaction? The work of social life is always a writing of and on the personal and the anonymous lives of people. It is in that most general sense an ethnography that may or may not yet be conscious of itself as such. To represent the life of people is to engage with them in the forms of marking, naming and calling out of differences that both separate and place them in touch. It is a working out of how each stands in relation to the other.

Imagine Jill engaging ethnographically, at work as a researcher, telling the story of her engagement with the work of doctors in a hospital. It's a Friday, late in April 2008, and I have just come away from shadowing a registrar on a day shift in an Accident and Emergency Department in a District General Hospital in a sprawling urban area within fifty miles of London. How do I represent what I have seen, heard, touched, smelled, felt and thought of the events that occurred during that ten-hour shift? How do I write it down? Shadowing and observing the registrar, as an ethnographer, I aim to walk alongside and 'be with' him in as many thinking, doing and saying spaces as is possible for me. There is at one level a 'motor intentionality' where 'the body senses that what it can and cannot do structures our perception of objects and space' (Pulido 2010: 38). Although not yet understanding fully the practices of the registrar, it was possible to build on what I could or could not do alongside him. With each step I gain a sense of what he can or cannot do as a comparison. The structures of what can be done are developed in relation to using all my senses to try to grasp what is happening from moment to moment, from one place to another, from one conversation to another, between one doctor to other doctors, between one doctor and other healthcare professionals and so on. I attempt to catch every innuendo of every dialogue, to pick up on body language no matter whose it is, and I try not to miss any nuance of any action that occurs. The theme I continually hold in some non-obtrusive corner of my mind is: 'What is it that I am not seeing?' This 'seeing' is used here to signify all the many senses involved in a witnessing, a witnessing that traverses its own boundaries into domains and standpoints in the work of participant observation. In certain contexts the term 'witness' implies an objectivity and a distancing from the reality that is occurring to others and to one's own self. Has the witness become spectator? Is the spectator aloof – a kind of anonymous observer who is distant from the emotions and experiences that are happening to others? What stand does the spectator take on what is happening to one's spectator self? Has spectator become witness, and in witnessing is there then a more particular, emotional engagement? Such questions are at work in mapping representations against reflections on experiences. The reflections operating at a cognitive level work to produce representations for analytic purposes.

Two kinds of intentionality are thus working alongside each other: motor intentionality and cognitive intentionality. Where the motor intentionality is located in the real of being-in-the-world in terms of what the body can and cannot do, cognitive intentionality works these experiences to draw out ways of representing what is experienced and done and to imagine what could be done. In each case attention is directed towards the objects that appear to consciousness through action and thinking. By asking questions, thought is directed to the details of experience, examining it from a variety of angles to identify what is common amongst the variations and whether the representations being produced are 'in touch' with bodily motor intentionality. It is not simply a matter of varying an object, say a geometrical one, a triangle in the mind, and identifying that no matter whether one side or two sides are elongated and angles varied, so long as the three sides made of straight lines connect at each corner, it remains within the definition of a triangle. It is also about relating the possibilities of the triangle to what can be done in the world. In making a triangle the body is implicated, skills of the physical manipulation of different kinds of material are built up. Rather than speculations being trapped within a Cartesian ego that cannot go beyond its own thoughts, a Spinozan approach refocuses from the I-Think to the body and its interactions with the world about in terms of what Merleau-Ponty describes as a tactile I-can or cannot do in relation to the perceived, felt world about. What can be done is placed as the contents of a representational category. These contents placed under a particular category can be tested out through dialogue with others to 'see' if the same contents, the same 'I-can do x' works for others. The contents cannot just be placed in any fashion, randomly. There is what may be called a lived body resistance as it engages with the materiality of the world about as well as a cultural resistance and what I can do is modified by the practices of what others can do in relation to what I can do. There is not an absolute freedom to do as I imagine: 'Merleau-Ponty points out in his critique of Sartre's extreme view of freedom that mountains are tall for us, and that where they are passable and where not is not up to us but is a function of our embodied capacities' (Dreyfus 1996). Furthermore, we respond not only to the physical world about, but also to the cultural world. Dreyfus, referring to J. J. Gibson, writes that he, like Merleau-Ponty:

> sees that characteristics of the human world, e.g. what affords walking on, squeezing through, reaching, etc. are correlative with our bodily capacities and acquired skills, but he then goes on, in one of his papers, to add that mail boxes afford mailing letters. This kind of affordance calls attention to a third aspect of embodiment. Affords-mailing-letters is clearly not a cross-cultural phenomenon based solely on body structure, nor a body structure plus a skill all normal human beings acquire. It is an affordance that comes from experience with mail boxes and the acquisition of letter-mailing skills. The cultural world is thus also correlative with our body; this time with our acquired cultural skills.
>
> (Dreyfus 1996)

The work of the social sets into relation embodied realities as a foundation for representation in terms of motor-intentionality or body structure, skills developed in relation to bodily capacities and skills directed specifically to the cultural. These three forms of intentional organisation criss-cross each other but there is no specific reason why they should crystallise into representational signs having a unique meaning for all people at all times in all places. There is an ambiguity essential to each. As Merleau-Ponty points out, even in the sensation of clasping one's own hands, the sense of which is touching and which being touched oscillates. So, meanings slip and slide. How then can an interpretation be fixed?

Gesturing towards writing

Getting in touch is essential to ethnographic writing. It is a matter of being with, of walking and working alongside until meanings are written in the flesh, in the behaviours, in the aesthetics of seeing as others see and in the ways of naming, classifying, forming associations and organising sequences of thinking and talking about the world. Reflected in the anecdotes, the stories, the histories, the myths of people are the ways they cast themselves as members, as agents, as subjects, in relation to each other and to the history, the vision of who they really are and the kind of work they inhabit, the place they call home and the community they try to build. Also reflected in the narratives are how they cast 'the others', the 'them' who are different and the extent to which this difference is an opportunity to make friends or is a potential threat that creates enemies. In short, how is a world constructed through the ways in which people are directed towards each other and towards the objects of consciousness that stand as representations of the things (whether conceptual, physical, real or imagined) of their world and as tools within their world(s)?

Case studies may show the extent to which instances, individuals, particular forms of organisation, sectors and systems mesh with the totalising visions, the idealisations of 'who we are' and 'what we do'. Or they may pick up on counter-vailing practices, values, identities and forms of social organisation. Such an approach would provide a means of evaluating practices and the consequences or outcomes of practices against the idealised or desired visions and thus identify possibilities for action either to 'improve' the quality of practices to meet the idealisations or to subvert them in the intention to create alternative visions. The writing then focuses attention either on the presentation of the case as a representation of the degree to which actual practices fit with idealisations or a representation of the emergent possibilities for counter-representations that are generative of counter organisations. By exploring the concept of 'real' in the relation between representation and 'thing represented', between experience of being and the semblant to be played, the work of creating objects and subjects through the powers of living beings is radically presented. It is presented, then, not just as a possibility for making a difference but for actualising it. The work of writing the difference involves the generation of publics open to the slipperiness of meanings and the alternative interpretations that can be made.

Chapter 6

Interpretations – and deconstructions

How do you interpret 'a child'?

It is hard to ignore a child. There are immediate calls to care, demands to respond. A child cannot be handled in just any way. Body is oriented to body at that level of motor responses skilfully shaped in the process of looking after a child. Beyond that, of course, there are the cultural meanings of child. Jung saw the child as an archetype of renewal, hope, the future. In the UK the Victorian myth of the child is of fairytale innocence, albeit children of the lower classes were simply cheap exploitable labour. The value of 'child' takes on further determinations when in a system where boys are valued higher than girls, or vice versa. When is a child no longer a child? At different times and in different cultures the age of criminal responsibility, for marriage, to be a soldier, to vote, to work have differed. Indeed, Ariès (1963, 1973) saw childhood as a social construction that was non-existent in medieval times. De Mause (1975) in his psychoanalytic-oriented history of childhood presented a very dark picture of abuse and violence towards children. In his view, childhood was a nightmare from which we are only just awakening. Pollock (1983) argued against the thesis of the invention of childhood and child abuse. De Mause (1975) responded to Pollock's and other criticisms with further arguments and evidence. In particular, he picked up on her methodology that he called an argument from silence: if parents did not mention forms of abuse in their diaries, or report it in newspapers, then none were committed; thus childhood was largely a happy experience. In Pollock's view there has been a broad continuity of 'childhood' throughout the ages. Hence she also criticised Ariès thesis that the concept of childhood is a relatively recent phenomenon. Grant summarises various views:

> Either Ariès was wrong or he was misunderstood, according to different scholars. He was wrong because numerous researchers have discovered sufficient evidence to establish that conceptions of childhood as a unique stage of life existed in ancient Greco-Roman society, early medieval Europe, and the Middle East, among others, and that Ariès' notion of parents as

'indifferent' to their children is less than nuanced if not mistaken. The premise that there are universals in parenting and childhood that transcend time and space infused Linda Pollack's *Forgotten Children: Parent–Child Relations from 1500–1900* (1983), one of the first battle cries in the litany of texts that have advanced the 'continuity' thesis in opposition to Ariès claims. Ariès has been misunderstood, some argue, because he was not purporting that childhood per se did not exist but that it had a very different meaning in medieval Europe. Hugh Cunningham contends that Ariès supposed provocative assertion that 'in medieval society the idea of childhood did not exist' in fact represents a mistranslation of the French word sentiment." Many scholars call for a rapprochement between the change and continuity theses. As Nicole Eustace, the author of an intriguing entry on 'Emotional Life,' aptly states: 'Just as claims of radical disjuncture in the emotional lives of early modem and modern children now seem unlikely and exaggerated, models of undifferentiated continuity appear overly simplistic, not to mention ahistorical' (p. 314). Yet few would argue with the fact that an intensified focus on the rearing and regulation of childhood has indelibly marked modern American and European societies.

(Grant 2005: 472–3)

Cunningham (1998) had commented that Ariès had certainly had a profound impact on the history of childhood; indeed, his intention was to convince readers that there was, in fact, a history. The 'mistranslation' that Cunningham referred to above was:

> The English version of Ariès' book contains the famous statement that 'in medieval society the idea of childhood did not exist.' The word 'idea' was in fact a translation of the French sentiment, which conveys a very different meaning.
>
> (Cunningham 1998: 1197)

Was this a mistranslation, a creative reading or indeed a reading that attempted to find the 'real' meaning to convey? However, on a further look at the uses of the term '*sentiment*' in French, other possible translations arise, related to 'opinion' and 'thought', depending on the context. For example, '*donner le sentiment de faire*' is translated in wordreference.com as 'to give the impression of doing'. In the online discussion forums on the word '*sentiment*' can be found an exchange over its best possible translation in the context of '*et nous serions très heureux de pouvoir entrer en contact avec vous, afin de connaître votre sentiment sur notre gamme*'. The words in bold were causing the translation problem. One translator offered 'and we would like to get in touch with you to know what you think of our range', adding 'or "to know your opinion ..." – I don't think "feeling" sounds natural here'. Another translator offered 'feedback'.

Where 'idea' in the Ariès translation perhaps pushes the line of thinking too far towards 'concept', the feeling tone of 'sentiment' can move towards thinking in the sense of the general feel of public opinion or mood. Regarding an issue concerning the mood of the public, we might ask, 'do they have an idea of what is going on'? Is what Ariès is trying to express more generally an 'idea' than a feeling, perhaps more broad unarticulated opinion than mood? Perhaps 'concept' was too strong an implication drawn from the use of 'idea', but it could be argued *sentiment* as 'idea' does not 'convey a very different meaning'. It depends on context and upon the evidence of use of a given term. What seems to be trying to be conveyed by 'idea' is more of an attitude towards children that did not exist and that in turn could not be conceptualised as such. Whatever is the case, upon the issue of the 'concept of childhood', the battle lines have been drawn between the protagonists. And these have been drawn on issues of interpretation in relation to the kinds of data that are or are not permissible. What is at issue is the representational value of the term 'idea' in relation to the value of the term '*sentiment*' in English and in French both in the present usages of the terms and in their usage in medieval times. All that remains are various forms of documentary evidence: diaries, entries in official documents, reports of various kinds, works of fiction, essays and other forms of academic and non-academic writing. What gets included and what does not? The criteria vary from writer to writer, researcher to researcher. If for de Mause the history of childhood is a nightmare but for Pollock it is the history of a continuity, very different analytics, frameworks of representation and agendas are in play, each making a claim and forming arguments to sustain an assertion of truth, or at least to provide enough argumentation to shift the balance of opinion from one side to another. In each case, then, the interpretations being made destabilise representations of the 'real' drawn from the data chosen as the basis for evidence of a 'real'. Where is the point of 'authority' to make a decision?

In religious texts that authority may be located with 'God' or at least with those considered legitimate interpreters of the word, especially when the original 'word' was in a language no longer spoken, or not spoken by the congregation. Interpreters are again particularly important when the question is asked of an ancient holy text, 'But what does this mean for us today?' This is no longer just a matter of translation from one language to another, but from one culture to another, from one discourse to another. The authority, then, is with the legitimate discourses prevalent at a given time with a given audience. Interpretation is thus a work of localising and making relevant texts that had been created for other purposes, in other contexts, in other times in relation to a present legitimising discourse or discourses.

However, what if the text is a literary document, or an autobiography or a diary? The authority here is surely with the author alone? Yet, what the author 'really intends' cannot with full certainty be recovered from a text. We have only the text, not the life of the mind. In Arendt's terms:

Seen from the perspective of the world of appearances and the activities conditioned by it, the main characteristic of mental activities is their invisibility. Properly speaking, they never appear, though they manifest themselves to the thinking, willing, or judging ego, which is aware of being active, yet lacks the ability or the urge to appear as such.

(Arendt 1978: 71)

There is then an essential indeterminacy at the heart of interpretation. When does the invisibility of a mental act become a deliberate act of silence? Or indeed when does silence denote an unconscious repression of a mental act? Agamben (2004) for example recounts telling Derrida of his discovery that there is an issue with the translation of a famous statement on 'friendship' – o philoi, oudeis philos, 'o friends, there are no friends' – a topic for a book that Derrida at the time was still writing. The issue was that a correction had been made, which produced a different meaning – oi (omega with subscript iota) philoi, oudeis philos, 'he who has (many) friends, has no friend'. However:

Since I had immediately informed Derrida of the results of my research, I was astonished, when his book was published under the title Politiques de l'amitié, not to find there any trace of the problem. If the motto – apocryphal according to modern philologists – appeared there in its original form, it was certainly not out of forgetfulness: it was essential to the book's strategy that friendship be, at the same time, both affirmed and distrustfully revoked.

In this, Derrida's gesture repeated that of Nietzsche. While still a student of philology, Nietzsche had begun a work on the sources of Diogenes Laertius and the textual history of the Lives (and therefore also Casaubon's amendment) must have been perfectly familiar to him. But both the necessity of friendship and, at the same time, a certain distrust towards friends were essential to Nietzsche's strategy. This accounts for his recourse to the traditional reading, which was already, by Nietzsche's time, no longer current (the Huebner edition of 1828 carries the modern version, with the note, 'legebatur o philoi, emendavit Casaubonus').

(Agamben 2004: 3)

Such issues in destabilising texts in forming interpretations add a sense of 'shiftiness', of mobility through which any given representation becomes unstuck. It is in this place of shiftiness where interpretations can be offered. There are two possibilities at this point: to search for the key, the code through which all will be resolved; or to explore the range of possibilities, noting the disagreements, the gaps, the blurs, the silences and the possible connections with other texts, other discourses, other signs. The one strategy closes down to a final, certain meaning. The other opens up, delighting in non-closure. However, 'between' them is another possibility. It is where the difficulties met in exploring the concept of the 'child' and the possibility of 'friendship' are articulated as a real-politic.

The real-politic of interpretation

Who is my friend? For the political theorist Carl Schmitt the fundamental axis upon which politics is built is the friend–enemy relation. It is in placing people, communities, peoples, faiths, nations on this axis that the undecidability of interpretations solidify around taking sides. In a representational system that sees only friends and enemies, what characterises the one from the other? As Agamben points out, the term friend does not act like a predicate such as 'red hair', since there is so much variation amongst people who could be called friends. Nor is it a performative, like the words 'I do' perform 'marriage'. The 'friend' acts more like a name. but not so much like a proper name – more like an insult. It is a pure experience of language signifying being. Once designated, then certain expectations are associated with the 'friendship' in terms of forming sides, engaging in alliances against the common enemy and overlooking faults in the interest of the greater friendship. There is called into being a logic of friendship where friends of friends are friends, and where families of friends are friends.

This analytics of the friend–enemy politics can be seen at work in a speech given by Obama on 19 May 2011.

> For decades, the conflict between Israelis and Arabs has cast a shadow over the region. For Israelis, it has meant living with the fear that their children could be blown up on a bus or by rockets fired at their homes, as well as the pain of knowing that other children in the region are taught to hate them. For Palestinians, it has meant suffering the humiliation of occupation, and never living in a nation of their own. Moreover, this conflict has come with a larger cost to the Middle East, as it impedes partnerships that could bring greater security and prosperity and empowerment to ordinary people.
> (*New York Times*, transcript; (http://www.nytimes.com/2011/05/20/
> world/middleeast/20prexy-text.html?pagewanted=all)

Reacting to this speech, Joseph Massad (Associate Professor of Modern Arab Politics and Intellectual History at Columbia University) wrote an in-depth Opinion article for the Al Jazeera online site on 30 May 2011. The title was 'Are Palestinian children less worthy?' Immediately underneath this title was the subscript: 'Although Palestinian children endure lives of suffering, Obama's love for their Israeli counterparts knows no limit'. Title and subscript then set the scene in terms of the agenda and framings. A fictionality versus a reality-of-fictions circumscribing a number of complex and contentious issues is set in motion. It is this reaction by Massad that will be a core reference point for explorations of what is at stake in interpretation during the following sections of the chapter. Does Obama in this speech, and by implication any other speech, have a 'concept', a 'sentiment' of the Arab child?

There is a presumption at work in the speech and the article of a universal principle that all children are innocent and should not be harmed. As Massad writes explicitly, '[i]nnocence and childhood are common themes in Western political discourse, official and unofficial'. Thus, his title is a direct challenge to that principle, questioning its operation in the real world and, in particular, the real world of being a Palestinian child living in the Occupied Territories. Massad argues that Arab children, especially Palestinian ones, are exceptions to this universal principle. In effect, the world turns a blind eye to the existence of any apparatus – any dispositif – that projects and inscribes 'evil' on to children from a particular birthplace and on to parents of a particular nation-state. In short, the story of the violence perpetrated against them 'remains ignored, deliberately marginalised, and purposively suppressed both in the US and Western media – and in Western political discourse'. In his argument he points to historical evidence from Zionist terrorists in the 1930s when grenades and timed mines were used in public spaces; the massacres of 1947 to 1949 when entire Palestinian villages were targeted and – in today's parlance – were ethnically cleansed; he includes Israel's War of Attrition against Egypt in 1970 and cites documented historical events where children in an elementary school in Bahr al-Baqar were killed; he then moves on to the 'first intifada' from 1987–1993 followed by the 'second intifada' of 2000–2004 and finally to the Israeli attack on Gaza in 2008. In Massad's view, '[t]his exhibition of atrocity is not simply about regurgitating the history and present of Israel's murder of Arab children for the past six decades and beyond', but it 'demonstrates' a deeper 'obscenity'.

The trouble with interpretation is that, like opinions, everyone has one. How can the 'truth' then be demonstrated? And 'obscenity' acts rather in the same way as 'friend', 'insult' and 'offence'. However, the obscene evokes something of what Kristeva called the abject, and the abject has a particular relation to the child and to the territory of the clean that is the child's 'own territory, edged by abject' (Kristeva 1982: 5). In being born and pushed out, in vomiting and excreting, in dying there are the experiences of boundaries – insides and outsides, thresholds and limits – to the body, the living and the clean. The abject resists definition but can be variously thought of as 'a massive and sudden emergence of the uncanny' (Kristeva 1982: 2), the affectual response of 'a dark revolt of being' directed against a life-threatening threat that 'seems to emanate from beyond the possible, the tolerable, the thinkable' (Kristeva, 1982: 1); 'an enemy of language and the Symbolic' (Hook 2003: 8). The abject is 'at the border of my condition as a living being' and a corpse, any corpse, is the worst vehicle for the abject, since it is 'that thing that no longer signifies anything. I behold the breaking down of a world that has erased its borders' (Kristeva 1982: 3–4). As a further and graphic example, there is an interesting use of the abject in relation to the real and symbolic terror caused by the attack on the Twin Towers of the Trade Centre by Semetsky (2006) when associating it with the symbolic imagery of the Tower in a deck of Tarot cards. In the Tarot imagery two terrified figures are propelled off a Tower by a strike of lightning. In Semetsky's (2006: 5) terms. 'The two beings on the card have built the tower – and sealed it at the top; there is no entry or exit. They have imprisoned themselves in their own creation – the rigid, phallic, mental structure – and the only way out is through the agency of a threatening, violent breaking force that would necessarily bring along a traumatic, abject, experience.' In their fall – they are pictured as still falling – using Kristeva's own words, Semetsky describes them as 'beset by abjection' (Kristeva 1982: 1). In a deck of cards that, as a collection of symbols, creates a system of representation that shuffle out interpretations of futures, its meaning or value is located in a desire for certainty – or at least a degree of predictability – in uncertain states of affairs. For those that do not believe, the compelling imagery may be located in other analytics of experience. The question for each is what is the 'truth' of the writing?

Truth in the sense being employed here does not have as its automatic opposite 'falsity' or even 'lie'. In falling from the tower, is the truth that one is about to die, that one is alive in the infinite moment, or that terror has sucked out the sense of life? 'So far so good' goes the old joke of the falling man overheard reassuring himself as he passes each floor of the skyscraper: it's not the fall but the landing that's the problem. In the Heideggerian sense, we are all in the state of being thrown into existence, and there is neither guarantee of an infinite fall nor of a good landing. It is the story being told by the falling man that provides at least moment of hope, resignation, nihilism or panic. As in Vonnegut's story 'The Sirens of Titan', even if it is discovered at the end of days that the Great Wall of China was really a message and that a crash-landed alien space traveller had manipulated human history to build it in order to say 'send spare parts', then life will have at least been a part of some purpose. The search for meaning is ubiquitous, and as Victor Frankl (1963) wrote, without belief in some meaning, people can lose the will to live. It was a theme he addressed in his accounts of people imprisoned in the Nazi concentration camp of Auschwitz. There is an existential connection with a text that is experienced as essential to be able to cope with a particular reality. It provides meaning that is greater than the otherwise tragic, or dreary or transitory or trivial engagements of everyday life. To understand an anecdote, an exchange of conversation, or some account of day-to-day life requires a reading behind the text, but the 'behind' depends upon the criteria by which a textual or narrative choice is made as 'my story', or 'our story' or 'their story' as the story that sustains all other stories. This text may intrude into countless other texts appearing as clichés, constant repetitions of key words or phrases that stand for a whole story, in the way that Ted Hughes (1976) wrote of a single word from a well-known story – like, for Christians, 'manger' – being so charged that uttering them would bring to mind the whole story. Riffaterre (1978) pointed to constants or repetitions in poetic texts that similarly indicated the existence of some other code or text necessary to make sense of the poem being studied. When people speak or write the language employed is not simply a straightforward statement mimicking the real. In some philosophies of science there has been the aspiration to create an unambiguous language through which reality could be exactly represented, as in mathematical languages. Even here, the systems are not perfect. Gödel (1992) famously proved the incompleteness of any complex system. Given that particular observations can only be interpreted through a theoretical framework, Duhem (1954) argued that particular observations providing no support for a particular hypothesis do not disprove overall theoretical frameworks since they will entail a multiplicity of hypotheses. If some or indeed many of these have been borne out by observations, then the one failure does not necessitate overthrowing the whole complex of theories. Both arguments point to an essential undecidability. Effectively, the same observations can support mutually exclusive interpretations or theories.

Politically, there is an argument from 'nature' that individuals in the natural state are 'savage', interested only in their own satisfactions (Hobbes 1651). In conjunction with the classical economic arguments concerning the functioning of markets where only the fittest survive and the later Darwinian arguments concerning the evolution of species to produce a social Darwinism, the 'facts' of human nature can be seen as evidence for contemporary neo-liberal market and political theories and interpretations that guide contemporary policies. Alternatively, observations of 'nature' can show co-operation between individuals and species. Indeed, Kropotkin (1904) developed from his observations of animals in the wild a conception of 'mutual aid' being the significant factor in evolution. Furthermore, the concept of division of labour itself, stemming from Adam Smith (1776), can be seen as presupposing the cooperative organisation of work just as much as it pre-supposes competitive markets where specialisation leads to productivity that outperforms people who created the whole product rather than contributing to only one small part of it. Indeed, although Smith has been appropriated by neo-liberals for proposing a market free of government interference, there are many counter readings of Smith, one of which being Smith as a critic of capitalism (Tribe 1999). Smith also proposed a system of power and thus the realities of politics and police (1762) in maintaining a market. Whether the world is composed of greedy self-serving egos or co-dependent mutuality-seeking egos is not open to observation alone. Rather, as imaginative beings who have a voice, it is in the ways in which voice is organised that the world becomes, and becomes 'legible' for one or more possible interpretations and thus a legitimating stimulus to action.

Legitimacy legibility and illegible children

Structurally, being placed in the position of the child is to be inferior in social status and excluded from public domains of debate, decision-making and action. However, structure is never quite stable. In post-structural terms, there is no centre even if there is a dynamic towards the framing of structures as if they were stable. Where power seeks to be the centre of organisation, voice seeks to create the conditions for its inclusion and thus disturbs and displaces the centre of power that in turn seeks to tame voice to become a form of orchestration, a 'singing from the same hymn sheet'. In nineteenth-century novels of bourgeois families their civilised children typically are expected to be seen but not heard, and servants visible only as machines are visible. Their 'innocence' is that of being not yet ready to assume power. Bourgeois women – as wives, mothers, marriageable daughters, widows, spinsters, aunts, cousins – take their value in relation to the men as centre of power. That is to say, they have no democratic 'say' in their daily life. Where the bourgeois children may look forward to taking their place in adult society, servants, whose value is 'value to the family', knowing their place, only have their places (kitchens, stables, store rooms and all the other structures of support), their margins, and their interstices for working out an alternative, perhaps parallel arrangement between themselves. When a child, a woman, a servant tries for visibility and audibility as a voice to be reckoned with, it can be regarded by power variously as insubordination, hysteria and nonsense. Something of these structured places and systems of value remain as rhetorical and discursive resources for interpretation. They can be seen at play in the media manufacture of the innocence of children and the re-versioning of the place of servants as the place of employees that in turn goes along with the taming of the voice of citizens in 'democracies' and consumers in markets. It is, of course, one resource amongst many. And any text, any speech, any conversation is likely to draw upon many resources. A text referring, whether explicitly or implicitly, to another text is often called intertextuality. It enables what Althusser and Balibar (1970) called a 'symptomatic' reading of a text where:

> The symptomatic reading makes visible the suppressed discourses, the naturalized power relations, the systems of exclusion which allow the text to make sense in particular ways. Having recognized a symptom, readers should not read it literally, but rather as a sign of something else that is going on. This helps me to search and to recognize the presence of more than one discourse in a text, and to explore the absent conjunctions that divide it into a multiplicity of meanings, if these complement, suppress or displace each other thereby truncating each other's development. The symptomatic reading will be effective in so far as it divulges the undervalued event in the text it reads. Here, my aim is not to present the substrate of a 'worker identity', but using the rhetorical activities and narrative strategies of the informants in order to open up the possibility of thinking the pragmatic application of singularities toward the construction of new universes of reference for subjectivation. The reader is also an active participant in the meaning of the text in a potentially endless process.
>
> (Commisso 2006: 177–8)

The child is located in many texts and discourses – fictional, legal, religious, political, sexual – and these discourses multiply position and construct the meaning that 'child' is to have in a given speaking, interactional and writing context. That is to say, the 'child' is overdetermined as the 'object' of a multiplicity of discourses and texts. Each discourse and text presents a 'surface' upon which can be written a variety of agendas. This can be illustrated through Obama's use of the discourses surrounding 'the child' to present a particular political agenda in his speech to the American Israel Public Affairs Committee, AIPAC, delivered at this US–Israeli lobbying group conference on 22 May 2011. Massad's reading of this speech provides further opportunities to inscribe 'readings' into the text of the speech. As Commisso pointed out above, producing readings – and thus inscribings – is a 'potentially endless process'.

The context, then, for this speech is highly political. At the time of speaking, Obama was facing re-election the following year. It is widely known that favoured presidential candidates can receive significant funding from the wealthy and powerful American–Jewish community – in particular, those who were likely to be on or close to this Committee – a fact that Obama publicly acknowledged in his speech. He needed to win this particular audience over both for himself in relation to his re-election and for his party. Of critical importance, then, were the kinds of discourses deployed by the committee and the wider Jewish communities to define, reinforce, protect and further their interests both in the USA and in the Middle East. To achieve his campaign goal, Obama would then have to inscribe his electoral agenda onto the surfaces afforded by these discourses. Several such key 'surfaces' are established in the following from the speech when Obama raised the issue of the desire for a safe and secure homeland:

> We also know how difficult that search for security can be, especially for a small nation like Israel in a tough neighbourhood. I've seen it firsthand. When I touched my hand against the Western Wall and placed my prayer between its ancient stones, I thought of all the centuries that the children of Israel had longed to return to their ancient homeland.

The desire for security is a key psychological and political 'surface'. That is to say, there is a solidity that is experienced most forcefully when there are threats to an established framework, say 'a small nation like Israel' that is the guarantor of a common and a particular sense of identity. The threat is the 'tough neighbourhood'. It is upon people's desire to maintain the guarantor of secure identity that Obama can gain a handhold. Such a 'surface' is identifiable in terms of its resistances that enable and retain the traces of impressions, marks, inscriptions. He attempts to write himself 'first hand' into this surface of 'security', this guarantor of identity, with a touch 'against the Western Wall', itself a symbolic and ancient physical surface, written with prayers, a history of longing, a desire for origins – the homeland. This desire for the homeland is inscribed with the legitimacy of heritage and innocence of children.

It is with this innocence of childhood that Massad opens up the surfaces of the discourses implicit in Obama's speech. It stands as a symptom for these other discourses, elsewhere yet very present, through which he constructs his reading. At first sight the mention of the 'child' appears to be a small detail in the speech. It acts like the 'ungrammaticalities' that Riffaterre (1978) sees as the indicators of some other text that is required to make sense of a poem. In Massad's reading, what is missing from the speech are the Palestinian children and their longing for a homeland that guarantees their identity, their heritage. In a real sense, the children are either legible or illegible according to their identity, their heritage, their security of nationhood. These conditions for legibility enable Obama to position himself at multiple political levels, giving legitimacy to his own agendas for re-election by the American people and to the agendas of his major potential campaign funders.

Dispositifs of interpretation

There remains a question when adopting and adapting Agamben's (2007, 2009) formulation of the dispositif as the particular network of relations between discourses, organisations and material resources that can be called upon when facing some urgent demand, problem, issue where 'we're all in this together' and 'on the same side' against some threat or to realise some opportunity. It is produced when recalling Saussure's metaphor of the two sides of a piece of paper where one side is the signifier and the other the signified, any cutting and framing of one side will impact on the 'contents' of the other side. Who defines which side is which?

The question of sides became imperative in the Middle East during the year of 2011 when the solidity of political arrangements within and between states was threatened by protest and demands for 'freedom', 'human rights' and 'social justice'. As described in Chapter 2, Eisenhower's (1961) warning of the power of the rise of the military–industrial complex was prescient and has transformed into a global framework of powers that include the new communications technologies that impact upon every aspect of everyday life and its forms of social, economic, cultural and political organisation. Such forms of organisation do not become a 'dispositif' until directed toward the resolution of a given problematics. Thus in 2011, how was interpretation of Middle Eastern and world affairs to be manufactured to enable particular agendas to be maintained and secured? Any speech by Obama as the representative of the American State, the 'leader' of the 'Western World', is an immediate focus of media attention and examined for its probable interpretations in order to decode its 'message' and its implications. The function of the media as a dispositif for Obama's purposes is potentially in competition with the purposes of other forms of organised power both within America and globally. However, if Obama in turn is part of the dispositif of a globalised, if American rooted, corporate-financial-industrial-military complex that includes telecommunications media, then the words spoken take their meanings from authorising codes that are located elsewhere than a simple application of dictionary meanings and grammar to the text of the speaker. When Ted Hughes (1976) wrote of the electrical charge that could bring into life a whole narrative from the mere mention of one of its well-known and symbolic images, he expressed the power of stories to organise the mind and generate an effect. Historically vital narratives are part of the machinery through which people are organised and self-organising. It is not a matter of re-telling a whole story, but of deploying significant historical images in relation to present agendas.

When Obama deploys the phrase 'the children of Israel' there is felt the electricity of an Old Testament naming, immediately positioning and framing the specific audience of AIPAC along with the multiple audiences of media networks in America and globally. Alongside that implicit narrative is a description of present circumstances, present structures, present characters and settings that parallels the way Riffaterre sees the relation between fiction and truth. In a given text he concentrates on:

> the actualisation of structures, the ways in which models are fleshed out with the description of characters and settings, and the representations of the thoughts and speech of these characters. In short, I am concerned here with the diegetic implementation of narrative models, which is achieved through the complementarity of the narrative and of the descriptive, a mutual dependency that can roughly be expressed by saying that the syntax is narrative and its lexicon, descriptive. The solution of the truth-in-fiction paradox evidently lies in redefining referentiality. Whereas referentiality assumes an actual or potential relationship between language and reality, we have to hypothesise that this assumption suffices only so long as it respects the rules of representation that exist in any language and with which all speakers of that language are familiar. Words may lie yet still tell a truth if the rules are followed.
>
> (Riffaterre 1990: xiii)

The phrase 'the children of Israel' acts, in Riffatterre's terms, as a kernel, or matrix, that can be fleshed out drawing upon the rules and the principles by which structures can be actualised (its syntax) in conjunction with a lexicon or vocabulary containing descriptive terms or categories through which a world is mapped out and travelled. If the referentiality of the fleshed-out narrative of the 'children of Israel' 'assumes an actual or potential relationship between language and reality', then there is the possibility of a truth being articulated in relation to that narrative. There is also the possibility of deception, illusion passing as truth. Interpretation, then, involves a decision on the referentiality of a text or discourse together with a judgement as to whether grounds can be found to claim that it expresses a truth according to the rules. But what rules?

For some, the rules may be defined in terms of a 'Big Narrative'. It is a narrative that provides a model to explain everything from the origins of the universe and all its worlds to the intricacies of everyday life. If it is accepted that there is a divinely revealed Big Narrative then it cannot be questioned, only interpreted according to the rules, rules applied by those ordained divinely. There is a parallel structure for the grand narratives of Science. Here, the place of the Divine may be occupied by the scientists, the scholars, the philosophers of the exact sciences, constructed upon systems of mathematics, logics and geometries that underpin the search for the general theory of everything. If science rules, then, the government of people can be organised through the principles and practice of scientific management. In a sense, it is the end of politics, since there is nothing left to discuss, or, in Hegel's terms, the end of history. Indeed, some saw confirmation of the end of history in the fall of the Soviet Republic (Fukuyama 1992). Others, however, saw different rules at play. Notably, Huntington (1996) saw not a clash of politics but a clash of civilisations expressible not in terms of reason and science but in terms of beliefs, values and ways of life. When the attack on the Twin Towers of the World Trade Center on 11 September 2001 had taken place, the event was interpreted by Bush as a war between alternative ways of life where the anti-Western alternative was composed of an Axis of Evil supporting terrorism. Alternatively, as some pointed out, it could have been interpreted as a crime, a terrible crime against humanity. In Chomsky's view:

> Was there an alternative? There is every likelihood that the Jihadi movement, much of it highly critical of bin Laden, could have been split and undermined after 9/11. The 'crime against humanity', as it was rightly called, could have been approached as a crime, with an international operation to apprehend the likely suspects. That was recognised at the time, but no such idea was even considered.
>
> (Chomsky 2011; http://english.aljazeera.net/indepth/opinion/
> 2011/09/20119775453842191.html)

A different analytics is generated according to the choice made between a generalised war on terror and the prosecution of a specific crime. Different dispositifs are required to address the urgent demands of each. For the war a global 'friends–enemy' logic reinforces the political world order. For the crime, the logic of a criminal investigation involves the search for evidence, the identification of the participants of the crime and bringing them to justice in a court of law under the law. In the war on terror the law was suspended, a state of exception was declared, and 'extraordinary rendition' meant that people could be captured and flown to friendly states for interrogation where the rules of interrogation involved torture. Guantanamo became the reality and the symbol of this process, where prisoners were kept outside the law, without legal representation and without knowing the evidence against them.

Interpretation, as it were, flows along the lines authorised by the dominant analytics, constructing political, social, economic and cultural realities in ways that reinforce – and legitimate – the power structures of the world order. In Riffaterre's (1978, 1990) terms, the 'friend–enemy' logic acts as the kernel or matrix pointing to a hypogram, the reference text, required to understand a given text like Obama's speech to AIPAC, or the tragic accounts of men and women killed in military action whether they are soldiers or civilians and the glossing over of 'collateral damage' where children and their parents are wiped out without a word and without count. There is in the war against terror a diffuseness of the enemy. Its referentiality does not pinpoint a specific state or a specific army. Rather, the enemy may be 'within' as much as 'without'. The truth of the referentiality of 'terror' is that it is potentially everywhere. It generates, as it were, a paranoid analytics. Anything and everything can be referred back to its persecutory logic that requires, not discussion, not democratic debate and decision-making, but shock and awe, overwhelming power, to maintain the boundaries between the good and the bad, the friend and the enemy. It is the Leviathan (Hobbes 1651) not as a State governing a people and a territory, but as Dominion over all. Where the State had its territory and empire had its colonies, Dominion decides who is the enemy, who is the friend globally and thus commands the political and authorises a 'true' interpretation. This is decisionism, in Schmitt's (1996) terms: the state of affairs where the sovereign power, the State, or here the Dominion, decides the fate of all. Dominion is thus the opposing political figure to democracy. What today seeks Dominion engages as if in the final struggle. The enemy, in this sense, is whatever prevents dominion. It is everywhere, particularly in the nature of the human being. There is then the issue of how liberal, if at all, politics should be. It was a question debated between Schmitt and Strauss, two figures who have influenced contemporary politics. The focus of the debate was on Hobbes' view that people were dangerous but educable. Education, of course, could open the way to freedom and in particular, the freedom to challenge dominion.

> If humans are morally base, if they are inherently sinful, if they are inclined to do wrong not only as a result of natural instincts but also because they enjoy doing wrong, then humans are in need of 'dominion.' A state that is agnostic with respect to the moral, theological, aesthetic, etc.—that is, a state that leaves judgment and action over these spheres to its subjects— does not exert sufficient authority over its subjects to forestall the civil war conditions that beset Weimar Germany and to prevent the crisis of the state in general.
>
> (McCormick, 2011: 179)

There is then a tension between the freedom of the individual and the stability of the state. For example, the self-serving ego of the free market has little interest in the state for anything other than to defend and enforce rights to private property and the freedom to accumulate wealth. However, if egos are socially constructed and thus dependent on others for the organisation of work, security and welfare, then education, rather than a threat to stability and security of community and the state, becomes its essential support. Rather than the freedom to dominate others and the world about, there is the freedom that underpins inclusion of one's voice along with all other voices in public decision-making through work and political decision-making. These are then alternative principles for the development of organisational structures and processes through which local, national and global community may be developed. The analytics of each differ as do the dispositifs available to respond to urgent matters. Where the analytics provide the ontological structuring of a perceivable and manipulable world, the dispositif provides an effective response to a particular problem or problem structure. In that sense, then, the analytics provides the way in which the elements of a world can be identified, described, organised and worked according to the needs and interests of people and the dispositif is the actualisation – the syntagms, as it were – of the relations between the elements to produce a specific effect or outcome. Under a Dominion analytics a decisionist syntax would produce instruments to manage and limit the freedom to present and act upon alternative visions of the state and its relations to the political, economic, cultural, social and personal lives of people as the basis for the organisation of everyday life. The object of Dominion is the body as the instrument and symbol of its mastery. As in Chapter 1, dominion over the body is evidenced in the body techniques, the 'flagging' and the 'branding' that can be read as the submission of the subject to the State, the Corporation, the Religion. As such, its logic stifles critique but produces criticism of any body that shows its difference and in particular its resistance, its protest, as 'deviance', 'indiscipline', disobedience and the failure to perform 'correctly'. From the point of view of the Dominion, there is no alternative. All people are in a sense Children of the Dominion. The Children of the Dominion are innocent until corrupted. The greatest internal danger is 'growing up', where growing up involves an independence of mind, freedom to pursue goals and in market economic terms, the freedom to pursue self-interest. Such growing up involves temptations that individuals must learn to overcome if the Dominion – whether financial, corporate, monarchical, religious, dictatorial – is to persist. All threats are then treated as subversion, perversion and a danger to security.

The obscene interpretation

Under conditions of Dominion, any expression, any demand for a democratic voice is obscene since it underwrites the development of alternative interpretations as a basis for working for alternative futures. The Dominion creates what may be called a regime of policing in the way that Rancière describes it:

> The police is thus first an order of bodies that defines the allocation of ways of doing, ways of being, and ways of saying, and sees those bodies are assigned by the name to a particular place and task; it is an order of the visible and the sayable that sees that a particular activity is visible and another is not, that this speech is understood as discourse and another as noise. It is police law, for example, that traditionally turns the workplace into a private space not regulated by the ways of seeing and saying proper to what is called the public domain, where the worker's having a part is strictly defined by the remuneration of his work. Policing is not so much the 'disciplining' of bodies as a rule governing their appearing, a configuration of occupations and the properties of the spaces where these occupations are distributed.
>
> (Rancière 1999: 29)

What appears is either innocent and modest and thus appropriate to the police or offensive and obscene and thus has no part in the whole. In the policing of world order some are on the side of innocence and others on the side of obscenity.

What, then, is the innocent and the obscene interpretation of the 'child'? In his article Massad (2011) focuses on the interpretation and use of 'innocence', pointing out that it has 'often been invoked to illustrate the innocence of Israel', a theme employed by Barak Obama on 4 June 2009 in his Cairo speech when, speaking to the Arab audience, he said: 'It is a sign of neither courage nor power to shoot rockets at sleeping children, or to blow up old women on a bus.' In other speeches, Massad writes, he has referred to the fact that Israelis must live with the fear that their children may get 'blown up on a bus or by rockets fired at their homes' and cope with 'the pain of knowing that other children in the region are taught to hate them'; that the US and Israel 'both seek a region where families and their children can live free from the threat of violence'. For Massad, excluded from this search are the voices of the people and children of Palestine and the wider Arab world. There is then a sense, in the public speeches of the US and of Israel, of being in it together, of having similar desires for their families and children and of striving for the same dream, the 'hatred' being located on the other side.

Massad documents other examples to support his argument that the Palestinian child is worth less in a system of values organised around the political logic of friend and enemy. In particular, in his speech to AIPAC on 22 May, Obama said: 'We also know how difficult that search for security can be, especially for a small nation like Israel in a tough neighbourhood.' From this, Massad makes intertextual links with anti-Black American white racism with the use of terms like 'tough neighbourhood' – a term first borrowed by Binyamin Netanyahu to refer to the Middle East over a decade ago – wherein Arabs are the 'violent blacks' of the Middle East and Jews are the 'peaceful white folks'. There is the sense of a historical layering of texts where one interpretation feeds on another as sides are constructed to explain a position. The obscene for Massad in Obama's speech resided in the one-sided sympathy with Jewish children without showing sympathy for the Arab children killed over decades. However, the obscene is also the part that has no part of any side. It is in that sense outside of the police, as Rancière calls it, a term that Adam Smith (1762: 290) equated with 'the attention paid by the public to the cleanlyness of the road'. Yet there would be no state, no side, no organisation without it. Each individual as a member of the multitude that composes a population is not reducible to a part of the system that has a clear function. The multitude is not a part of the system. Only when individuals are organised and lose their identity as 'the masses' are they then a functioning part of a system. It is the multitude that all 'sides' fear as obscene because in the unbridled multitude they lose their dominion. It is the move through this 'obscenity' determined by each side that is involved in making a difference.

Gesturing towards writing

Writing interpretations shows that what is at stake is not a whole world, but worlds. Adopting one interpretation is to exclude the life of another. Ethnographic writing, then, seeks what is made alive and what life is threatened by the interpretations made. The writing engages with the pure and the dirty (Douglas 1966), the innocent and the abject, and explores the conditions of interpretation that enable an unbridling of meanings. There is then a permeability of boundaries as between cases and within cases. It is not just about writing a case but writing a case otherwise as a way of seeing otherwise and as a means of opening the possibilities for action.

The case of a critical absence, a silence, something missing signifies another place where the key may be found. What is not being looked at? How is attention diverted? How is the visible policed? A counter case may be drawn from the patterns of diversion by crossing the boundaries of 'good taste' or 'good order', or 'common sense' maintained in the symbolic and spectacular performances of leaders, role models, stars. Case studies, then, can be written as contested and contestable spaces for interpretation and action through which the boundaries define the limits of the 'real', the 'real-politic' and the possibilities for making a difference in everyday life.

If action research is written to show how differences may be made in specific situations, and if radical research (Schostak and Schostak 2008) sees that change as a catalyst for the emergence and proliferation of democratic publics, then writing radically generates the textual resources for the inclusion of excluded interpretations. What is at stake for people?

Chapter 7

Risking Theory and Explanations – realising difference

What is at stake in writing are the impacts on people and their environments of the theories and explanations through which differences are made. A theory or explanation is in a sense an interpretation that has or seeks total dominion over people and the physical world. It demands that there be no alternative. That total dominion is achieved through an analytics that knots categories of the real, practices and resources into a sensual seamless reality. Threats to this reality, and thus those whose power and security is invested in the Dominion, triggers and unleashes the available dispositifs to settle the problem and bring things back to 'normal'. Outside of that dominion all is meaningless. This meaninglessness is the 'evidence' that is needed to throw out challenges and exclude voices. A particularly clear example was a key feature of a 'debate' between Charlie Wolf (named as a conservative), Dean Baker (co-director of the Center for Economic and Policy Research in Washington) and Camille Rivera (a Wall Street demonstrator from the United New York Organization) broadcast by Al Jazeera's *Inside Story* (Al Jazeera 2011b) on the purposes of the Occupy Wall Street protests of autumn 2011. Camille Rivera starts by describing the anger of people at the crisis, concluding that 'big banks and corporations need to take responsibility, that people are tired of going into their pockets and suffering from what is not their responsibility but the responsibility of our government to help us create jobs'. Charlie Wolf is asked by the interviewer whether he agrees:

> No, it just sounds intellectually fallacious … Listening to Camille just a second ago made no sense, if this was something said in a class I would have kicked her out the classroom … er … you know you're petitioning for jobs so we're going to protest and we're going to hinder the people who actually create the jobs. This makes no sense to me. Uh, you know, Wall Street for all its faults and it does have faults are still the people who are the job creators. The problem here is you have a White House that is standing in the way with massive tax rates and uncertainty with what they're doing and that's why capital is being held back.

Dean Baker found Charlie Wolf equally meaningless, saying 'I'd throw him out of my classroom,' and continued:

> No one forced these banks to make money on these loans, they were making bad loans because they knew that they could give them over to Goldman Sachs have them anything packaged off into mortgage backed security and sold everywhere in the world. These people are absolutely right to be outraged. The banks are better off than ever. We see their corporate profits are at a record share of GDP. The financial sector share of corporate profit are a new record high bonuses are as high as they've ever been and yet we still have 9.1 per cent unemployment. We've known how to deal with unemployment for 70 years. Everyone who took an econ-intro class learnt Keynes. It's an outrage that we don't have a government that can get its act together to get the unemployment down. We know how to do it: it's really simple. Yes people are absolutely right to be outraged.

In turn, this led Wolf to exclaim: 'You're actually talking Keynes and you want me to take you seriously?!' And thus the impasse is complete.

In these extracts from the exchange the protagonists justify their comments, make their exclamations and provide their solutions based on the theoretical models that for them identify the causes, explain the economic malaise and provide the knowledge required to effect solutions. At stake here were two fundamentally different theoretical explanations concerning how to solve the economic crisis and the legitimacy of who is able to make the decision. A theory has an objective value when it 'predicts', organises to determine outcomes, identifies causes, origins, reasons, and brings order to what had seemed chaos. However, the particular subject value of a given theory or explanation also depends on who benefits and who loses from is application. Evidence in each case may be called upon. Yet all evidence is multiply interpretable and the decision depends upon who has access to the means to make and enforce a decision. For those who adopt a neo-liberal, monetarist approach to markets, like Charlie Wolf, 'the market doesn't lie''' Hence, it is only the unfettered market that 'decides' through what Adam Smith (1776) called 'the invisible hand'. As Wolf went on to explain, in his view, governments should get out of the way of the wealth producers who through their creativity produce jobs, products and services give us the quality of life that we enjoy. Accepting such a theory and its explanatory power has wide-ranging implications for the organisation of our lives. Its implications are the opposite of the Keynsian view proposed by Baker. Indeed, Baker's views can be seen as a misinterpretation of Smith (Baum 1992; Samuels and Medema 2005). For the one interpretation, it is a matter of reducing the interference of government and getting out of the way of businesses. For the other, it is about regulating the way business is done to ensure a level of fair play and intervening when the markets are in crisis. Between them is a space of struggle where explanations are at war. The options for each side include reducing the status of explanations to being just an interpretation or opinion, to being ideological and thus political, to lacking knowledge and thus in need of education, or to being meaningless and thus needing to be expelled. The broadcast debate, if it can be called that, was intended to represent the different interests at stake. Thus each member was a representative – or semblant – playing a role: the interviewer 'neutrally' represented the kinds of questions that an audience would ask; Camille Rivera represented the protestors; Charlie Wolf represented conservative neo-liberal market explanations; Dean Baker represented the Keynesian alternative. However, what was left out?

The writing project, the people and its cast of semblants

The writing project is a work, in the broadest meaning of the term, to explore how voice and truth are realisable in public. In this sense, 'truth' is the term employed to make a difference. It is through the expression and contestations of voices that truth is recognisable as a public 'real'. In this approach, the truth is whatever resists arbitrary interpretations of voices that express the reality of their experiences. The work of writing involves inscribing the multiple truths and reals that people express as 'their life', 'their complaints', 'their injuries', 'their hopes', 'their demands', 'their interests'. But how is this work to be organised?

The people either as active agents of their own lives are the source of inscriptions or as passive objects of manipulation are the material to be inscribed. There is, then, either a writing down, or a writing up. The debate between Wolf, Baker and Rivera illustrates both. The debate was mediated by a broadcast channel, Al Jazeera, that at the time had no broadcast outlet in the USA except via the internet. Yet Hillary Clinton, during the early months of the Arab Spring in 2011, recognised that it was providing a better-quality service than the equivalent American broadcasters (Wolf 2011). In effect, broadcast media serve the need of Power seeking Dominion to 'write down' explanations and thus to manage people engaging together to 'write up' alternative explanations.

Digital technologies, however, are no longer limited to being broadcast from a centre. Peer-to-peer technologies such as the mobile phone and the computer linked to the internet provide direct wired and wireless contact between people. Social networking applications provide support for anyone to broadcast across the internet. Hence, more threateningly for centralised Power, broadcast content is no longer monopolised by states and corporations. The technologies are open to creating the conditions for mutual coordination and organisation globally without a symbolic centre of leadership. In this way, people without access to or being members of formally constructed, hierarchical organisations of Power, can create the conditions for spontaneous, dynamic, even if ephemeral, forms of organisation. By extension, through the peer-to-peer digital technologies and their social networking capacities the multitude has access to a dispositif supportive of multiple types of organisation to meet particular demands. There is thus a form of 'writing up' where demands can be written into widespread popular organisation that in turn can be the basis of creating forms for the localisation and dynamic interlocking of countervailing powers to the forms of organisation of centralised Power. Each may attempt to 'write off' the powers and organisations of the other. Power itself may be either hard as in a tyranny or soft as in an elite managed corporate market democracy. Soft power has what Bernays (1928) called its 'invisible government' that stands behind the symbolic power and face of an elected President, a Prime Minister. The real power, however, is the organised aggregate power of the multitude. If the multitude takes their aggregate powers into their own hands against Power, then revolutions take place. For Power to have Dominion, then the taming of the multitude is essential.

The writing project that seeks to make a difference is organised around how power is effected by people and how it is taken away from them. Central to this is the construction of the 'public' space for voices that can be heard and that are not 'meaningless'; the space for people to be seen and not rendered invisible; the space where people can debate, decide and act. Within this public a cast of characters appears, each adopting a role according to the kind of power to which he or she has access. The particular analytics of power and the public that prevails at a given time generates the possibilities for identifying and naming a 'cast'. Hard Power in the form of Dominion will generate its masters, enforcers, dupes and slaves as well as those who resist and sacrifice themselves for a difference. Soft Power will have all these, but in the guise of some explanatory reason as to why power must be organised as it is, that has to be believed and, indeed, desired by the masses. The cast is constructed as Hard Power and Soft Power, each seeking to discipline the multitude and to prevent or manage the emergence of a public. An actually existing democracy of powers has yet to be created, but a writing project can at least outline the conditions for its castings of characters to come into existence. Each in turn has his or her different explanations and theorisations of the 'real' as supports to the ways in which powers are lawfully organised throughout a given society and its territory.

Each form of explanation provides a way of structuring a writing project. Under Dominion, the writing project reduces data to evidence of the certainty of the Dominion. All is to be explained in terms that reinforce the stability, the security, the legitimacy and supremacy of the structure of Power and those who benefit from it. Under Democracy as the condition for the equality and freedom of all to engage in the decision-making that underpins the emergence of all forms of organisation, data emerges through a process of contested and negotiated recognitions by the voices that compose the public. The data in turn become the materials for evidence validating explanations. Writing for difference challenges any one explanation by identifying the range of possible explanations. The possibility of an explanation is grounded in voice. To make a difference involves identifying the range of alternative voices that can be counterposed with the legitimating voices of a dominant form of Power and organising these as a textual space for the audibility of voices and the evidencing of their views and explanations. Such a textual space is an education of the public in the sense of drawing out voices and drawing up the forms of organisation necessary for each to hear and take account of the other. This process is curricular in effect. That is to say, it involves a public reflection on experience that generates courses of debate and mutual learning as a basis for the formation of personal and public judgement, explanation, knowledge, decision and courses of action. Such a curricular form includes voices in a work of living together rather than excluding voices from the classroom.

Drawing up the textual public

Take the following interview extract:

> I think they know what they wanted to achieve, and they had an idea, do I really think they knew what was they were going into when they first started? No. They had no idea. Do I think that some of them have any idea now what they got into? No ... and I still think that they don't quite get what it is that they've achieved. They're very happy with the figures that are coming in and uh some PR and stuff but, I think they sort of expected these sites to just come up and just happen and you know and be happy and be fantastic and everyone would just love them, be no negative PR and I think that's been quite a steep learning curve for them. But have they learnt as much as I would want them to? No, if they continue to do such a 'hands on'. If they were quite content to say, actually we don't know anything about facility development, but you're the experts, and [name of organisation] you're the regeneration experts and uh manage by exception, but that's not the way they're set up to do their CSR, or this particular part of their CSR.
>
> (interview undertaken by JFS 2007)

This is the viewpoint of a person in a senior position in an organisation that is part of the 'voluntary sector' speaking about his or her role as a partner organisation in a Corporate Social Responsibility (CSR) programme of a major financial corporate in the private sector. It is clear that there is a difference of opinion as to how to manage a project. The difference of opinion provides an opening into the explanatory discourses that provide the reasons for courses of action. It is a symptom, as it were, signifying other texts, promoted by other voices providing explanations. The idea behind the project was to build sports facilities around the country, at approximately 200 sites. The budget started at around £30 million and built up to around £50 million with the input of another partner. There is both a CSR story as well as a story of how to work with disadvantaged young people and their communities. There are also stories about how such a programme should be managed and how data should be constructed, collected and processed as 'evidence' to construct explanations. Each is necessary to describing what went on, explaining what happened and developing theory that could encapsulate the process and its intended and actual outcomes.

The writing project becomes a textual space for making public the range of storied explanations including the rationale of its own textual production. The rationale, itself, is a collection of explanations drawn up as the supporting framework justifying the organisation of the research and its writing project. However, the rationale at the end of the writing process may well not have existed at the beginning of the project. The rationale changes dynamically in relation to the counter rationales raised by the range of voices discovered in the literature(s), the fieldwork and the discourses heard, overheard and engaged with in everyday living. At each encounter between the multiple explanations there is a borderline to be traversed if the voice is to be heard and the perceptual field of action seen as real by that voice is to be rendered visible. As in the gestalt image that can be perceived either as a duck or a rabbit, neither the one nor the other can be held together but rather oscillates, incapable of becoming a stable image of both. Whether it is the image of the child made visible by Obama's speech to AIPAC (Massad 2011) where the Palestinian child is rendered invisible, or the reduction of the voice of a protestor to 'meaninglessness' because his or her perception of events cannot be made visible as really existing or as legitimate phenomena within the governing political order of the market. To challenge this is to undermine the order of the world as the perceivable 'object' of 'my life', 'our life' and the things within it that are 'mine' and 'ours'. Such a world provides a certainty where 'the market doesn't lie'. To ask what truth it is telling, or indeed, to say particular experiences and events are its consequences that are undesirable to millions is to take away the certainty and the authority upon which the logic of a whole worldview is build. Charlie Wolf's denial of the meaning of the protester's views and his response that these views would lead him to kick her out of his classroom has its more sinister parallels in dictators 'disappearing' those who speak out against a regime, or indeed its seemingly less-sinister use of police strategies such as 'trap and detain' or 'kettling' to control protests:

> On April 15, 2000, according to court records, demonstrators had gathered in front of the Department of Justice on Pennsylvania Avenue NW and marched to a spot close to the International Monetary Fund on 19th Street NW. Police were very much a presence during the march. As the crowd headed toward Dupont Circle, where it was set to disperse, the activists were suddenly penned in on a side street by the police, according to Becker and court records.
>
> The department at the time justified the arrests by arguing that the officers were trying to prevent chaos in the streets. 'I apologise for nothing we did,' the then-Police Chief Charles Ramsey said at the time. 'They have the right to sue us just like they had the right to protest.'
>
> Along with the mass arrest, several plaintiffs in the Becker case alleged that they were beaten by D.C. cops. The court case produced a video that

showed a police unit charging a group of demonstrators and beating them in the face with batons. The officers had obscured their badge numbers. Another plaintiff said he had been injured with pepper spray and alleged that the cop's attack had been unprovoked.

'There was a police line in riot gear,' Becker remembered. 'They refused to let us go. We turned around and the police line blocked. We were chanting for almost an hour, "let us go!"'

(Cherkis 2011)

Since that time, the strategy of surrounding and trapping people has been used many times around the world. It is also typically accompanied by the use of other weaponry such as pepper spray, tear gas, water cannon, batons and rubber bullets. For example, Astor described a YouTube film of the Occupy Wall Street protests:

It begins with one police officer telling another, earlier in the day, 'My little nightstick is going to get a workout tonight' – presumably referring to his baton – and both officers laughing. Then it cuts to footage of several police officers standing in the middle of a crowd of protesters, who are penned in by metal barriers, and hitting a number of the protesters with their batons.

(Astor 2011)

Who can legitimately appear within a given space and voice their views is inscribed by the laws and customs of public order, circumscribed by organisation of the forces of order and ultimately enforced by weaponry against the bodily presence of individuals who are 'seen' as disturbing social order. What weaponry can legitimately appear and be deployed depends on the political and legal dispositifs that can be called upon:

A senior New York police officer accused of pepper-spraying young women on the 'Occupy Wall Street' demonstrations is the subject of a pending legal action over his conduct at another protest in the city.

The Guardian has learned that the officer, named by activists as deputy inspector Anthony Bologna, stands accused of false arrest and civil rights violations in a claim brought by a protester involved in the 2004 demonstrations at the Republican national convention.

Then, 1,800 people were arrested during protests against the Iraq war and the policies of president George W Bush.

(McVeigh, 2011)

The capacity to remove, arrest and injure bodies depends on the extent to which the everyday spaces of social life is militarisable. And this depends on what can legitimately appear and what can legitimately be rendered invisible, inaudible and meaningless. This legitimisation textualises spaces, that is, it makes them readable according to categories that can or cannot appear. This points to a perceptual basis for the analytics that flows from the relation between the visible and the invisible. Thus the power of any explanatory rationale is always derived from an analytics of the visible and the invisible, the audible and the inaudible and from what can and cannot be done. What fundamentally and radically appears is the body as a speaking, acting subject demanding visibility and audibility as a basis for action in a public space.

If there is a ground upon which to build an analytics of the real that incorporates all voices, then perhaps it may begin with something like Merleau-Ponty's formulation of the body as an 'inborn complex' which marked phenomenology's existential return to the body as constituting 'the locus of being in the world' (Morris 2008: 114; Merleau-Ponty 1962: 78–81). This being in the world is taken from Heidegger's 'being-in-the-world', the hyphenated structure of which 'flags the indissoluble reciprocity of our being, the world and the relation of being-in' (Morris 2008: 114). As embodied beings facing each other, located in the world(s) that people construct, experience of being located in a given world is translated through the inborn complex of the body. As described earlier in Chapter 5, the inborn complex is a kind of 'anonymous existence' or 'amorphous existence' (Merleau-Ponty 1945/1996: 347):

> Merleau-Ponty notes that this independent, anonymous existence asserts its presence even in the midst of the strongest and most personal sentiments – 'While I am overcome by some grief and wholly given over to my distress, my eyes already stray in front of me, and are drawn, despite everything, to some shining object, and thereupon resume their autonomous existence' (Merleau-Ponty, 1945/1996, p.84). Our existence qua subjective, conscious individuality is precarious and cannot be the ground upon which meaning in one's life is built – 'Personal existence is intermittent and when this tide turns and recedes, decision can henceforth endow my life with only artificially induced significance' (Merleau-Ponty, 1945/1996, p.84).
>
> (Welsh 2007)

And yet, the 'existence as subjective, conscious individuality' has its demands to be made public even to the point of extreme danger. Perhaps it is here that the in-born complex of the body plays the role of the 'real' that must be recognised by the 'personal' if a meaningful life with others in public is to be created. That is to say, there is something that resists all attempts to tame it, to reduce it to meet the whims and fancies of others no matter their destructive capacity to prevent it from appearing.

The textual public may find its *raison d'être* here in the body that is already always oriented to others, sensually composing a world of interactions and interfaces, where the categories of existence expand and refine with each touch, each sensation of pleasure and displeasure. The body is always ready in being directed towards things in the world. It is a sensual body directedness. In speaking the real of language, there is the tongue (*langue*) at play, tasting the air, feeling the vibrations of sounds, the roof of the mouth, the teeth, the saliva, the breathlessness at the end of a long utterance, the pause and the await for a response. The real of the tongue is that its techniques of languaging are always shaped by the perception of a community of others. There is here already the dimension of 'intersubjectivity', as Husserl called it, that precedes the emergence of a reflective individual ego. For Merleau-Ponty it is the *embodied* experience of intersubjectivity that precedes the emergence of the individual sense of being a subject. These are grounded in the experiences of reaching out, contacting, withdrawing, tasting, ingesting, spitting out – all such bodily acts through which the contents of a consciousness of particular things and particular others for a particular subject are composed. With each glance, each touch, each sensual relation with another a sense of the objectness of the thing met emerges over time, determining those features that do not change regardless of the changes in context, circumstances and variations in appearance. Identifying the features that do not change makes possible the mapping of those features over other objects that are potentially the same. If there is a fit, then they can be located as being in the same category, at least until there is evidence of an essential difference that breaks the condition of 'sameness'. The essential feature of consciousness for Husserl was its intentionality, that is, its directedness towards objects the features of which can be drawn out through a process of varying their appearance to consciousness and identifying what did not vary. It is a fundamental process of generalisation through which 'samenesses' can be identified and thus categorised together. The intentional construction of objects can be seen as an intellectual process of idealisation. Husserl called the process eidetic variation where the idea of the object is subjected to variations to see what the essential, that is invariant, feature of the object was. The sides, for example, of a triangle can be varied in length, but the feature that there are three sides cannot. In distinction to Husserl's concept of intentionality as the structure of consciousness, Merleau-Ponty saw it as founded by the body in relation to what he called the body schema:

> What is essential to the concept of the body schema, and what it shares with its Kantian predecessor, rather, is the notion of an integrated set of skills poised and ready to anticipate and incorporate a world prior to the application of concepts and the formation of thoughts and judgments. This kind of embodied poise or readiness, which Merleau-Ponty calls 'habit,' consists in a kind of noncognitive, preconceptual 'motor intentionality' (1962: 110). Habit is not a function of reflective thought, nor is it transparently accessible to reflection in pure consciousness, rather it manifests itself in the perceptual body as such: 'it is the body that 'understands' in the acquisition of habit' (Merleau-Ponty; 1962: 144).
>
> (Carman 1999: 219)

If this is so, then any explanatory structure of the real and of people's behaviours, their desires, their hopes are already founded upon a body inclined towards others and the physical environment to produce a world that is knowable, thinkable, touchable and manageable according to the concepts and practices of a community of expression and public debate, decision and action. A textual public is already in the process of construction – through the acquisition of 'habits' – as a perceptual and perceiving body organising and organised by what appears. Merleau-Ponty's 'habits' developed not through reflection, have an affinity with Mauss's (1973) body techniques described in Chapter 1. Merleau-Ponty's noncognitive, preconceptual motor-intentionality level together with Mauss's cultural level provides what may be conceived of as a matrix of inscriptions organising perception, bodily posture and behaviours and thus providing already inscribed surfaces for more deliberate cognitive acts. It is the threshold where schema become the scheming of surfaces.

Scheming the real

Merleau-Ponty viewed his body schema as an integrated set of skills. Carman (1999) distinguishes this from the Kantian schema that deal specifically with how an image appropriate for a concept is produced:

> Schemata, then, are rules or procedures that issue from the faculty of imagination and specify the construction of sensible images adequate to pure concepts of the understanding. It is the imagination that carves out the space of possibilities within which objects can appear to us at all as objects of knowledge. What allows schemata to mediate the discursive categories of the understanding and the passive intuitions of sensibility, moreover, is the fact that they exhibit the *a priori* condition underlying all representation, both conceptual and intuitive, namely time. For time is both the form of inner sense, to which all appearances must necessarily conform, and the sequence or duration that makes intelligible the implementation and execution of a rule or procedure.
>
> (Carman 1999: 219)

Carman argues that Merleau-Ponty rejected this 'intellectualist conception of schemata as explicit formal rules, since of course the very intelligibility of such rules would in turn depend on precisely the kind of embodied perceptual experience whose phenomenological features Merleau-Ponty is trying to describe' (p. 219). However, rather than conceiving such schema as deriving from the imagination, it is interesting to reversion them as a way of thinking about political schemings for the shaping of imagination to provide contents for concepts that in turn are employed in explanatory frameworks for the 'understanding', organisation and manipulation of perceptions and behaviours in the production of events or outcomes. Just as perceptions are organised into objects over time through a process of what Husserl calls eidetic variation or that Merleau-Ponty would see as the development of bodily habits, so explanations as to why *this* always leads to *that* are based on perceptions of constant conjunctions, as Hume (1772) called them. At various levels of rigour generalisations can be composed of 'x' happens *every time*, or pretty much *every time* someone or something does 'y', and thus a degree of causality is imputed. As each individual is oriented to others, then intersubjectively, each 'constant conjunction' can be corroborated by others who perceive the 'same' thing. Such 'everytimes', however, are open to manufacture, as in Lippmann's (1927) notion of the manufacture of consent, as discussed earlier in Chapter 2. Explanation, in that sense, can be manufactured across a network of individuals who are oriented towards corroborating the experience of each. Rather than a schema, it is a scheming aimed at bringing about compliance by transforming body-schemas into compliant body–mind techniques for the engineering of consent (Bernays 1947).

Manufacturing and engineering consent to explanatory frameworks that serve particular interests on the large scale is the business of governments and corporations. Creating compliance to their agendas requires dispositifs that can come into play at a moment's notice around any issue that threatens the agenda. At the broadest level, there needs to be some sort of agreement about whose interests are to be served. Taking contemporary developments in capitalism and the economic, social and political policy appropriate to create the conditions conducive to the growth and accumulation of capital, there has increasingly been broad agreement since at least the 1980s led by the USA (Harvey 2003, 2005; Norton 2004; Klein 2007; Wallerstein 2003; Arrighi 2007) among the visible and 'invisible' (Bernays 1928) governments of nations as to the necessity of a neo-liberal strategy economically tempered with either a neo-conservative or a 'modernising left' strategy politically. Until the banking crisis of 2008 this strategy appeared to be delivering for the very wealthy and for a sufficient number of the employee classes. However, in the immediate aftermath of the crisis, the gaps between the wealthy, the middle and lower income employee classes and the unemployed poor rapidly became ever greater and increasingly brutal. The explanatory frameworks providing the rationales for the delivery of wealth to all were under stress in the leading Western economies and within Europe there were fault-lines between the richer northern states and the southern states, in particular Greece, Spain and Italy, that to varying degrees had to be 'bailed out'. It is in such circumstances that the dispositifs underlying the application of explanatory economic and political rationale have to be reinforced with something much more coercive. It is here that the militarisation of space becomes effected whether internally through police tactics or externally through military tactics that seek to hold, control and dominate territory.

There is a series of determinations: states have dominion over the use of violence, corporations have dominion over employment, banks have dominion over money, churches have dominion over the story-ing of a final personal fate enduring 'forever', and media dominate the means of distributing interpretations along with PR over the manufacture and engineering of consent. Each of these presupposes a way of parcelling up the perceivable world, or an analytics that is generative of ontologies and the arrangement of categories of beings into ways that reinforce the perceptual world. Together they are the tools of a real-politic for the overdetermination of the minds and behaviours of people. It is a fixing into place, a setting of limits on variation. This real-politic is both a recognition of and a strategy for the management of fault-lines, splits and tears across territorialised textual spaces. Within these, discursively produced subjects appear whose identities are constantly under threat by the perpetual erosion of structures and boundaries without which mutations or transformations into something 'other', something 'new', would occur. It is this fragility of discursive constructions, then, that allows and enables either barely noticeable but progressive or violently disruptive changes that alter the nature of key categories of being. Whether such changes are seen as threats or as opportunities depends upon what is at stake. It may be that a subject's sense of identification with and security of being in a known and familiar world – their primal ontological security, as Laing might put it (1965) – is at stake, or perhaps more specifically their opportunities for employment and wealth are being undermined or advantaged, or perhaps the quality of their health, communities and environments are under risk. Whether out of fear for the worst or hope for the better, people can then be marshalled into 'sides', each possessing their explanations supporting the adoption of sides, neither understanding the other.

As in the 'flagging' of people described by Billig (1995; see also Chapter 1), people can be marshalled under flags, the symbols of religions, the shirt designs and colours of football clubs or, indeed, the brands of corporate products. Each can be wrapped in explanations that support the rationality or other motivations for choice. At the highest level of generality across peoples there are the key universals: freedom, justice, human rights, equality. Few would be against freedom when their own freedoms are placed at stake or hindered by disadvantages and inequalities of resources and opportunities. However, it is with the contents that these terms cover that the disputes begin. In exploring the power arrangements that marshal people into one camp or another, Laclau and Mouffe (1985) drew upon Gramsci's discussions of hegemony to provide their more post-structuralist explanations of the dynamics of political allegiances and the consequent impacts on identity formation. Although, as in the Arab Spring of 2011, masses of people from very diverse and previously antagonistic social positions may all come together under the banner of 'freedom' and 'human rights' to oppose and get rid of a particular tyrant, after the fall of that tyrant their divisions and old hostilities may then return. As 'rebels' or as 'protestors', the universalising slogan is 'we are all together'. Their identities are formed in relation to their universalistic stand and their unity of purpose to overthrow the unwanted tyrant. However, this identity becomes fragile once again when the tyrant falls. As in Egypt, during the protests at Tahrir Square, Christian Copts and Muslims acted together, supported each other, protected each other.

However, after the fall of Mubarak, the fault-lines could be exploited by the 'hardliners' attacking Coptic churches and as in the clashes between military and protestors that left at least twenty-four dead and many injured in Cairo on 10 October 2011 (Al Jazeera 2011c; BBC 2011). With each injury, subjective identities become realigned and divisions hardened. Universals in conjunction with particular injuries can be employed to explain actions and the formation of identities and sides. The injuries provide the motive for the demands for remedies that may be in the form of political and legal 'mechanisms' or 'procedures' required to address and resolve the causes of the injuries. This setting into relation universals, particular contents, demands, identities, sides, mechanisms, procedures and actions contributes to the development of an explanatory schema for the inscription of a public and its forms of organisation.

A schema is transformed into a scheme when particular interests are set above others with the purpose of subjugation or repression. If in the political, social, cultural and economic realms personal freedoms constitute a real, then injuries, protests and demands are symptoms of that real. The real, in this sense, is whatever resists arbitrary attempts to change it. The real in that sense is what gives explanations their force. To make a difference can only be accomplished through the traction that the real provides. That is to say, the real provides the surface upon which any course of action takes its place and produces its effects. No one has total freedom to do what they please according to their whims or desires since within a social grouping everyone must take into account the resistances of others and the physical world. Moreover, it is through organising together that freedoms are secured. Through people working together more of everything can be produced than could be accomplished by individuals seeking to satisfy their physical needs for food and shelter alone. As people specialise particular products or services their specific knowledge and skills grows and thus they can produce more than someone who tries to do everything. Through collective forms of work and in communities people can find friendship as well as share ideas and engage in new projects to enhance the quality of their lives. However, such freedoms obtained through co-operative and community living also entail compromises that in effect imply a reduction in freedoms, as specialisation in the division of labour brings about a sense of alienation from the totality of the work process.

In the pursuit of increasing freedoms there is, then, a trade off between the chosen forms of organisation to constrain or shape behaviours and the collective power to overcome other kinds of constraints thus producing new freedoms for people impossible to achieve alone. The key issue then is how the choices about the forms of organisation are made. Some forms of organisation may benefit some at the expense of others or may generally produce more hardship than benefit. The processes, mechanisms and procedures to be employed in making choices therefore become critical for the general sense of freedom for all. Where neo-liberalism privileges freedom it also abhors equality. Its criteria of justice focus on the freedom of individuals to pursue their own ego-centric interests as in the case of Ayn Rand's (1957) heroes of capitalism in *Atlas Shrugged*. Through a combination of hard work, talent and luck, their personal success and wealth is justified by the wealth and job creation that it is claimed the rest of the world depend upon. Their leadership and their activity is stripped away from and exalted above the productive work of people who are only hirelings and have no ownership of the product or service. The law then places a barrier between the owner entrepreneur and the employee. Work then loses the reality of its co-dependencies, its need for co-operation between many who accept their specialisations and limitations on some freedoms for the benefit of other freedoms. The explanatory model of neo-liberalism developed by Hayek and Friedman among others equates the freedom of the market with the freedom of the individual in a democracy. The economic demand for a product and service is essentially equivalent to political demands concerning the allocation of resources, products and freedoms. In effect, the social value of the individual rises in terms of the wealth possessed and the personal wealth made. The free market is thus in Walzer's (1985) terms a 'sphere of justice' allocating social value as well as economic and political value. However, Walzer argues that economics and politics are different spheres of justice and that there should be no leakage between them where value in one sphere influences justice in another sphere, as say, in large corporations funding political parties and the campaigns of particular politicians. There should, he argues, be an equality between the multiple spheres of social life without any one being able to influence any of the others. Hence a billionaire should not be seen as someone who automatically has standing in another sphere nor as someone who is able to use the billions to influence politics, religion, military decision-making, science, education or any other sphere of justice. Clearly, in practice, such leakage of influence and power occurs and is even promoted as essential to freedom despite all evidence of widespread social harm in terms of poverty, ill health and social breakdowns. Where a particular explanatory model serves the interests of the few rather than the freedoms of the many it becomes a scheme to manage the perceptions of freedom. Thus there is a proliferation of arguments and the rhetorics of persuasion.

Gesturing towards writing

Writing ethnographies as systems or as organisations, or at least fleeting arrangements of powers where people are directed towards each other in amity or enmity, focuses attention on the constant creation of the social and all its forms by people acting with or against each other. Rather than there being a fixity to human society that is to be discovered, writing draws attention to the acts that depend only on the collective power to enact, underlying the apparent regularities, consistencies and repetitions of social life. How then, collectively, do people – as a public – convince themselves or become convinced (which amounts to much the same thing) of their powerlessness?

The case of a collectivity at work, counterposed perhaps to other collectivities, can explore the multiple explanations and theories provided by the members. Whether it is an ethnomethodological (Cicourel 1964; Garfinkel 1967) 'rational accounting' of why things are done this way rather than that, or whether it is a dramaturgical approach exploring strategic interaction (Goffman 1970), or whether it adopts more psychoanalytic or philosophically informed approaches that seek to deconstruct the surface 'solidity' of 'facts' or more radical politically approaches – the case both composes and decomposes according to the views of people into the ways their powers to act are variously managed, promoted or repressed.

The work of research to bring about change or generate differences is then caught up in the ever-changing matrices through which power is multiply channelled. This matrix is inscribed on people to construct the textualised public(s) that maintain a social order or bring about change. The key question for any action research project is the freedom to act and how this is frustrated or set going by the discourses, the texts or more generally the inscriptions on mind and flesh that shape an identifiable 'public' as either a phantom or as effective. Writing then follows the courses of action adopted, the conditions under which they are undertaken and the effects that they produce, or seem to produce, to 'explain' why this and not that.

Chapter 8

Persuasion and Arguments – de-mystifying the rhetorical tools

Arguments exploit the margins between the certainty of explanations and the openness of interpretations. Between them is rhetorical play. At stake in building an argument are the steps that take a debate between a multitude of voices from how questions of what and who can be represented, how representations are created, how they are employed through to questions of what counts as reliable, valid evidence for explanations and theories that can provide the basis for action. Each voice may claim a truth or question the truth of others. At stake for each voice is a perceived reality and how that reality confers the protection of interests, the ability to make demands, make decisions, form policy and take action. The role of an argument is thus to persuade about the truth of some description, proposition, analysis, theory and their combination as an explanation, justification and even the inevitability or fatality of consequences, as summed up in Margaret Thatcher's famous phrase 'There is no alternative.' However, there is always an alternative if other ways of perceiving reality are permitted. And this depends on including the voices of others in debate. In the real-politic of everyday life attention is manipulated to exclude the appearance of competing views of 'truth' in order to focus attention on the one explanation that is 'real'. Drawing on his experience of reporting from war zones, Rosen called such manipulated realities artificial green zones. The green zones in occupied territories are secure compounds.

To and from the green zone

In his experience of the Iraq war, Rosen writes:

> Throughout the occupation, almost no journalists actually inhabited the Green Zone. They stayed in green zones of their own creation, whether secure compounds or intellectual green zones, creating their own walls. The first green zone for journalists was the fortress around the Sheraton and Palestine hotels in Baghdad, which was initially guarded by American soldiers and later by Iraqi security guards. The *New York Times* soon constructed its

own immense fortress, with guard dogs, guard towers, security guards, immense walls, vehicle searches – so too did the BBC, Associated Press, and others, then there were was the Hamra hotel compound where many bureaus moved until it was damaged in an explosion in 2010. CNN, Fox, Al Jazeera English had their own green zone, though freelancers like myself could rent rooms there.

(Rosen 2011)

The argument, then, is that the data collected by the journalists who stayed within their intellectual green zones was already managed by the defensive procedures, practices, mechanisms and resources required to keep them safe. The red zone is where the people are, where they live and where the danger and violence of their lives in a war zone is experienced. Thus journalists

did not just hang out, sit in restaurants, in mosques and husseiniyas, in people's homes, walk through slums, shop in local markets, walk around at night, sit in juice shops, sleep in normal people's homes, visit villages, farms, and experience Iraq like an Iraqi, or as close as possible. This means they have no idea what life is like at night, what life is like in rural areas, what social trends are important, what songs are popular, what jokes are being told, what arguments take place on the street, how comfortable people feel, or what sorts of Iraqis go to bars at night. Hanging out is key. You just observe, letting events and people determine your reporting. They also did not investigate, pursue spontaneous leads, develop a network of trusted contacts and sources. Dwindling resources and interest meant bureaus had to shut down or reduce staff, and only occasionally parachute a journalist in to interview a few officials and go back home.

This 'just hanging out' is a way of enabling the development of closer relationships with the ways people behave, the social, economic, political procedures they do or do not have access to, the resources that are available or lacking and the impacts of conditions, circumstances and the acts of others on their lives. Indeed, in Rosen's view, 'The average person anywhere in the world goes to work and comes back home "knowing" little about people outside his social class, ethnic group, neighbourhood or city.' In short, the conditions of everyday life make it impractical for anyone to have first-hand contact with everyone else even in a small town or city let alone the world. In that case, Anderson's (1983) argument is that our communities are imagined rather than real. Journalists, as Rosin argued, are central to the construction of the imaginary communities of social life as well as to their de-construction. At the eruption of a crisis or the continued attention to on-going issues, the available dispositifs – for example, media, PR, social workers, community focused charities, schools, community policing – engineer damage limitation and work to repair the structures, mechanisms and practices necessary to the maintenance of power or to the acquisition of new powers and dominion of over new ways of being, new territories for colonisation, new resources and scenes of action. However, Rosen's 'average person' does not have access to such well-established dispositifs, hierarchically managed to maintain elite controls. Nevertheless there are countervailing forms of organisation traditionally available: families, friendship groups, work colleagues, professional associations, trades unions, faith communities, clubs, gangs. Contemporary media add to these by providing the means of peer-to-peer communications through social networking applications. There is thus a potential to create dispositifs that are not hierarchically organised but are effective in co-ordinating the actions of thousands, even millions, of people to target particular issues and bring about specific outcomes.

These alternative ways of gaining access to the lives of people and constructing what can be perceived and made known provides the conditions for an ironic structuring of the visible, the audible, the tangible in relation to the 'invisible', the 'inaudible' and the 'intangible'. It is here that the politics of interpretation and explanation come together in creating the conditions for arguments that persuade this set of circumstances, experiences, values, attitudes, beliefs to be real and not that set. If an interpretation is conceived as being 'true' in all possible worlds, then it is accepted as an explanation having universal dominion. However, where such a claim for an explanation is made and there are countervailing claims that point to evidence of the contrary, then these may either be dismissed as 'meaningless', or repressed and kept out of sight and hearing by the media that address and 'capture' the attention of the majority or at least those that have the power to harness the physical and mental powers of the necessary number of people who are able to manage the rest. The role of management has become central to the organisation of both the private and public sectors.

The argument of management

New managerialism has reduced management to the generic skills and competencies considered common to all forms of organisation whether schools, chocolate manufacturers or defence industries. Since managerialism claims to be rational and directed towards the most efficient use of economic resources, there is no need for further democratic discussion when it is used to 'modernise' 'old-fashioned' or 'outdated' forms of organisational practices. In the private sector it can be employed without recourse to democratic debate because the 'owner' – which may be a corporation as a legal 'person' – has every right to do as they wish with his, her or its property. Public sector organisations are 'owned' as government property and thus an elected government can again make decisions about the forms of organisation to be applied. These decisions that are made by the elected 'representatives' of the voices of people reduce the public to 'opinions' to be shaped into the forms of consent required by elites to manage the 'public'. This is the public Lippmann referred to as a 'phantom public' (see Chapter 2), a public by definition incapable of making decisions about complex, specialised and difficult matters. If the democratic is then equated with the economic, operating freely, then any interference by a government to regulate it, or to distort it through state ownership of utilities, or the provision of services can be interpreted as anti-democratic. In that sense, the democratic is outsourced to market forces, or more particularly, to the economic actors as legal persons, whether they are single individuals or transnational corporations.

In this argument, the more that government owned organisations are privatised, the more there is democracy. In short, the argument is: as people express their preferences through the mechanism of demand, so suppliers will seek to meet that demand, the price reflecting exactly how much people are willing to buy at a given price and how much suppliers are willing to produce at that price. As prices go up, people will progressively stop buying. If suppliers supply more than people are willing to buy, they will be left with stock until they bring the price down again. At some point there will be an equilibrium between buyers and sellers and, so the argument goes, resources and rewards for production will have been allocated at the optimum level. If this is true for all goods and services then there would be a perfect allocation of resources and rewards according to people's demands and the firm's ability to supply. There is then no need of government because all resources are allocated according to the effective demands of people, that is, what people are willing to pay. Indeed, since the consumers in the market are also workers they are thus organised to meet all their personal needs in the best way possible. Again, there is no need for government to arrange any of this. Where there is a need for government it is only for such necessary factors as security and the protection of property rights. Such a perfect operation requires certain assumptions. People would need to be fully aware of market conditions otherwise they could be fooled into buying poor-quality goods and services or those that were not adequate to their needs. People would have to be motivated to seek the maximum profit, otherwise they might sell too cheaply or not work hard enough. There should be no barriers to entry to or exit from a market, otherwise better firms might be kept out and poor firms protected. Moreover, there should be no monopoly powers either on the side of the firms or on the side of the consumers otherwise they could manipulate the market. And if there is to be real competition between producers of the same good or service in order to ensure only the most efficient firms survive, then there should be no discernible difference between the goods or services being offered except in terms of cost and price. These assumptions that underlie market economics are extremely exacting and rarely, if ever, in effect in really existing markets, particularly markets that are global. In order to attain them, there would need to be strict regulation. The consequence of such market conditions – real and imaginary – is to loosen all personal and social bonds as people compete with each other and look after their own interests. For some this is worrying in terms of losing traditional values that have no function in a market dominated society. Hence, it is argued that the market needs to be buttressed with traditional and religious virtues that again do not require government intervention since the values demanded are only those that have always been available in good families, the church, national pride and the military that defends these. Neo-liberalism often thus entails a neo-conservative return to such values and the institutions that sustain them as a source of stability.

What is excluded from this line of argument is the fuller articulation of the powers of people through their inclusion as voices that count in all the organisations and institutions that allocate resources between competing ends and the rewards of work. Since a multi-national corporation is a legal person, it has rights of ownership and is able to make decisions through its shareholders and the board of directors about how to structure its own internal organisation, its operational procedures and allocate rewards. Since the thousands of people who work within the organisation are employees with no rights of ownership, they have no legal entitlement to participate in decision-making. Since they are only one of the factors of production, employees are tradable as 'labour' and thus their 'price' is set by market forces not by entitlement to a share of the rewards of their work. Trade unions, then, in this model, as with any labour regulation set by a government, becomes 'red tape' or a barrier, inhibiting the market price and tradability of labour. Labour has thus been fully separated from work, the organisation of work, its product and its rewards. Rather than being able to engage in the discussion and decisions about work, its organisation and the just distribution of rewards, labour has only to be managed or engineered to perform efficiently. This has major implications at every level in personal and social life. How these implications are traced in the day-to-day conversations, interactions, practices, forms of organisation and events are fundamental to the formation and presentation of arguments. The writing of research becomes radical when its argumentation is about opening textual spaces for the inclusion of voices by which to create alternative and countervailing ways of being together without losing the uniqueness of voice. What is at stake is being able to seek alternative sources of legitimation and enter them into debates rather than defending the status quo that perpetuates injustices. Writing then involves creating the steps between ideas and actions that realise difference and thus brings to the fore what is at stake for individuals as actors within their communities that are impacted by the trans-community structures and processes operated by corporations and governments.

The strategic stakes

In any argument what is at stake is the range of voices admitted, how they are included and represented in the processes of debate and decision-making within which arguments are formed and accepted or rejected on the basis of being 'objective', 'valid', 'reliable' and 'natural'. With each new voice, there is a shiftiness to representation that challenges pinning everything down in a way that has total dominion over the 'real', a totalitarianism that allows no perceivable alternative. A new voice is a new perspective shifting debate, challenging categories, expressing alternative demands. Each challenge disturbs what had been settled, the agreed norms, the habitual practices. Whereas the democratically textual public – as described in Chapter 7 – develops arguments from the voices of all and thus is creative of new forms of organisation, a phantom public is subject to the engineering of consent through public relations, advertising, news manipulation and schooling. In terms of what is at stake for sustaining neoliberal schemes, manufacturing consent involves hijacking the spaces of shiftiness created by new views, and rewriting them in the name of perpetuating the continually moving happiness and desiring machines (President Hoover, as cited in the BBC 2002 documentary *Century of the Self*; Deleuze and Guattari 1972) and maintaining the freedoms and the power of the elite few within private domains, away from interference from an active public or a government acting on their behalf. Since representation creates the 'visible' from which an aesthetics, an ethics and a politics of the real can emerge, it lurks between the public and the private, constructing the gaps and knots in this virtual terrain. Rhetorical strategies can alter the virtual appearance of this landscape in order to stack the odds in favour of seeing the world this way – say as a neo-liberal – and not that way – as socialist. Of course, rhetoric can be used to persuade otherwise.

What, then, is at stake for research supporting the freedoms of people is to lay out the kinds of competing arguments, the strategies of persuasion and the ways in which an audience can be transformed into an active public as a condition for the possibility for critique, decision-making and action in all spheres of life. This, then, is a framing argument, a rationale for writing up research. What it excludes is the creation of the conditions for the possibility of domination by elites in any sphere. In all stakes there is a choice and reasons for the choice. In making the choice, then, at each step the sub-arguments will be inflected to support that choice. At each point of inflection, there is the possibility of the shiftiness of representational categories that embeds slips and slippages of meaning. There is a sense in which the very language employed is always just out of control. As in Derrida's poignant words: 'I have only one language, it is not mine' (1998: 1). And yet,

> I remain in it and inhabit it. It inhabits me. The monolingualism in which I draw my very breath, is, for me, my 'element'. Not a natural element, not the transparency of the ether, but an absolute habitat. It is impassable, indisputable'.
>
> (Derrida 1998: 1)

The impasse – that limit of impassability and indisputability – relates to our 'absolute habitat'. Reconnecting Derrida with the phenomenological discourses of Husserl and Merleau-Ponty, this habitat is the place for the emergence and construction of the 'life-world', that realm of experience that (Schutz 1976) lays the ground for a phenomenological sociology, regarded as the primordial realm that is always taken for granted until further notice. It is a realm dominated by pragmatic habits and routine ways of behaving and Mauss-ian body techniques that are inscribed deep into the body and its pre-cognitive ways of being directed towards the other, receiving and organising impressions from the world about. In another shift it becomes the habitus of dispositions, structuring structures and schemas of Bourdieu (1977). The work of language is to create our human spaces, our dwellings, our home, our world. That is, it creates an address – or addressable spaces – where we live, where we can be found and where we can be identified. Within a realm of addresses, calls, demands, pleas, seductions can be targeted and sourced. However, effective power within this circuitry of addresses depends on the deployment of resources available to enable a 'voice' that sets the workings of language in motion. In economic terms, to have a voice is to have effective demand, that is, the money that can be used to purchase: the more money, the more 'voice'. Where the public is reduced to 'consumer', its voice is available to be manipulated through the logic of a must-have culture of demand, where only the latest up-to-date model or version of the product or service counts. Where the public is reduced to employee, their behaviour is managed through the logic of becoming attractive and compliant to the demands of employers, since without employment they cannot take their place in the logic of the happiness machines. This complementary logic provides the hooks – or addresses – necessary to manipulate everyday language and thus everyday reasoning to keep the desiring, happiness machines in constant consumption, constant labour and thus always in a state of dependency on those who provide employment as well as the desirable products and services. It also directly feeds the bonuses and bank accounts of the executive management, owners and shareholders of private businesses. It is the rhetorical structuring of attention to objects, practices and identities that is essential to the maintenance – or subversion – of ways of seeing and thus of explaining the realities of the world and consequently of what is reasonable to expect, hope for and accomplish.

Rhetorical address

Framing creates the conditions for managing attention for particular interests and thus for what is able to appear as an address. A text, whether written or spoken, is addressed to and constructs an audience, that is to say a public. In order to convey message and sense, the writer or speaker will have decided upon the key issues (the agenda to be addressed), identified the main strategies for drawing attention to key factors for a given 'side' (framing), researched some background to the issues (reviewing the literature), collected and processed data in order to map the issues relevant to the agenda as a basis for theory and action. The speaker or writer has something to say and it is x and not y or z. But constructing a public able to 'receive' 'x' and then communicating x to this public is no simple matter. Every analytics adopted in contestations and debates between people will define 'x' differently, structure attention differently, and hence intend to structure the public differently. In effect there are many publics competing for attention and the right to decide and to act, that is, for the right to be an effective public, a right that, in the long run, may only be settled by might. All publics involve debate concerning explanation and argument about how and why action is needed. Some seek consensus, others seek to be inclusive of disagreements as a basis of creating new forms of social organisation that value the differences. In seeking consensus a real work of consensus building may take place, or it may be for show only and hence a work of generating the spectacle of a 'public' is undertaken. If the public is for show only, the explanation and argument to persuade the public to see x is framed rhetorically in order to load the dice towards the end-game of getting x across. If it is about consensus building then there needs to be an openness of intention that allows all concerned voices to enter into debate and participate in decision-making. However, there are times when consensus is not possible. It depends on the nature of the issue in debate. If for example, it is a question of how to manage the allocation of scarce resources across competing ends, then an economic framework is required. The principles under which this market should operate would need to be considered through public debate to ensure that it operates freely and fairly. However, not all goods and services, even if they are scarce, may be deemed appropriate for a market solution.

There are certain goods and services that are essential to the preservation of life, for example, food, water, shelter, health, care of the elderly. Others may be essential for the operation of a complex society and so may be considered utilities, for example, energy, water supplies, transport and communications infrastructures. Some may be thought of as essential for the development of people and society: education, law, the arts, the sciences. And finally some may be thought necessary for security: police, military. How such essentials are to be defined and undertaken may be thought the province of politics and hence public debate and decision-making rather than the play of demand and supply in markets. In this case, the definition of the 'public' – that is, whose voices are included and count – becomes critical in terms of who is addressed, what is addressed and who is able to make an address. The framing of the conditions of address define the kind of society produced. At one extreme it is only the Tyrant who can make an address. All others are simply audience, expected to be obedient. At the other it is the radical democracy where all voices are to be included and since, as Arendt (1998) points out, with each birth there is always a new perspective to be included, the critical reflection on democratic structures, practices and processes is an unending project. In between, there are conditions of degrees of freedom and equality of voice. Each political form will involve different rhetorical strategies. To move from one to another involves a rhetorics of de-framing, that is, a process of perceptual change so that voices become either audible or inaudible, persons visible or invisible and things tangible or intangible depending on the direction of the move. Writing as a research and educational practice then involves mapping the conditions under which publics are constructed and exploring the implications for social organisation and the impacts on persons and individual freedoms and their effectiveness to engage their voices in public arenas.

The strategic work(s) of rhetoric(s)

When a writer or speaker deploys analogies, metaphors and story-ings thought appropriate and useful to stack the deck of values, attitudes and beliefs in order to bring the mind's eye of the public to a focus – with like-mindedness – on the issues and problems deemed by that individual to be at stake, it is a strategic work of persuasion. In its propaganda mode, it works to manufacture realities that reinforce a particular set of interests. In its function as stylistic adornment it can be valued as 'beauty' or as 'frivolous' but in each case as superfluous to the argument or explanation that is assumed to be 'neutral', or as 'speaking for itself'. In the sense to be employed here, rhetoric is a work that alters perceptions, understandings, generates 'sides' to a debate, opens or closes possibilities and thus sets the conditions for action, for making a difference.

In linguistics the techniques of rhetoric are divided into two major categories: scheme and tropes. In the scheme the pattern of words is changed from what would be normally expected – examples include parallelism, antithesis and climax, parenthesis, ellipsis, alliteration, assonance and chiasma. In everyday life, these schemes can be recognised in the patternings of activities and action in terms of the kinds of association formed between people as friends, allies, enemies or in the management of formal and informal work arrangements. Changes in the normal or expected patterns of work have ranged from the imposed break up of work into its specialist component skills and competencies to the transformation of the hierarchical management of tasks into the formation of small project teams that decide among themselves how to manage a particular task. In this sense the rhetorical scheme provides a basis for the scheming that results in the manufacture of consent, a consent that may well be contrary to and dangerous for the well being of people and the development of mutually beneficial forms of social organisation. Alongside this, however, there are the frameworks and processes of tropological thinking through which 'consent' can be imposed, seduced or challenged.

A trope involves wordplay where a word is used outside of, or in excess of its literal or normal form or meaning. The word 'trope' stems from the Greek *tropos*, with its connotations of to turn, to direct, to alter and to change. The word has been turned away from its usual meaning. Take, for example:

> Race, as a meaningful criterion within the biological sciences, has long been recognized to be a fiction. When we speak of 'the white race' or 'the black race,' 'the Jewish race' or 'the Aryan race,' we speak in biological misnomers and, more generally, in metaphors. Nevertheless, our conversations are replete with usages of race which have their sources in the dubious pseudoscience of the eighteenth and nineteenth centuries. One

need only flip through the pages of the *New York Times* to find headlines such as 'Brown University President Sees School Racial Problems' or 'Sensing Racism, Thousands March in Paris.' In 'The Lost White Tribe,' a lead editorial in the 29 March 1985 issue, the *New York Times* notes that while 'racism is not unique to South Africa,' we must condemn that society because in 'betraying the religious tenets underlying Western culture, it has made race the touchstone of political rights.' The *Times* editorial echoes Eliot's 'dissociation of sensibility,' which he felt had been caused in large part by the fraternal atrocities of the First World War. (For many people with non-European origins, however, dissociation of sensibility resulted from colonialism and human slavery.) Race, these usages, pretends to be an objective term of classification, when in fact it is a dangerous trope.

(Gates 1985: 4–5)

Tropes more than organise thinking about the world; they construct the ways in which a reality may be perceived and the objects in this reality rendered visible, invisible, audible, inaudible, tangible intangible – in effect, they constitute worlds. They make worlds thinkable. From the Renaissance, rhetoric began to be organised in terms of four master tropes: metaphor, metonymy, synecdoche and irony.

One of the most striking and least examined aspects of the four-trope series – the 'master tropes' of Vico and Kenneth Burke – is their inherent movement through a fixed course: from metaphor, the preliminary naming operation, to metonymy, the process of reductive manipulation and formalization, to the integrative, macrocosm/microcosm relationships of synecdoche, to the final awareness within the series that all of its processes have been relativizing turns, the whole process ironic. On this view, the tropes become 'moments' of the tropology itself, which is not seen so much as a set of forms or categories, as a system, indeed the system, by which mind comes to grasp the world conceptually in language. The order in which the tropes present themselves in this system is strictly and logically entailed. That is, to speak of the 'four master tropes' as a tropology necessarily invokes the sequence of the series, which thus represents a narrative curriculum with its own propulsive forces.

(Kellner 1981: 16–17)

For Kellner (1981: 27):

the four-trope system of renaissance rhetoric ... represents a form of knowing, of grasping a concept ... that not only accords, whether loosely or strictly, with many theoretical systems of knowing, or coming to be known, as in Vico, Kant, Hegel, Marx, Croce, Foucault, Goethe, and many others, but which also possesses an inherent narrativity."

To come to know takes time and effort and thus is narrative in form. This narrativity of the known that is named, elaborated in terms of its parts, and organised into wholes is a course of reflection on experience. This course of reflection is named as a 'curriculum' that essentially has the structure not so much of a progressive future oriented knowing, but a knowing that progresses only by re-inventing or re-naming its past. Lacan described this structure in terms of the future anterior: in terms of what something 'will have become'. When Libyan protestors in Benghazi on 15 February 2011 came out on to the streets, this was not then known as the start of the revolution. When on the 23 October 2011 liberation was declared, it was as a return to and thus a re-naming of its 'beginning' in Benghazi. And from its beginnings a whole series of events, activities, incidents can be brought together into a whole and named as parts of the revolution. The term 'revolution' acts as a refracting lens through which all the different 'colours' of the revolution pass and are integrated into the whole, the resulting 'white light' through which each part is 'seen' as an element of the whole. This rhetorical process of refraction is named anaclasis. It is the process that Martin (1982) sees as being undertaken by Kellner (1981: 17), where:

> The rhetorical studies of the past three decades have prepared the ground for the appropriation that Kellner concludes: a return of the tropes to their proper meaning by refraction of their varied colours through Kant's Principles of Pure Understanding to reveal the white logic of their literal source, and the discovery that 'the order in which the tropes present themselves' in the fourfold succession of metaphor, metonymy, synecdoche, and irony 'is strictly and logically entailed'.

The Libyan revolution can be placed into a yet wider narrative, the globalising story of democracy and its relations to the free market. Each such narrativisation draws upon the refractive capacities of key namings – revolution, democracy, free markets, neo-liberalism, socialism – to draw everything into a way of seeing, of thinking, and of generating knowledge about what is seen as the basis for action and the development of the identities of actors. However, to make a difference in the way of seeing, to bring a change in the practices and the ways a society is conducted, requires a countervailing practice. Once the revolution has been named, it is no longer a revolution but a framing that stabilises, that orders, that generates explanations in re-interpreting what were once isolated activities and incidents into a great event or a stage in the great event. In short, it employs the rhetoric of mastery, a different rhetoric than the previous rhetoric of mastery, but nevertheless of mastery. Yet, if the characteristics of the democracy that the revolution sought to bring about are freedom with equality of voice, then it must incorporate the countervailing voices to the new mastery. Democracy takes on an ironic structuring in the sense of including countervailing voices, that is, voices in disagreement. Rather than a refractive integration into white light, it is reflection or a breaking into different colours or views. Rather than a pedagogy of consent to a dominant view, it is a radical teaching involving a rhetorics of antanaclasis, a term 'connoting opposing definitions rooted in competing theories' (Ratcliffe 2005: 137) that in turn find their place in a public that aspires to be a totality of all voices, including all but not in subjection to a consensus. More strictly, antanaclasis is a form of punning, where the same word is repeated but with different meanings, much like the repetition of freedom, equality, democracy by voices having different views as to their meanings. With each new meaning voiced, there is a shift in perception, in what can appear. And as Arendt suggests '[j]ust as appearing beings living in a world of appearances have an urge to show themselves, so thinking beings, who still belong to the world of appearances even after they have mentally withdrawn from it, have an urge to speak' (Arendt; 1978: 98), thus making manifest what would otherwise be an excluded but essential part of the appearing world.

Arendt's tropology of appearances has its movement into meaning through metaphor, where 'the criterion of logos, coherent speech, is not truth or falsehood but meaning. Words as such are neither true nor false' (Arendt; 1978: 98). If the move is from logic to meaning, 'implicit in the urge to speak is the quest for meaning, not necessarily the quest for truth' (Arendt 1978: 99). To think, then, requires a resource of words that are already meaningful, 'in order for the mind to, as it were, travel through them' (Arendt 1978: 99). Reasoning silently with oneself is the way in which we 'come to terms with whatever is given to our senses in the everyday world of appearances – the need of reason is to give account' (Arendt 1978: 100). In our quest for meaning we name things, appropriating them and 'as it were, disalienating the world into which, after all, each of us is born as a newcomer and a stranger' (Arendt 1978: 100). However, paradoxically whilst naming renders the world less strange to ourselves, the act of naming kills the thing being named since it renders it an object subjugated by a subject inasmuch as the name does not come from out of that named entity's being. Naming it brings it to 'word and appearance' and thereby to the mode by which it is given meaning in language (Schwenger 2001: 101). This naming process, then, is metaphorical and its result is to produce a double as it were of the world, a dead thing of named representations that live only when drawn upon by the thinking, speaking body, a body that is also doubled by representations and in that sense deadened and awoken. Each naming, each calling of a difference between one 'thing' and another and 'within' one thing, creates a spacing of difference, a nuancing that reduces, fragments and systematises metonymically the relations between things and their parts in the world of appearances.

In demanding speech in a public of speakers, the mind holds onto the world of appearances by its doubling composed of analogies, metaphors and emblems even though it has of necessity withdrawn from that world. For Arendt, these 'guarantee the unity of human experience' (Arendt 1978: 109) – it is thus the rhetorical move from the metaphorical (a fusion or uniting of unrelated things) through the metonymic (substitution of related names) to the synecdochal that elaborates a world of entities and draws the parts into a whole. Through its metaphorical modality, language 'enables us to think, that is to have traffic with non-sensory matters, because it permits a carrying-over, metaphorein, of our sense experiences' (Arendt 1978: 110). This, however, for Arendt is no Cartesian split because metaphor unites non-sensory matters with sensory ones. It allows 'the transition from one existential state, that of thinking, to another, that of being an appearance among appearances, and this can only be done by analogies' (Arendt 1978: 103). Language, however, is not 'as adequate' for the functioning of the invisible mental activities as are the senses for 'their business of coping with the perceptible world' although the metaphor improves things (Arendt 1978: 112). In other words, language not only kills, but as a medium for manifestation it is at its limits where '(e)*very mental act rests on the mind's faculty of having present to itself what is absent from the senses*' (Arendt 1978: 75–6 [italics in the original]). As seen previously in Chapter 5, representation makes present what is actually absent – it re-presents what is absent – and this is the mind's 'unique gift' (Arendt 1978: 76).

This gift, however, is coercive and seductive to the extent that, recalling Derrida, the gift is of a representational language that is not mine. For Lacan, language had an 'eximate' (intimate + external) relation to the individual. Through language and its rhetorical framings a world is always already intersubjectively and analytically organised as a condition for appearing and knowing. To meet a particular communication issue a tropological process combines a particular analytics (Chapter 4) with an available dispositif (Chapter 4) to manage what appears. Like Rosen's (2011) war correspondents, in order to escape a specific way in which the visible and the invisible is managed we have to leave our comfortable places:

> One reason for the failure of journalists to leave their green zones may be a combination of laziness and aversion to discomfort. But in Iraq, Afghanistan, other developing countries and areas of conflict in some countries, you have to leave your comfort zone. You might prefer an English-speaking whiskey-drinking politician over six hours of bouncing along dirt roads in the heat and dust in order to sit on the floor and eat dirty food and drink dirty water and know you're going to get sick tomorrow, but the road to truth involves a certain amount of diarrhoea.
>
> (Rosen 2011)

Truth here is not logical truth but the truth of witnessing, of 'being there', of being in danger, of being in abjection. It requires an existential commitment to 'bringing to appearance' an otherwise repressed or imperceptible voice to a public in a way that announces the existential conditions of its 'truth'. In this case, it is a dis-placement, a transgression of comfort, to occupy a space of uncertainty, of potential danger with a return to occupy as a voice, a new space in a public constructed to receive the new(s).

As speaking beings we create narratives in which we cast ourselves as actors and as agents whose identities can be constructed, manipulated and codified for particular purposes. When these castings are naturalised as reality, they become mystical. That is to say, the representations in repressing the real, replace it. Such replacements are the stuff of ceremonial, religious and political speeches. When Obama wove the narrative of his own life-story, and that of his wife, Michelle, into the American Dream in his 7 November 2007 speech in Bettendorf, and again in the El Dorado Speech of 29 January 2008, the biographical accounts were positioned as no longer a personal narrative but as one that is universal and political. The speech is inscribed in the history of rhetorical practice, the promise of the American Declaration of Independence and spoken by a black man seeking the presidency it alludes to the 'I have a Dream' speech of Martin Luther King.

Drawing on an ancient rhetorical practice brought to its contemporary form by the pioneering public relations approaches of Lippmann and Bernays, Obama wrote himself into the narrative of pioneer Americans: the story of starting from nothing, being from poor working-class origins but still able to attain the heights of becoming president of America. In Lippmann's sense it painted a fantasy dream-world perpetually haunted by the hope, indeed the promise, that everyone can achieve their dream. The dream worked for him and for Michelle and so 'it can work for you' is the message. In short, 'vote for me and you will see your American dream fulfilled'. The tropological process is established by linking the one story of his family metonymically with a listing of particulars that all have in common 'the dream' and the dream synecdochally defines 'America':

> Our family's story is one that spans miles and generations; races and realities. It's the story of farmers and soldiers; city workers and single moms. It takes place in small towns and good schools; in Kansas and Kenya; on the shores of Hawaii and the streets of Chicago. It's a varied and unlikely journey, but one that's held together by the same simple dream.
>
> And that is why it's American.
>
> (Obama, El Dorado Speech, 29 January 2008)

The end point of Obama's tropological process is a self-transformation where existentially his person is both representative of and masked by the symbolic appropriation of the American Dream. In turn, the existentially lived personal histories of each believer become inscribed in the Dream of the Dream Giver. There is a sense in which he is the fulfilment, a sentiment clearly stated in his acceptance speech:

> If there is anyone out there who still doubts that America is a place where all things are possible; who still wonders if the dream of our founders is alive in our time; who still questions the power of our democracy, tonight is your answer.
>
> (Obama 2008b)

He becomes split along an axis between the existential and the symbolic. And so, at a later date, as President starting the long journey to re-election, in a speech to AIPAC, another dream is invoked in relation to the common purposes of America and Israel at the time of the Arab Spring when international relations and dominance in the Middle East are becoming uncertain. It is a dream of a home: 'When I touched my hand against the Western Wall and placed my prayer between its ancient stones, I thought of all the centuries that the children of Israel had longed to return to their ancient homeland.' In his countervailing story of the killing of Palestinian children, Massad (2011) lists the deaths that have occurred from the 1930s, which included 'the Zionist blowing up of Palestinian cafes with grenades (such as occurred in Jerusalem on March 17, 1937) and placing electrically timed mines in crowded market places (first used against Palestinians in Haifa on July 6, 1938)', to the present, and asks 'Are Palestinian children less worthy?' In Obama's speech, it is the symbolic master, not the existential person, that answers when asked more generally 'How do you interpret a child?'

Gesturing towards writing

Tropes are not superficial but are ingested to become substantially who we are. They compose us as a people. Through their very repetition across different contexts, places and times, their very anticipation becomes the surface on which new chapters in the story of a person, a nation, a people are written.

Writing an ethnography of 'home', of the myths that prefabricate futures and capture people to play out identities in actions across prefigured territories as their purpose for living, reveals the choices to be made between the person as living being and the life of semblance already mapped, awaiting its staging by its *dramatis personae* where each member has the voice only of a semblant. The ethnography may explore how the writing of home deep upon the embodied surfaces of minds and across territories is accomplished by an analytics dramatised as friend and enemy and organised against ever-imagined threats or opportunities as dispositifs ready either to deal with emergencies and dangers from enemies or to achieve success and wellbeing with friends.

Each case studies the splits, gesturing between the experienced powers of people to create in freedom and the prescribed identities, behaviours, and actions of organisations – whether formal or informal – designed to meet real or imaginable needs, demands, and interests whether equally or unequally. Each instance of an organisation, a dispositif, a threat resolved or a goal achieved reveals the extent to which people lend their powers to the organisation, or the mobilisations of machineries that create the effect of a dispositif or withdraw them, voice resistance and engage in counter-organisation to write alternative possibilities, ways of seeing and acting.

How, then, is the action of action research already prescribed by the myths of organisation, of home of friend and enemy? How in the minute details of everyday life are these driven down into the designs to 'improve' social action? If the evaluations that take place of 'improvements' achieved are articulated within the prevailing rhetorics of 'the good', then where is the space for a critical public to voice alternative evaluations and make alternative demands?

Chapter 9

Being Critical – achieving critique

Between the dream and the reality of people's experiences, irony prepares the ground for disappointment and the emergence of alternatives. These alternatives can provide the means to critique the dream; they can also be seen as a focus of criticism in relation to the dream as an expression of 'the good'. The good society is what is at stake during the periods of crisis, where confidence in the 'good' is shaken by events or under threat through a play of interpretations that have no point of anchorage. In the call to topple a tyrant or a monarch, the leader who filled the place of power is toppled, leaving it empty. In democracy, this space is permanently, as Lefort (1988) called it, the empty place of power. It may be occupied by presidents and prime ministers, but they have no permanent right to it. The real occupants are the 'people', or at least those who have voting rights. However, as already argued, the people and their access to the public are highly problematic terms framed by the organisation of power to shape opinion, reduce choice and limit access to the resources and mechanisms through which power operates. This potentially creates the conditions for criticism of the operation of democratic processes. However, there are different views as to the meaning and practices appropriate for democracy. These alternatives then create the conditions for critiques. Thus, as a brief distinction, criticism may be directed towards the operation of a system, whereas critique challenges the system itself. That is to say, critique challenges the basis upon which a way of seeing, a political and social order, a legal system, or a way of working, allocating resources and distributing wealth has legitimacy. Critique thus opens up dangers for those who have interests dependent upon a particular way of life embedded in a perceptual order, or as Rancière (2004) calls it, a police order. It is a term that evokes an older sense of the term 'police', a sense that Adam Smith pointed out:

> has been borrowed by the English immediately from the French, tho it is originally derived from the Greek πολιτεια signifying policy, politicks, or the regulation of a government in generall. It is now however generally confind to the regulation of the inferior parts of it. It comprehends in generall three things: the attention paid by the public to the cleanlyness of the roads,

streets, etc; 2nd, security; and thirdly, cheapness or plenty, which is the constant source of it. When Mr. Lamonion was constituted Intendant of Paris he was told by the officers that the king required three things of him, that he was to provide for the neteté, surete, and bon marché in the city.

(Smith 1762: 290)

Distinguishing the two senses of police is useful. At one level, it refers to governance, the politics of good order where each part in society contributes to the whole. Only the people as a mass of individuals, a multitude, are 'outside' of the part–whole relationship, since the people as such have no functional part in the order of the whole. They are the dis-assembly of the whole and its parts. Yet, of course, they are a part in the sense that that neither the whole nor its parts could exist without them. The danger of disassembly is thus always present unless there is a policing in its narrower sense, employed to keep the population in awe, as Smith (1762: 416) might say. Thus the police is not simply reducible to the police force as an organisation of the state; it is the organisation of governance itself that keeps all in their place as functional parts of a whole. In a sense, the policing is a state of mind as much as the force – moral, physical, psychological – that others may bring to bear.

The criteria for critique, if it is to be unbiased to any one interest group or another, must then of necessity step outside the police to act out of a principle of the inclusion of all voices from all people (at the level of the dis-assembled multitude) both freely and equally. Since each voice speaks from a particular location for particular needs and interests, then it follows that no one voice is identical to any other. If all are to be free and no one disadvantaged, then each voice must be treated equally and taken into account in all decision-making and consequent action. The forms of radical democracy (Laclau 2005; Mouffe 2005; Balibar 1994) and its ethical positions (Critchley 2006) variously proposed aspire to the construction of a public space inclusive of and supportive of difference. This is an approach that aspires to take into account people as 'multitude' (Hardt and Negri 2000; Badiou 2005) and as individuals who are free to work together to aggregate their powers in freely formed associations to achieve mutual benefits. Such a dynamic public is a fundamental threat to all forms of elite power consolidated to coerce the behaviours of the masses.

Neo-liberalism negates one of the terms essential to the aspiration for a radically free democracy – equality. In the market place the freedom to make choices is dependent on the wealth to back those choices. The less wealth, the less freedom to act. The essential instability that results requires strategies to manage the discontent and injustices that arise from systematically produced inequalities. Conservative, traditional values were able to manage the experience of inequalities either through an appeal to religious values of the virtues of poverty and rewards in heaven or to traditional values of knowing one's place and being content with one's lot. With the industrial revolution creating wealth for and expanding the class of merchants and industrialists, this wealth itself became a sign of virtuousness justified through what Weber (2001) called the protestant work ethic providing a religious justification for capitalist accumulation of wealth. As capital became more mobile through the globalisation and increased speed of market transactions with every advance in communications technologies, capitalism produced increased global and local inequalities, the break up of family and community lives and the fear of social unrest. Neo-conservative strategies sought to 'balance' the freedom of the market with a degree of 'equality' – or rather, less of a gap between the economic classes – and a return to the values of the family, patriotism and work as a virtue. Neo-conservativism provides a means to justify an inequality judged necessary to reward and motivate hard work and the talented. The hard-working talented become the experts that Bernays (1928) called the 'invisible government', the ones who really rule over what Lippmann called the 'phantom public' (1927), that is, the citizens whose votes and opinions have to be shaped and their consent manufactured or engineered through the techniques supplied by the social sciences. Given the funding of the main political parties by wealthy benefactors, the place of power – as Lefort (1988) called it – is at least displaced in the 'public' mind. That is, rather than its visible and obvious central presence in the elected president or prime minister, it is to the side, and unelected.

The 2008 financial crisis and its aftermath revealed the extent of the power of financial institutions 'too big to fail' and of financial markets able to cripple and punish the economies of nations. The place of power, in this sense is located outside the nations themselves. For Lloyd Blankfein, Chairman and CEO of Goldman Sachs (one of the key too-big-to-fail institutions), as reported in The Sunday Times (9 November 2009), he is 'doing God's work' in making markets and making money. In the inquiry into the financial crisis (Meltdown 2011) he defended himself from accusations of the Chairman of the inquiry, Phil Angelides, by saying that all the investors were professionals 'who want this exposure'. This was contradicted by emails from a Goldman executive, Fabrice Tourre, saying he was selling to unsophisticated investors, that is, 'widows and orphans that I ran into at the airport'. What was being sold were Credit Default Swaps (CDS) that constructed

> More and more leverage in the system. The whole building is about to collapse anytime now ... Only potential survivor, the fabulous Fabrice Tourre ... standing in the middle of all these complex, highly leveraged, exotic trades he created without necessarily understanding all of the implication of those monstrosities [sic]!!!
>
> (Quinn 2010)

The values and attitudes of traders were further underlined during a BBC interview with Alessio Rastani: 'Personally, I've been dreaming of this moment for three years. I go to bed every night and I dream of another recession.' It is through the volatility of markets typical of recessions, that traders can make money. In Rastani's view, The governments don't rule the world, Goldman Sachs rules the world' (Delingpole 2011). Given the extent of Goldman Sachs' funding of political parties in the USA and UK together with the funds given by other powerful financial institutions, Bernays' invisible government continues to occupy the place of power, with only phantom presidents and prime ministers passing through as the symbolic face of 'democracy'. At the back of the symbol resides then an extension of what Eisenhower called the industrial–military complex to include the globalised financial corporations that is able to decide and act without recourse to democratic legitimisation by calling a state of exception in order to protect vested interests. It is increasingly being argued that there is a permanent state of exception politically (Schmitt 1985; Agamben 1998, 2005; Butler et al. 2000) and now economically that is employed to justify the erosion of freedoms politically and the imposition of 'austerity measures' economically. There is thus a double operation of the privileging of market freedoms and the denial of that freedom for all through the reinforcement of inequality that provides the grounds for criticism and for critique. Inequality is justified either by a social Darwinist-like rationality as being the natural result of human differences in talent and self-interested struggle to win or as the result of differences due to how hard people are willing to work and to take a risk. In each case, there is the belief that not only is there no alternative the inequality is just, because the best have been rewarded – as in Weber's 'puritan ethic', or Blankfein's work of God, or the market's invisible hand does not lie – thus, through a calculus of demand and supply driven by the profit motive, the best of worlds is produced.

This calculus of economic reasoning underlying a notion of the good society provides a basis of criticism internally to the system by arguing that if the system is not working it is because the market is not free due to government inter-ference. It can also critique alternative views in terms of its criteria of 'freedom" and of the justness or fairness of inequality based on the values of hard work, the courage to take risks and the application of talent. Countervailing critiques would then need to explore the notion of 'freedom' in relation to 'inequality' and the impacts of the injustices and suffering brought by inequality and thus argue for the application of further criteria such as 'humanity', 'rights' and 'care' for others. At stake in such debates are the competing views as to whether there is some essential human 'nature', a vision of the 'good society' or some overarching set of humanly established or divine laws that establish the boundaries for behaviour.

These debates emerge within and if taken into account are constitutive of a public space. For Mouffe (2005), this public space has the function of reducing antagonism to agonisms, that is, from violent disputes that are settled by trials of strength, to the voicing of countervailing views and demands that take the place of the use of violence to settle conflicts through democratic processes and procedures. In Hegelian fashion, the first inscribes mastery and servitude (through some form of slavery or indebtedness) if not death; the second inscribes freedom with equality of voice across a multitude that agrees to accept the results of its deliberations. Each provides a symbolic ordering of the personal and the social through which a society is composed from particulars into some greater organised totality, whether or not that totality is a stable unity or a dynamically changing heterogeneous complex impossible to reduce to some self-identical whole. Of course, one may hope to impose some sort of fixed unity over such a complex system, but it will fail even if it from time to time produces a satisfying sense of control. For example, regarding the 2008 crisis, its aftermath and the question of why no one in the mainstream of economic forecasting saw it coming, Martin Wolf of the *Financial Times* commented:

> You will never foresee these things because the system is ultimately just too complicated for anybody really to understand. The economy is an extremely complex, uh, adaptive system and in fact I think it is the most complex system we know. It has the complexity of billions of people engaged producing billions of products over time and space. And they are people. And because they are people, they are subject to all the emotions of human beings both euphoria and panic and all the rest of it collectively and individually. Such a system will generate very complicated phenomena and, uh, it will very often be very difficult to interpret them.
>
> (Martin Wolf interviewed on *Meltdown* part 4, 2011)

In the view of the commentator for the *Meltdown* documentary:

> The failure to agree on new international financial rules will allow big banks to play one country off another to see where they can find the most lax regulation. Many believe the competition between New York and London to be the financial capital of the world was a major contributing factor to the 2008 meltdown.

In the absence of global governance, then each territory is subjected to mutual competition rather than mutual cooperation. Thus in the view of Paul Martin (Prime Minister of Canada from 2003–6):

> Now the real problem that we face going ahead is that this same kind of pressure – where is going to be the financial capital of the world? – is going, uh, to come back once the crisis, memories of the crisis have faded. Um, Certainly Frankfurt and Paris are going to be back into the race. But so is Tokyo, so is Singapore, and so is Shanghai, and so is Hong Kong. And what I think may well happen at some point is that Shanghai and Hong Kong combine. Then you are really going to see a race that where's going to be the financial capital? And unless we have some kind of global oversight, it is going to be regulatory arbitrage, it is going to be a race to the bottom.
>
> (*Meltdown* part 4, 2011)

The world, then, is composed of territories governed by laws that in turn are subjected to the complexities of the economic market that force territorial competition to create the most favourable conditions for global corporations. These become the symbolic masters of the global markets, or, as Rastani put it, 'Goldman Sachs rules the world', and so according to Blankfein is 'doing God's work'. Smith's (1762) comments on the role of the police to keep good order in the market place now sound ironic as government's bow to the freedom of markets to dictate policies.

Symbolic fields

The symbolic, with its rules of reference, division, comparison, combination and substitution, enables systems of exchange, the determination and the calculation of value within or across whatever spheres of human activity, whether these are for example, economic, political, religious, cultural, aesthetic ethical or linguistic. When Blankfein says he is 'doing god's work', whether jokingly or seriously said, there is an implication of a central purpose, a unification, an order and cohesion brought about by the reference to God. This reference locates all human activities as well as all beings under the unifying central activity: God's work. It governs a powerful symbolic framework covering all fields of action, not just financial transactions.

The internal complexity and openness of the symbolic is reduced and fixed by being dominated by key metaphors that replace the real with something that in representing a reality – e.g., the work of God – disguises, represses or excludes all the particular material entities and interactions that comprise the complexity of the real and are always open to alternative namings, explanations and interpretations. It is here that the move is towards a psychoanalytics, in producing a master metaphor or signifier that centres the symbolic under its name (say God or Great Leader) or universalising demand (say freedom or Human Rights).

The symbolic field that psychoanalytics opens up relates the social – in its broadest sense, that is, a collective life through a variety of forms of organisation with the multitude of others – to the psychological, the life of the embodied self that knows itself only through reflections with, alongside and against others and otherness. What is critical is how the multitude is formed and fashioned – or schooled – into a mutually reinforcing perceptual world of self, others, forms of social organisation and boundaries that discriminate, include and exclude. The body techniques and 'flagging' of the body described in Chapter 1inscribe the social deep within the body, shaping its powers just as the thinking body works on the social for its living needs and interests. In one sense, the elements and forms of organisation of the symbolic are empty. Their relation to the real is fluid. Nothing sticks. The signifiers and signifieds of Saussure's view of language operate through the tongue, lips, nose, breath, throat, chest; and through fingers, hands, arms of gesticulations or the nods of the head, the looks and winks of the eyes, the lifted eyebrow, the posture of the body and the expressions of the face;

as well as the ways of walking, the clothes worn, the cut of the hair, the presence or absence of make-up, the scent or perfume of the body. The meanings that they signal and address to others are already there as an intersubjective resource before the birth of the individual. Thus, located in what both Lacan and Kristeva call the Symbolic, these significatory practices impose meaning and convey it through language, a dynamic system of signifiers and signifieds that are at once arbitrary and defined only in terms of being different from each other.

Born into worlds of language(s) that emerge from the use of signifiers and signifieds to distinguish one thing from another, we are as much fashioned fashioned by them as we – collectively – fashion our worlds. Once we learn to speak we, as speaking beings, live in and of material and textual worlds that offer or suffer themselves – as we offer or suffer ourselves – continuously as inscribable surfaces. This then is what comes to be known as the real, a real composed of surfaces of inscription that through their materialities receive impressions on their resistant but inscribable surfaces. At one level there is no split in the perceptual real, we do not have a sense of separation and apartness from it. Yet, the complexity of the real and its interactions with and effects that follow from how inscriptions can be made cannot be fully encapsulated. Thus there is a disjunction because the real cannot be represented since in its totality it is 'insignifiable' (Hook 2010: footnote 10, p. 19 of 34). However, it is not just the totality that cannot be represented but the very in-its-selfness of the materiality – for want of a better term – of the physical world.

Kant drew a distinction between the phenomena that appear to consciousness and the noumena that are the 'things' that cannot be experienced in themselves. Only their appearances can be experienced and known. Most intimately, this relationship is experienced between the body and the processes of thinking and reflection mediated by the realm of language and tropological processes leading to the forms of rhetorical and discursive construction and symbolization of the real. The discursive – like water over the beach, leaving its impressions but with no exchange of their separate substances – runs up against the body that resists and refuses 'the contractual exchange of signifiers' and so stands 'outside of discourse' (Hook 2010: 3 of 34). With its 'density' and 'gravity' this body-in-excess, this 'ecstasy of body ... cannot, will not, be sublimated into signifying space' (Hook 2010: 3 of 34). The words chosen here are significant for their connotations whether of 'excess' or of its near rhyme ecstasy, which provide a tension between a sense of too much and of extreme in the production of a state of being outside of oneself, a jouissance, perhaps, that places this within a psycho-analytics, Lacanian or otherwise. It is here in these excesses, on these thresholds, at these limits separating a self or an 'us' or some other identity from an otherness that spaces for the plays of difference open up through which the radical can emerge and claim a stake in bringing about change. The ecstasy, the too much, radically inserts into the range of the perceptual, other sights, other voices, other 'realities' that are potentially threatening to the stability of a given state of affairs. Boundaries against ecstasy, against too much, too far circumscribe a territory of the safe. Territorial control can be accomplished through a gathering of all the elements into a whole so that they become transformed into parts signifying the whole the boundary of which is the territory. Any disturbance of the process leads to criticism that in turn leads to enforcement through threats of punishment. The crucial question now is how to articulate and explore the excess, the threshold and the limit in order to better understand and utilise such spacings for radical thinking and action. How can one touch upon – think, speak of and act upon and play with– such abstractions?

Playing fields

In a project focusing on Corporate Social Responsibility the 'abstraction' of the limit and the excesses of views were concretely experienced as the defendable territories of gangs:

> There are three main areas we are dealing with: sectarianism, territorialism, and racism. To be honest, take sectarianism and racism out and territorialism is the main cause for conflict isn't it? What we said was that all the other things e.g. 'Oi you xxxxx xxxxxx what are you doing here?' come up after the actual incursion on territory, it's always the territory that comes before the other points. So I think that's a really good point that Gary has made as [area name] has such a stigma attached to it.
>
> It's all territorial. We have two Pakistani groups literally divided by one street, called [Upper] Road, and if you live where the MUGA is you're classed as 'top end' and if you live past [Upper] Road you're 'bottom end'. And top end and bottom end are constantly in conflict. I think that like Gary said the fact that you don't have that so much right now because of what we're doing now. I'm also working in partnership with the [youth organisation] at the moment and they have got an Astroturf over at [area name]. So that's the bottom end catered for ... [develop organisation] and the [youth organisation] have such a great partnership relationship, we are working together to try and integrate the two areas by using these two sites. That's actually working really well now and I think what Gary has said is a really good point, as the kids are saying 'I'm going to the MUGA or going to the Astro', and that's being said a lot more.
>
> (interview by JFS undertaken 2007)

The territories were named by the gang to remake the geography – the symbolic field – as theirs, as familiar as their playing fields. The remaking is essentially a process of 'toponymic inscription' (Rose-Redwood et al. 2010), that is a play of names, necessary to the construction of identities, the organisation, the control and the meaning of a territory:

> In early April 2003, a mere two weeks after the initial invasion of Iraq,

US troops commandeered Saddam International Airport, and the US Central Command swiftly renamed the complex 'Baghdad International Airport' (Woznicki, 2003; USA Today, 2003; Hunt, 2005; Pike, 2007a). The renaming of Baghdad's airport marked the opening salvo of the US occupation, which continues to reshape Iraq's toponymic landscape today. New US military camps and bases were given names that resonated with righteousness, such as 'Camp Freedom', 'Camp Liberty', and 'Camp Justice', and other toponyms were taken straight out of the American geographical lexicon, including 'Camp Arkansas' and 'Forward Operating Base Manhattan' (Pike, 2007).

(Rose-Redwood, Alderman and Azaryahu 2010: 454)

The gang territories are mapped over the official names, the boundaries created are a shared imaginary construction that are real in their consequences for a play of identities and actions. Under the impact of the project another work of re-naming took place through the re-territorialisation brought about by the new Astroturf or MUGA that has entered the discourses of the young – 'I'm going to the MUGA or going to the Astro' – enabling and permitting them to change their patterns of behaviour and play other games. Since there is no necessary connection or fixity relating the symbolic to a material real, then there is nothing to prevent the slip and slide to create new metaphorical 'namings' to mark out the symbolic fields of people's lives, except the determination of people not to change.

Under the name of sport and the metaphorical 'level playing field' – a term often used by the project members – people as individuals, as particulars, it was believed, could be re-collected, re-organised under a commonly valued name. This, if it works, is a critical move. There was then the possibility for identity critique – that is to say, a prior identity is radically altered and judged in some way. This alteration goes beyond a physical variation, say, as the legs of a chair are lengthened or its back shortened while still keeping the essential features of a chair. New conditions open; the chair, as it were, has the possibility of transforming into something else, of taking on a new name and being something else, something 'better'. Like the concept of the friend as Agamben (2004) analysed it, the toponymic inscriptions are linguistic events that are experienced as having effects on the real. So, as the friend is set into relation with an enemy, the political as Schmitt conceived it is inaugurated, creating the friend–enemy axis that Reagan exploited as the Evil Empire, Thatcher as 'the enemy within' and Bush Jr as the Axis of Evil sponsoring a terrorism across territories so generating the conditions of possibility for an endless War on Terror under a State of Exception.

Renaming under friend and enemy, if it is to create the new fields of play, must impact the imaginary in terms of how the world is actually perceived and made nameable by the application of an analytics. Then, in terms of how the world is walked, worked and played, the categories, programmes, discourses, routines and formulae of the analytics recreate the world as divided into sides. The key antinomies of Friend and Foe underlying the national and global political orders are driven right down to the day-to-day territorialisation of communities and gangs. Each gang has its friend–enemy logic overruling and homogenising the multiplicities of differences through which a sense of the good life and the good order required to produce it is alternatively constructed by members. Each side has its 'laws' its different rationalities whereby each transforms the other into the enemy, the 'sucker' or the nothing who can be ignored. Each has its resources, its mechanisms, its forms of organisation and methods of maintaining order over territories – its dispositifs – that can be drawn upon as threats arise. Critique acts on these dispositifs through which territories are established, maintained and controlled by disturbing and challenging their limits, boundaries and certainties to enable the emergence of other possibilities. Each disturbance, each challenge brings strenuous activity to restore the 'normal', as well demonstrated by Garfinkel's (1967) ethnomethodological strategy of 'causing trouble'. When the tacit assumptions of what is normal, what is supposed to happen were shaken in Garfinkel's studies by asking questions out of place, or by acting out of order, people responded emotionally, even violently. The apparent trivialness of responding to such everyday gambits as 'Hello, how are you?' with the attitude of a scientist asking for further elaboration such as 'Do you mean how am I in my health, my work, my finances, my …?' would typically lead to anger. There was an excessive response well beyond the normal play of events. It is as much, perhaps more, through the apparently trivial, the tacit rules of polite behaviour, or the rules of mutual indifference rather than overt coercion that the symbolic dominion of a territory is enforced.

It is at these limits through which the everyday is maintained that the conditions of possibility are open to or threatened with change. And yet the limit – 'this essentially abstract, insensible, invisible, and intangible thing' (Derrida 2005: 98) – announces that 'this limit must be reached, must come to be touched' and to pass the limit of meaning, of the known, perhaps it follows that 'one must change sense, pass from sight to tack' (Jean-Luc Nancy, ' The Sublime Offering' cited in Derrida 2005: 98). Rather than the certainty of routines or formulae, there is a fumbling sense, a feeling around until either there is a new practice and a new way of seeing with an alternative tact, or a new way of returning to the old way of seeing, a falling back to a default practice. As in the sports research and its programme of changing the symbolic fields of communities, there is an intrication of agendas – corporate, charitable, community – that in a sense wrap around the undertaking, defining it step by step as the project, or programme composed of many projects, progresses over time. At first, the outlines, the steps that needed to be taken, the detailed design to meet day-to-day organisational issues were fuzzily understood by the managers:

> it kind of felt a little bit kind of fumbly, it felt a little bit like we know what we want to do but we're not quite sure how we get there. And I guess a bit of this, you know, we're looking to launch September, you know we've done a pilot, we kind off know what we want to do but actually, the enormity

of it, I don't think anyone quite understood how big a project this was. I almost feel that once people saw the project rolling out it was almost like well this is the easy bit now and actually it's not, it actually just kept growing and growing.

(interview by JFS 2007)

What was at issue for this member of the bank's project management team in getting to grips with the project of building 200 sports facilities was its size, its continuous growth and its escape from the grasp. How then could a text be created that would become the programme? In one view, the normal default position of the bank, it was about defining outputs, deciding deadlines, generating mechanisms for feedback to ensure the kinds of effects that could be reported back to higher management and for publicity purposes. That is, it was about throwing a familiar symbolic map over the targeted terrain. In a second view, it only emerges through the multiplicities of voiced experiences, demands, interpretations, explanations, and impacts upon lives. It is in this possibility that a critique that escapes dominant symbolic fields can emerge into new symbolic playing fields. What is the nature of this text that is critique and not just criticism?

The two texts – the one of criticism, the other of critique – involve quite distinct tropological or figurative practices that promote alternative ways of seeing as a basis for action. But each seeing is also a touching – as in 'their eyes met' or 'her eyes touched mine'. Recalling Derrida's Jean-Luc Nancy, 'one must change sense, pass from sight to tact', the process has both a literal and metaphorical effect. It is the place where the figurative touches the real of sense, work and the political life of the everyday. Figuratively creating alternative ways of being and acting with others involves radical research practices (Schostak and Schostak 2008, 2010) designed to explore and to make a difference in terms of what can be seen, heard, felt and done. However, the playing fields of the bank were not of that kind. They were more about transforming the world under its own view of itself. Choosing to invest charitable monies in building and developing sports in communities was part of the bank's process of managing its appearance in public:

So what is it that we do that allows us to show ourselves to the world? For the world to know what we're about. And because it's about the world and knowing what we're about there's an increasing desire for us to have a focus on something that demonstrates what our business is about. So, you know we're good at financial stuff; well maybe we've got a duty to do something in the area of financial education, inclusion, and all those sorts of things. And we know we need to do better in that direction, so what is it that we do there?

(bank project team member, 2007)

This member of the management team drew upon the analytic resources typical of a financial institution, its way of figuring itself and practicing in a world of familiar objects, objectives and activities that can be incorporated into a policy:

So instead of just Corporate Social Responsibility being primarily about shouting about all of this stuff that we do – and then just, 'well we do some stuff in the environment and we do some stuff in supply chain' – but quite unconnected messages, we got a focus on corporate responsibility that said, we're actually about becoming a responsible banker. That's kind of who we try and be as a business. And that should inform what we try and do with our corporate community investment properties, well, some of our corporate community investment properties.

(bank project team member, interview by JFS 2007)

The bank was able to draw upon its internal resources – its internal machineries – to meet the perceived problem that its CSR messages were too dispersed and disconnected. It drew together a project team that was able to call upon its internal public relations agency, its project management knowledge, its internal discourses of volunteering and its mechanisms and resources to enable bank employees to volunteer time and effort in a given charitable cause, its legal department, its accountancy services and so on to form a dispositif targeted at delivering the sports programme.

Few outside of large corporations have the freedom to deploy such resources. The intention is to create an identity – responsible banker – and linking this directly with action that goes beyond 'shouting about all this stuff that we do'. The project team then unified the smaller particular charitable activities under the heading of the programme that it could then, with one voice, one appearance, promote nationally and internationally under the figurehead of the programme. The tropological strategy of the programme was to unite all its activities under images of sporting heroes, community sports and good works. In short the central images metaphorically represented the abstract CSR programme and simplified into graspable friendly images the whole complexity of the day-to-day local, national and global financial business activities of the bank as a socially responsible enterprise.

Spacing(s) and the articulation of powers and critique

The nature of criticality for Arendt (1978) becomes clear in her reference to Eichmann not as monstrous but as ordinary, and whose everyday manner was of 'thoughtlessness' (p. 4). It is in the use of '(c)lichés, stock phrases, adherence to conventional, standardised codes of expression and conduct' that 'have the socially recognised function of protecting us against reality' (p. 4). Such resources of discourse map the symbolic fields of everyday functioning, rendering them manageable. In that case, a question occurs: 'Could the activity of thinking as such, the habit of examining whatever happens to come to pass or to attract attention, regardless of results and specific content, could this activity be among the conditions that make men abstain from evil-doing or even actually "condition" them against it?' (p. 5). It is in the support that the metaphor lends to thinking about the real that also creates the conditions for their unthinking repetition as clichés that map over and take the place of the real and critical attempts to experience it anew. If metaphors associated with visual perception drive the imagination, and if in Arendt's terms, the metapherein – the process of the metaphor – permits a carrying over of sense experiences to the material realm of things then the limit has been figuratively touched. At this point, there is either a withdrawal from the limit or a breaking through, or perhaps an oscillation as the new and old figurative playing fields struggle for dominance over the 'thingness' of the material reality, the reality that resists and escapes all attempts at its capture in representational nets and is in that sense, untouchable.

Changing sense, whether in terms of the nature of the sensory perceptions or relating to the sensible, entails a shift, a movement to another plane of being, a transformation – what may be called a space-ing, where one 'thing' passes from one state into another. In this way, some untouchable is announced in a touch. For Derrida it is the case that:

> nobody, no body, no body proper has ever touched – with a hand or through skin contact – something as abstract as a limit. Inversely, however, and that is the destiny of this figurality, all one ever does touch is a limit. To touch is to touch a limit, a surface, a border, an outline. Even if one touches an inside, 'inside' of anything whatsoever, one does it following the point, the line or surface, the borderline of a spatiality exposed to the outside, offered – precisely – on its running border, offered to contact.
>
> (Derrida 2005: 103)

Except figuratively, there is no possible synthesis of the real and the figurative or the symbolic nets through which our social realities are mapped out for mutual co-ordination of our activities – the relation between them remains contingent and heterogeneous.

There is always between them a 'space', announced, for example, by Lacan's placing of a bar between the signifier and the signified. In trying to see the construction of any representation of the real, any figurative totalising of the real into an image, a symbol, there is a recalling of the 'spacing' between the representation and the real. The fragility of the relation between a figurative grasp of the real and the real itself is where criticism and critique mark out the choices to be made between the criticism that bolsters the figuratively constructed pictures of the real or the criticism that subverts them to make place for a whole scale critique that goes to the founding metaphors of the old figuration to make way for alternative 'groundings'; or, indeed, as Gasché (1986) might put it, to enable a 'groundless ground' in order to construct an effective public from an otherwise disasembled multitude. Criticism and critique work to shake the fixity of the sense of the real, the symbolic nets that define the fields of everyday routine behaviours and so raise the fundamental question of how the sense of the real may be re-configured to meet the individual and collective interests of people, of 'humanity'. It is through the recognition of 'spacings', of the boundaries between representation and real, the re-constructions of figurative formulae for 'seeing' a real, that the possibilities for alternatives arise as well as the resistances to any alternatives by those who have vested interests in the maintenance of a particular view by the 'public'.

The public may be figuratively defined as described in chapter 4 as a phantom public, a public whose attention is open to be shaped by public relations, or coerced and policed through a kind of mental kettling; or the public may be defined as the multiplicity of voices engaged in a debate about 'figuring' the real, a debate that opens the possibilities for alternatives figurings. For example, in the public relations exercise that accompanied the promotion of the bank's sports programme, it was learnt from a range of interviews, from attending meetings, that there were deadlines to achieve at every stage of the development of the programme. Each deadline had an output, a deliverable. There were deadlines for signing the contracts between community groups, local authorities and the bank, that was the major funder of the programme. There were deadlines governing the build, deadlines on involvement of target groups in sports activities. There were forms to fill to gather data on defined 'outputs' at each site. Each deadline and its prescribed output provided a powerful control of attention, its patterning over a schedule of deadlines, a kind of delivery pulse. However, there were differences of opinion expressed by the community focused organisations charged with providing advice and strategies for community regeneration. There was also a difference in language employed, albeit each was a language of expertise. For the bank, the schedules of deadlines and the defining of outputs meant control. For the organisation involved in regeneration, it meant the illusion of control since there was always the unexpected. For them projects had to grow communally otherwise they would not be owned by the community. The bank, however, saw the issue as ensuring compliance and thus of driving it downwards to the community groups. Thus, from the point of view of community groups, they could level criticisms as to how effective the mechanisms employed by the bank were in achieving compliance to the schedules. For example:

> we've had changes in reporting, not being communicated, it's been unclear, um, I don't think lessons have been learnt or uh you know it's difficult, what I found difficult actually from my perspective coming in is um the decision-making process which you know the ... basically being a reporting mechanism ... if someone comes to me with a question I can't, there's no way I can give them a response 'cos I have to go to [name] who has to go to [name 2] and [name 2] appears to be the only person who makes any decisions ... It kind of overlooks the skills, knowledge and experience of people that are involved in the programme, I think to the detriment sometimes but, uh, the structure of the programme, you have to work within that framework. You just have to get on with it really, don't you?
>
> (interviewee is a member of a partner organisation reflecting upon involvement in the latter phases of the programme – interview by JFS)

There is in these criticisms the glimpse of an alternative, but also a resignation that the alternative cannot become effective. Without the organisation to make effective critique there can be no move beyond a complaining or resigned recognition of spacings as a creative source for the new, thus, no agonistic voicing of alternatives and so no politics for the organisation of debate as a resolution to violence. In short, there is no 'spacing' allowed in the bank's organisation of work, no challenge to the system of categories through which work is made specifiable according to schedules and outcomes and no mechanism by which to engage in the deconstruction of the rationales and ways of seeing that compose the bank's view of CSR, communities and the undertaking of projects. Without spaces for difference, there is only dominion, that is, total coverage.

Without spacing there is no 'room' for the articulation of powers, there is no place for the powers of individuals to work together in the creation of projects and their preferred forms of social organisation across the domains of politics, economics, law, education, health and culture. Rather, as in the case of the bank framing its control over individual projects, there is the aggregation of powers – as in a synecdochal process described in Chapter 8 – resulting in the symbolisation of Power as Leader, System and State that dominates territories and practices restricting change, restricting anything 'new' that is not already in the image of the 'old'. The really new in any change involves some degree of crisis, perhaps a fatal degree of crisis in the 'old', the 'stable', the 'political order'. Was it there following the crisis in the financial sector of 2008? The political and social mood of large sections of national populations towards the banking system changed dramatically. At the height of the crisis and in the aftermath, there were many calls to regulate financial institutions following judgements that they acted irresponsibly. The threat to the global markets and national economies meant they had to be bailed out by taxpayers. Furthermore, adding to resentment, the 'culprits' continued to take large bonuses for their personal profit. Yet, what were the real available mechanisms, the real public spaces, to enable people to articulate their criticisms or their more fundamental critiques? The exercise of the individual powers to protest led to retaliation by police and military powers and for many imprisonment, injury and even death. Both criticism and critique in their different ways make a demand for change, for the realisation of the new. Where the spacings for this are overseen by coercive policing both in the military and Rancière's broader sense of the term, then until the structures of this policing are effectively challenged, there is no change, and all criticisms and critiques are meaningless. Achieving critique means achieving the systematic spacings where people can join together in public debate in the place of power(s) where each voice can be heard and incorporated in decision-making and action. How then can the new, the novel, the risking of difference be broached?

Gesturing towards writing

Ethnography in writing of people, writes of the ways in which powers are assembled and figured to constitute a sense of 'us', of 'friends' and, indeed, of 'enemies'. It explores the ironic syntheses of an unutterable real of experience with the symbolic maps by means of which powers are co-ordinated and organised under a practice of namings to articulate a sense of 'home', of territory, of places to play both prescribed and alternative games.

If the routine maps of practice are blown away by thinking, then to explore a case of territorialisations and their possible re-territorialisations requires focusing on the ironic syntheses that enable both fixity and fluidity, conformity and dissension. Where the unnamed is metaphorically claimed under a name, there is always the hope and the fear of its thoughtful de-fusion. In that arises the possibility of re-spacings, re-namings, re-claimings and re-actings. Can action research be designed to inscribe the new, the novel? Can a radical move be made? Or, are we capable only of ironically writing in jest?

Chapter 10

Being Novel – risking difference

Making a difference implies a 'new', a 'novel' in at least one of various senses. At one level it might arise as a product of criticism; at another as the outcome of critique. Or it may be a personal experience where, for me it is new albeit well known for you. Or it can be about practices that were once denied but now possible. More existentially, it may be about patterns of attention and inattention that enable a new awareness, even a new world-view. These latter have a sense of the Copernican revolution, the shift from dominion by a 'religious' order to a 'scientific' order, or vice versa. Creating the novel involves allowing the conditions for new spaces to emerge. It is not about sitting and awaiting the eureka moment. Nor is it to be found in the lost sense of the whole, or a once-upon-a-time fullness of being to be rediscovered and recreated. The source of the new is always in the act that steps out of the routine that long since lost the requirement for a thinking agent. It is not about whether something has been done before. The new is always new for someone, somewhere, as an expression of self-discovery, of being with others, of working together engaged in a mutual project or more generally of employing ideas to make a difference in the material, social and psychological worlds of people. In that sense, the possibilities for the new, the novel, are endless.

Becoming an actor engaged in thinking the new, the starting point is always now, with these conditions, these circumstances, these resources. That is, we begin with our powers in the place we find ourselves. And that can seem so small and confined, so lacking in the power adequate to the job. It is easy, perhaps, to think the new in a big organisation that has the resources to make a difference and to prevent differences being made. How does a thinking subject emerge in an environment that is overdetermined with the controls and surveillance mechanisms of organised Power? How does one bring the act of thinking to bear upon current circumstances in a context dominated by competing organisations of Power serving elite interests? And how then can thoughtful acts be undertaken?

A question of thinking community

Reflecting again as a member of a team at Manchester Metropolitan University researching the aspiration, the practice and the legacy of a national and indeed global sports CSR programme of a major bank, questions haunt the representation, the interpretation and the generation of theory about its impact on people. It is a haunting because of its ironic framing. How can the powers of people to engage with each other and the world about be liberated under the Power of a major corporation? The writing demands a re-thinking of community and its relation to Power. As such it is a case within a global ambition to inscribe anew the conditions of an effective global public.

The theme of 'community' is implicit if not always explicitly central to any exploration of writing. To act in the world is to inscribe meaning onto the material, social and psychological surfaces of a 'people'. Each act draws attention, aligns responses to it or away from it, is the occasion of interpretations and the expression of interests, rejections or demands. For example, at one point, in the legacy report for the bank, it is written that how a community is seen may change due to the construction or upgrading of a sports facility:

> Once built, it has the potential of changing the kinds of scenarios that are seen around the community, for example:
> So at the moment we've got the scenario where kids are hanging around with nothing to do. Or, they're hanging around on the current pitch causing a nuisance, OK and we've also got projects such as street football that [name] United get involved in. So they're running activities. We've got our own project called street games, which is very informal recreation, on a recreation ground or a little pitch with a couple of coaches, with a youth worker that goes along. And it's generally done at times of the day when kids are hanging around with nothing to do or causing trouble. So it's quite targeted.

Each scenario is an element, the physical and visual manifestation of the day-to-day stories of young people and those who live in the community, work with them or try to control them. The new scenarios opened up by a project point to the life and career trajectories of people where new kinds of futures open up for individuals to pursue:

> It ties in quite nicely to Positive Futures, well very nicely, with Positive Futures the monitoring and evaluation of which has recently been renewed and part of it, the new phase going forward, it's as much about the story of the young person or the journey of the young person involved in the project as it is bums on seats and a numbers side. So the project we're running it [the monitoring and evaluation exercise] will go right through the project trying to capture that softer outcome and the story behind it.

An example is a piece of work we're planning to do down there with partnership support so we can extend the amount of work that we do and that the [name] facility is going to be fantastic for that. Whilst you have the two spaces, the renewed area which is two multi-use games areas and next to that you have also an unused pavilion which is in perfectly good condition but is just pretty much unused. Which has a small kitchen area, a meeting area, and it has some left over pool tables and football tables from a former youth club. So part of the work we're looking at is how can we use the whole site. How can for example NACRO deliver sport activities on the court outside but then Millennium volunteers come in and do a juice bar and PAYP (Positive Activities for Young People) come in and run a drop in centre; or connexions come and give an advice centre. Therefore we can cater for a huge number, a range of young people, not necessarily the ones that are just interested in the sport and are confident enough to go and get involved in that but provide support and a full range of activities and support for these young people to use the whole site.

It is through social involvement that people are affirmed in their identities, their sense of confidence and their sense of self-value. This can be reinforced through changes in community 'infrastructure'. It changes the possibilities for 'encounters' between people, the development of positive social identities and the actions and events that then can then take place:

In [place], at the skatepark project, since that was done just before Christmas, the police have come back to me and said verbally over the Christmas, New Year and January period, the number of incidents, as they call them, has dramatically dropped just because [in their view] of, literally, the skatepark being built. The actually the young people that are using it are local young people that aren't brilliant at skate boarding but they're local, and they're not causing problems elsewhere. And that's always been the case with the pilot funding for the football, is in the evenings, dragging people away from the street corners and the shops causing problems and to give them something positive to do, potentially making them healthier, even though half of them are probably stood around smoking than playing football. But at least they're out of trouble and they're doing something positive rather than negative.

So we're looking to build on that with the other projects as well. And we do work quite closely with the sort of community beat officers on these particular areas because they're really the police officers that can give you the most in terms of what's actually going on, on the ground. Stats from the police aren't brilliant because stats only give you an incidence and the time of the incident. It doesn't tell you if it was involving a young person, old person, what was actually going on. It's private, confidential information. It's literally a load of numbers. Whereas the actual beat officer can tell you the ins and outs of what's going on in that area in much more detail so you get anecdotal information which I suppose could be taken down in written evidence to support the evaluation.

(MMU Team 2007/8)

An initial perception is provided that sees young people as 'hanging around'. They are targeted in order to make a difference. This process of targeting is placed within a process of narrativisation composed of 'scenarios' that actors engaged with a 'community' identify as something to work with or upon. As local community workers, always seeking funding opportunities, their work is shaped by the policies and resources made available. In this case, the resourcing that the bank's programme provides fits with the government's Positive Futures policy which, like the bank, looks for measurable outcomes:

Our evidence

- In 2010–11 over 57,000 young people attended Positive Futures projects, involving nearly one and a half million contact hours
- Thanks to Positive Futures, thousands of young people are now in education, training and employment
- In 2010–11 young people were recorded as achieving over 38,000 positive outcomes, that's an increase of almost 30% on the last year
- Recorded outcomes ranged from improved behaviour, self-confidence and self esteem through to returning to education and gaining employment.
- In 2010–11 young people achieved nearly 10,000 qualifications

(Positive Futures undated)

Accompanying the 'evidence' there are some illustrative 'stories' of successful outcomes, like 'Kate's Journey' into work with a Positive Future's corporate partner. Alongside the statistics, then, are the 'soft data', the captured stories of effects on young people. These are snippets from the stories that qualitative research methodologies uncover from the interviews and observations of fieldwork. They tell of change. The depth of detail, however, is missing.

In the details, narratives describe characters in action whether this is with, alongside or against each other. In any course of action, a person's power to effect change is only as extensive as his or her reach. An individual can physically reach out, touch, grasp and manipulate something and can move around to get within distance of other things. To communicate, other people have to be within range of the voice. The difference of physical reach between one person and another is very little. It is through the combination of individuals, tools and technologies that their powers can be magnified. The value of a community to its members, then, is evaluated according to the extent it enhances the powers of each individual in meeting his or her needs, interests and demands, if not immediately then in the medium and long term. How a community is organised to meet the requirements of its members matters in terms of how benefits and hardships are distributed. If, as Margaret Thatcher maintained, there is no society, only the self-interest of individuals, their families and 'good neighbours', then the underpinning logics of organisation is of competition for the private accumulation of resources to which others are prevented from having access unless a good neighbour takes pity on the less fortunate. In the Positive Futures rationale this logic underpins the good neighbour-like focus on the education, skilling and the shaping of the behaviour of individuals to put them into a position to compete in the labour market. Each community initiative, whether it is government, charity or privately sponsored, is shaped by the overriding political, economic and managerial contexts, forms of organisation and practices through which resources and opportunities are allocated. The sports facilities therefore were just another means by which to organise efforts with football or some other sport as the lure.

What constitutes the 'new', the 'novel', within such a framework? It is first of all a question of how community is being thought. It can, in policy and developmental terms, be thought of as a series of partnerships where each partner either delivers something that attracts young people or works with young people to reduce nuisance and increase their usefulness as citizens of a market society. The 'newness' consists in both services not previously in existence in the area where a 'community' is presumed to live. The research and its evidence then becomes a 'new' account of this newness, describing its effectiveness as well as actual and potential limitations.

In this sense, 'community' is a kind of metaphorical roofing over a territory unifying it for policy, research and reporting purposes, and the 'new' is simply the latest articulation of policy and the impacts of various interventions. However, to rethink community involves a radical re-writing of what 'community' is capable of signifying and meaning in practice in terms of the patterns of attention and inattention through which the 'powers' of individuals are targeted, harnessed and organised.

One of the common reasons for entering into community is for greater security, each being able to collectively aggregate their powers for defence against some threat. Another reason is to combine talents, knowledge and skills to organise more productively in work to make the goods and provide the services people need. Then there are the more social and cultural reasons of friendship, love and entertainment. Thus community is formed through the needs for co-operation whether for security, work or other psychological, social and cultural reasons. This is not to say that there will be an absence of conflict, but that conflict itself is a reason to develop community responses to settle disputes without violence or at least through community sanctioned violence. In community the powers of individuals are directed to common ends in an expectation of mutual support. Drawing on the notion of intentionality as discussed in Chapter 5, powers are intentional in nature and are thus generative of subjects and objects made meaningful and in terms of what can be effected from the direction of powers. How the object of powers resists or changes in ways that are unexpected or to be discovered becomes a definition of a real that is independent of any single or combination of individuals' powers to make it perform arbitrarily (cf. Tragesser 1977). Any new intervention, any new way of working, or new form of social organisation and cultural product that follows from the exercise of powers has to be valid, reliable and representative of the needs, interests and demands of members of the community. It is in that way that the outcome becomes objective for all rather than subjectively desired by some subgroup. There is therefore a directedness of each member towards the others. To be a valid member involves a mutual recognition of each as having a voice in all matters to do with the collective organisation of social and work projects. A valid organisation, then, is one that is inclusive of voices from all members of a community in its operational projects. By this measure, privatisation inscribed through its principles, philosophies and practices of exclusion and the exclusivity of proprietary rights is a denial of community voice and thus of an effective public within the physical, social and cultural domains and territories of operation of the privatised organisation.

This contrast in positions and their consequent evaluation of the audibility and effectiveness of voice in different forms of organisation and social spaces can be written in many ways. Any writing of community can be reduced to the political forms of communism, socialism, communitarianism or cooperativism and their historical examples; just as any focus on the private can be reduced to exploitation by the self-interested powerful elites through market forces and capitalism. The alternative logics that animate an analytics elaborated through the inclusion of voice in the creation of an open and public space of community or its exclusion and privatisation bring about the conditions for possible choices:

> I think today the world is asking for a real alternative. Would you like to live in a world where the only alternative is either Anglo-Saxon neo-liberalism or Chinese–Singaporean capitalism with Asian values?
>
> I claim if we do nothing we will gradually approach a kind of a new type of authoritarian society. Here I see the world historical importance of what is happening today in China. Until now there was one good argument for capitalism: sooner or later it brought a demand for democracy ...
>
> What I'm afraid of is with this capitalism with Asian values, we get a capitalism much more efficient and dynamic than our western capitalism. But I don't share the hope of my liberal friends – give them ten years, [and there will be] another Tiananmen Square demonstration – no, the marriage between capitalism and democracy is over.
>
> (Zizek interview 2011)

A claim is made by Zizek that presumes a surface, an open world surface, where a range of alternative demands can be inscribed. The claim is that 'if we do nothing' then something we do not want will be inscribed. The 'we' in question is the critical space for the new.

The we in question

Writing the 'we' either places all individuals or some who align themselves with a particular interest or demand under its name. A place of privilege is given to 'We the People'. It is a declaration that assumes the powers of all people and aligns them to bring about a co-ordinated action. It is in that sense a democratic act that pertains to and encompasses all people over a given territory, in this case 'in Order to form a more perfect Union, establish Justice, insure domestic Tranquillity, provide for the common defence, promote the general Welfare, and secure the Blessings of Liberty to ourselves and our Posterity, do ordain and establish this Constitution for the United States of America' (Charters of Freedom, undated) It is a powerful writing.

From the place of privilege, we-the-people act to bring about a range of desired outcomes through the institutions of executive power and the organisations through which that power is applied. As such the "We the People", as a tropological framing of the masses, is causative of all the forms of social organisation required to deliver on the constitution. Through the free and equal inclusion of all voices there is a radical inversion of places from the sovereignty of a single voice dominating and subjecting all other voices to the sovereignty of the collective voices, a people. The collective voice of democracy is thus a primal ground upon which all else is to be built. All the institutions and forms of social organisation that are subsequently built call upon it to demonstrate that they are valid democratic forms and can reliably deliver on the inscripted demands of the constitution. As in the case of religious texts, the ancient writings need always to be interpreted for particular circumstances at particular times. There is an opening then, for a form of re-writing as 'interpretation' that must always show its validity as an interpretation of the founding script and demonstrate that what is done in the name of the valid interpretation is a reliable deliverance of the founding demands. The argument in chapter 2 proposed by Lippmann and Bernays' for the re-writing of democracy as government by experts can be re-read here as both a novel strategy that contributed substantially to the development of the Public Relations industry as a necessary support for capitalism and also as a necessary structure to manage 'we the people' by enabling governments 'get their message across'. As Lippmann's phantom public (1927) a covert re-inversion of elites over 'we the people' was enacted. At one level, they were seen as representatives of 'we the people', doing their bidding. At another, they could inscribe their own agendas upon 'we the people' by, as Lippmann called it, the 'manufacture of consent' through the employment of contemporary psychological and sociological research and research methodologies. Rather than 'we the people' subduing the elitist, self serving demands of the rich and powerful, the elites in the guise of representatives, could perform an inversion of terms and subdue, tame and shape 'we the people' in their 'best interests'.

At a grammatical level, this is a chiasmus. As Connor (2010) puts it, a chiasmus is a 'figure consisting of two parallel clauses, in which the order of elements in the second clause inverts the order of the first: when the going gets tough, the tough get going: ask not what your country can do for you, but what you can do for your country'. The first provides a model of how people ought to behave under difficult circumstances, say, in the context of austerity measures to reduce a national deficit. The second of these two illustrations of chiasmus was famously used by Kennedy in his inaugural address of 20 January 1961. In the move of emphasis to 'what you can do for your country', there is an echo of Kitchener's First World War call to arms: 'Your country needs you!' Or, in American terms. 'Uncle Sam needs you! In each case, the subject position of 'country' – and Kennedy taking his position as legitimate leader and representative of that country – is placed above the individual and the collectivity of individuals who are set apart as 'you', not collectively unified as 'we'. Kennedy in the position of leader – in the place of 'Uncle Sam' – makes a further appeal as leader of the Western World: 'My fellow citizens of the world: ask not what America will do for you, but what together we can do for the freedom of man.' There is the implication here that America is in the dominant position as a subject to be petitioned by the subject citizens of the world. However, there is a higher-level 'we', where America is positioned as not the lone deliverer, but the fellow subject in a united world struggle for freedom. The play of subject positions, echoes, partitionings and universalising terms is fundamental to managing attention and thus of rendering what is to become visible and what remains invisible. These systems of visible and invisible foci of attention and inattention create the play of light and shadow, smoke and mirrors, the familiar and the uncanny and the sense of dangers glimpsed at the edge of consciousness, the night terrors of a liberal conscience trying not to notice the huddled figure wrapped in blankets begging beside the cash machine. The new emerges in the tensions, the shivering of boundaries between the certain, the possible and the unthinkable. It is in this tension that the search for refuge is motivated to fill the uncertainties, to displace them by attention to safer categories, to cover them with more encompassing metaphors of the foundational rock or the whole-that-must-not-be-challenged.

Ironic structuring and its symptom

Each play between the visible and the invisible, the dislocating of boundaries to reveal possibilities for interpretation and action, generates an ironic writing where there is a double-sided surface between what can be inscribed and what can only be glimpsed at best. Regarded as illegible, it is reduced to being the detritus left over after the work of producing and thus swept away, or articulated only as symptoms to be 'cured', or as natural disasters that cannot be 'foreseen', or as acts of a god 'behind' the 'seens'. The ironic draws from those surfaces that are structured through plays of attention and inattention as surfaces of each other where one or more are 'visible' in relation to others that are 'invisible'. This relation between surfaces can be read as an intention to say something that involves an 'intention otherwise', that is, an intention that is discoverable only through clues. When Swift wrote in his 'A Modest Proposal' in 1729 that a solution to the Irish Famine was the boiling and eating of babies, his intention was to provoke attention to the tragedy of the famine and arouse humane action. However, the clues to this reading are not explicit in the surface of the text. It has to be read against some other inscripted surface. The irony explored in literary terms provides some clues to the ironies of lived experience that while lived may not be experienced as such in a given present circumstance and context. However, rather than the focus being around some suspected or presumed intention to say one thing but mean another, the structure of what may be called everyday ironies is that of the future anterior. That is, the meaning of a particular act at one point in time will be what it will have become at some future date as patterns of attention and inattention change, re-writing what can be seen from what was seen otherwise or in other terms at the time. For example, an event, say the initial protests in France in the late 1700s, or the self-immolation of Mohammed Bouazizi in Tunisia, could at the first moments be regarded as having no more than a local meaning. With the passing of time the one could be named the steps leading to the French Revolution the other the start of the Arab Spring. The initial acts require later inscriptions to compose a text that re-marks earlier acts as a 'beginning'. Rather than thinking these as a sequence of events historically overlaying surfaces of inscription from one time period to another, they can be re-thought as parallel 'realities' where events intrude from the one to the other. The everyday experience of Mohammed Bouazizi in Tunisia was not singular but could be read in relation to the texts of many lives

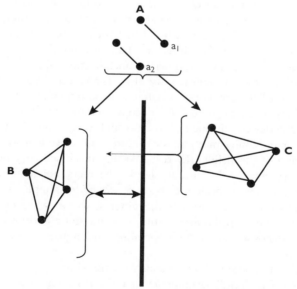

Figure 2 Mirror Groups (Schostak and Schostak 2008: 172)

which experienced their own hardships, their frustrations, their injustices and their despair. Take figure 2 above that schematically illustrates the boundaries constructed between different groupings.

Figure 2 can be read in many ways. In one reading, for example, Group B and C stand in relationship to each other as the 1 per cent and the 99 per cent, or the middle class and the underclass, or as one faith group and another faith group, or one gang and another gang. They are characterised in terms of a systematic inattention towards each other. The bar between B and C signals both a block (constructed through systematic inattention) and a double-sided surface where one surface doubles as the 'tain' for the mirror of the other, where the tain is what gives glass its power to mirror (cf. Gasché 1986). It may also act as a filter where each group is, say, darkened for the other, seen as shadowy creatures whose presence is a danger or seen as exciting and dangerous objects of desire. Each member of each group is directed towards each other, creating an 'interior' of the visible or perceptible. This directedness composes a 'mirror' of self acting in relation to others as each reflects, evaluates, encourages or rejects the actions and identities of the others through their comments and responses. A third group, C, seems to straddle the two. It is positioned to 'see' both sides. Possible groups that aspire to or at least claim such a perspective include national policy makers and professional political, social and cultural commentators and researchers. Such groups create their visions, their theoretical oversight, their methodologies for grasping and understanding what is at stake for the multiplicities of communities, interest groups and their complaints, injuries, vulnerabilities and demands. Whether it is a bank commissioning a research group, an ethnographer exploring the lives of people or an action researcher seeking to make changes 'for the better', they may perhaps start from a position of asserting a belief that their vision of the totality is sufficient for them to know the best interests of all, or claim that their methodology is sufficient to identify, draw out, describe, analyse and evaluate what is essential, typical, probable, desirable. In each case there is a vision of the totality and even if such a vision of the totality is presumed to be impossible it conditions the processes of representation, analysis, deconstruction, evaluation, decision and action. An analytics conditioned by the possibility or impossibility of a totality as a writing or inscribing machine has within it all it needs to perpetuate itself as a structuring of the visible, the real. 'Writing machines' may be constructed in various ways, imagined, conceptualised. The metaphor of the machine has from the beginnings of modernity been a way of imagining the operation of minds, organisations, societies and the physical world, whether with rational conscious intention as in the formulation of computer algorithms or through a Lacanian-like unconscious machine operating on language, or a Deleuzian-like desiring machine.

Fink (1995: 15), asking how unconscious thinking can happen, shows that Lacan draws upon Freud's arguments that the thinking in question is structured through the operations of condensation and displacement that Lacan re-formulates in terms of processes of metaphor and displacement respectively, and moreover:

> According to Lacan, the unconscious is structured like a language, and a natural language (unlike speech) is structured like a formal language. As Jacques-Alain Miller says, 'the structure of language is, in a radical sense, ciphering,' the type of cyphering or coding Lacan engages in when he superimposes numeric and alphabetic matrices on chains of pluses and minuses (altogether akin to the type of ciphering used in the machine language 'assembler' to go from open and closed circuit paths to something resembling a language with which one can program). To Lacan's mind, the unconscious consists in chains of quasi-mathematical inscriptions, and – borrowing a notion from Bertrand Russell, who in speaking of mathematicians said that the symbols they work with don't mean anything – there is thus no point talking about the meaning of unconscious formations or productions.
>
> (Fink 1995: 21)

The point, as Fink argues, is to discover the original traumatic signifier that subjects the subject, mechanically generating symptoms. Fink imagines a chance overheard remark by a young child's parents, 'and though he was still too young to understand it, it was nevertheless recorded, indelibly etched in his memory' (1995: 22). It is not the meaning that is heard but the signifier. It is only later, over the years, that the signifier will have come to mean something, as in the case of the death of Mohammed Bouazizi, which has grown in meaning and historical significance with the world's recognition and naming of the Arab Spring.

The act of the signifier, not the meaning, is what is critical in the first instance. It is the material force of sound, of striking, of feeling, of slicing, cutting or otherwise making a mark upon the sensible world. The bar in figure 2 [p. 151] can be read as such a signifier that cuts across the people to produce two 'sides'. The historical significance of the sides play out over time. The totality of all people being members of a single 'community' has been displaced by the creation of sides. From that emerge changed subject positions and reconfigurations of internal relations between people. No longer is a given individual able to 'reach' all others; no longer is there the possibility for all to work together. There is a separation imposed. The bar as signifier of separation has brought into being something new. On each side there is a new consciousness that 'we' are on this side, not that side.

The 'we' in question on each side places into question the totality as 'people' by creating parts of a whole in which the people have no part. If the whole is a capitalist market system, then one side, say B, may represent the 'bosses' as 'C' represents the employees. Although the people comprises the members of B and C, the people as such has no part in the system except re-defined as members of functioning parts of the system. If they are not members of functioning parts, then they are without use or meaning, and thus their voices can be excluded from key policy debates although they may be objects of such debates. As objects of debates they may be regarded as 'enemies within', 'criminals', 'underclasses' and variously scorned and despised. If the new in question is to be a radical inclusion of all voices in debates about common futures, then how the whole space of the social itself has been inscribed is to be questioned. In short, writing the new involves a mapping and a de-construction of the prevailing analytics with its categories of the real and the processes employed to reproduce itself through self-validating procedures and practices sealing over the splits and the symptoms of a repressed unspeakable real. In the last resort to prevent the ironic structuring of a real and its representation erupting into legibility, its cover-ups, its bound-aries are enforced – policed as it were – through threat and pain of violence. To have the courage to re-write 'we' and make legible the ironies that bind people's freedoms involves a quest for space.

Space in question

Fundamental to the novel or the new is the search for a space where people can meet and together do things they could not do before. What prevents finding such a space is the prevailing configuration of Power through which people are seduced to conform or are deprived of their powers through the force of law sustained by the threat of violence. The only effective countervailing power stems from the free and equal association of individuals who through debate and action are able to create ways of working and living together as a mutual project for the achievement their individual hopes and ambitions. Writing the new in spaces that are already configured with old ways of thinking and behaving demands radical beginnings. It demands the space to think.

MacDonald (2000) writes of Descartes' project of radical beginnings that in many ways parallels the difficulties of writing the new not so much as a project of reaching secure and certain truths about realities but of creating the conditions for new, more inclusive, more culturally enriching social forms. For his project, Descartes battled against the scepticism of his day that saw in the multiple opinions and disagreements of people proof of the impossibility of finding any secure way that human beings could come to the 'truth' on anything. Similarly, the multiplicities of definitions of the 'good' and the impossibility of agreement on the 'good society' can also be presented as a reason to impose order by Power. In Hobbes' paradigmatic writing of *The Leviathan* (1651) the awesomeness of such Power inspires so much fear that all are obedient to its demands – such was the effect that the 'shock and awe' strategy of the Bush administration's invasion of Iraq desired on 20 March 2003 after its 48-hour deadline. Such was the desire of military or police crackdowns by tyrants during the Arab Spring of 2011, or, in more diluted fashion, the overwhelming policing of protests in western nation states with baton wielding, mustard gas spraying and armour-protected police. For example, when there were 'Occupy Wall Street' protests in 2011 on campus at the University of California, Davis, the Chancellor, Linda Katehi, authorised police action that led to the use of pepper spray:

> Footage of the incident prompted immediate outrage among faculty and students, with the Davis Faculty Association saying in a letter on Saturday that Katehi should resign.
>
> 'The Chancellor's role is to enable open and free enquiry, not to suppress it,' the faculty association said in its letter.
>
> It called Katehi's authorisation of police force a 'gross failure of leadership.'
>
> At a news conference later on Saturday, Katehi said what the video showed was 'sad and really very inappropriate.'
>
> The events surrounding the protest had been hard on her personally, but she had no plans to resign, she said.
>
> 'I do not think that I have violated the policies of the institution. I have worked personally very hard to make this campus a safe campus for all," she said.
>
> Charles J. Kelly, a former police lieutenant in Baltimore who wrote the department's use of force guidelines, said pepper spray was a 'compliance tool' that could be used on subjects who did not resist, and was preferable to simply lifting protesters.
>
> 'When you start picking up human bodies, you risk hurting them,' Kelly said. 'Bodies don't have handles on them.'
>
> After reviewing the video, Kelly said he observed at least two cases of 'active resistance' from protesters.
>
> 'What I'm looking at is fairly standard police procedure,' Kelly said.
>
> (Al Jazeera 2011d)

What sort of space is this, and what does it presuppose about the conditions that have to be in place in order to make it possible? Recall Adam Smith's (1762) comments on the role of police in government. It is an integration of policy, with the management of the streets and the regulation of markets in the interests of business. Rather than Lefort's (1988) empty place of power following the fall of the Leader and the replacement of authoritarian rule by democracy, the police on behalf of government continually re-impose awe of a Power beyond the powers of people.

The re-occupation of space

If social space is constructed of multiplicities of connected relations, that is, where one individual is connected to one or more others, the more connections there are the more dimensions there are within the space that is occupied. Each individual, each group and each organisation is directed towards another within the dramatic occupation of a university space described above in ways that imply the existence of prior arrangements: not just a faculty association, nor just a university but a system of laws, regulations, principles, procedures and cultural practices that have emerged historically not just locally, but nationally and globally. Issues of 'open and free enquiry' are intertextually connected to Enlightenment texts, to issues of freedom of information, and to the foundational principles of democratic freedom and equality of voice. From such intertextual intermeshing of concepts analytical categories can be produced from the key binary of suppression versus free expression that nuance the boundaries between freedom and slavery, liberty and imprisonment, openness and secrecy. Leadership and policing are set into an oppositional relation that also realises their co-dependence. What, ultimately, is leadership without the underlying force to ensure followership? It implies the necessity of a central focus for a group, a community, a people through which they are structured. Leadership 'fails' when it has to have recourse to 'external' policing. A boundary between these concepts is implied, yet what makes it possible to draw upon this external use of force?

There is a wider notion of legitimacy at play where issues of 'authorisation' or the 'violation of policies', or the 'use of force guidelines' and of 'standard police procedure' signal mechanisms that can be deployed to deal with particular situations. Faced with protests, authorities have at their disposal these mechanisms aimed at preventing the emergence of alternative structurings of space from occupying the grounds of a university. Hence the critical concept of 'occupy'. It is the occupation of private grounds as a space for public protest that has led to the local crisis. It reveals the lines of connection between organisations that can be called upon by individuals who occupy positions of power that have been legitimated by the wider system. There is a design, however complex, dynamic and rough it may be, to social order that becomes most explicit and delineated in its contours and connectivities in such moments of internal and external crisis. The police officer talks of pepper spray as a 'compliance tool' that can be applied with 'subjects who did not resist', yet he talks also of 'active resistance'. Such categories pre-exist the specific incident, just as the roles and systems of roles of specific organisations and institutions that deal with issues of 'resistance' pre-exist as police forces, justice systems pre-exist the moments of their deployment. Alongside these are the necessary technologies, training organisations and industries that make the 'compliance tools'. And finally, there is the political organisation that legitimates other forms of organisation to make use of 'compliance tools' and there is the media through which this legitimacy is disseminated as 'news'. The categories and forms of organisation through which a real is made visible, audible, and manageable thus pre-exists and is available for its organisation into a dispositif that can be called upon quickly to deal with a specific incident, issue, problem. In interpretation of the meaning of the specific use of pepper spray an analytics of police order can be drawn upon just as it can be countered by an analytics of freedom. Each can draw upon pre-existing texts whether as guidelines, political constitutions, or the principles of academic inquiry and the wider literatures of religious, political and human rights. Within this intertextual complex there is the opportunity for multiple interpretations.

However their openness of interpretation and realisation in practice can be hindered, resisted and prevented by the access different actors have to assemble dispositifs to generate assent and support or overcome disapproval and impose particular interpretations.

What, finally, are the chances of re-occupying and transforming spaces for new forms of social organisation and cultural practice? In one view:

> A 50-state study in 2009, 'Who Pays?' found that California's 1 per cent paid taxes at a rate a quarter lower than its poorest 20 per cent did. On the other hand, students are ruled over by overpaid operatives of the 1%, whose orientations are utterly divorced from the spirit of public service. Exhibit A on the latter point is UC Davis Chancellor Linda Katehi, on whose orders the riot police were deployed. Katehi is both a member of the 1% and an overt supporter of police repression on campus. Although she has tried to disavow any responsibility for the pepper spraying of students, it has quickly emerged that she was a co-author of a report used to justify the recent repeal of a 1974 law, banning the police from Greek universities. That law was passed following the overthrow of a military junta. The repeal came just in time, earlier this year, to help suppress Greek protests against the imposition of harsh austerity measures.
>
> (Rosenberg 2011)

With the occupy movement a new text is being painfully written. It finds its legitimacy in the political paradigm being inscribed through the courage, confrontations, partial victories and tragedies of the Arab Spring during 2011. If the voice of protest proclaims itself as a vanguard of the new then including its demands as a legitimate voice in public debate, decision-making and action becomes a fundamental step in realising the new in social organisation. More generally, the inclusion of all voices is a fundamental principle in the systematic transformation of private into public space. There is then finally a critical role for radical research in writing up projects for sponsors or for publication that creates the conditions for inscribing the new voices into the realities of all forms of social organisation. But the new will remain in question until writing and inscription of all voices are co-extensive with the creation of public space globally. To do that, requires an escape from the policing of the boundaries between private and public space.

Gesturing towards writing

When ethnography describes how space comes to be occupied by people, then writing the novel is a challenge to the limits of occupation. At each limit and each crossing of limits, there is a struggle of validities from a multiplicity of viewpoints as each poses a 'truth' that another contests or denies. How are suppressed truths to be expressed? If there is to be an ethnography of change that includes the novel in people's day-to-day lives across the contexts of home, work and play, then what are the symptoms that signify unarticulated demands? It is not just a matter of describing what counts as community in the lives of people but what counts as the community to come. Is there an envisaging of an alternative community? What are the cultural and the 'thinking' resources available to people to address themselves to the work of organising differently?

These are perhaps questions for case study drawn from a reflection on the symptomatic sites that demand alternative texts to those that define the symptoms as 'disease', 'problems', 'break downs' to be 'cured', 'repaired'. Rather than action or evaluations research being designed to 'improve' the running of the machineries supporting social order, they can be re-conceived as exercises in thinking where the 'normal' categories of analytic regimes are reviewed for their ironic structurings and for the dispositifs drawn into play to police dissent and prevent their collapse. Case studies of how disorder is prevented may provide clues to the points where countervailing powers may seek to build the new.

Chapter 11

Organising – escaping order

A research-based writing project seeking to be inclusive requires a central organising strategy to map the text with the experiences of the real across a range of voices. Each voice will express its agendas, give reasons and provide accounts of its understandings, interpretations, knowledge of what is right, obvious or what is suspicious, hidden from sight and what is unknowable. This may be done with anger, studied neutrality or love – whatever the tone, the emotion, the force of expression or its tentativeness, through a voice others are touched in a mutual weaving of textual realities. Creating a sense of this interweaving in the writing project is vital to the lived reality of people's experiences. This is where sole reliance on or privileging analytical approaches that list out the categories and categories-of-categories fail. In this sense, it has to be said, all social realities are a stitch up.

The repeated word from person to person in a crowd, in an audience, in a protest march binds each individual into a voice. This repetition in rhetoric is called 'symploke'. Etymologically, this means 'interweaving'. The aggregation of the powers of individuals into a chanting, into a constant repetition over time, over locations, over contexts is constitutive of a force that resists any whim or fancy for it to be otherwise (Tragesser 1977). For Laclau and Mouffe (1985) it is through such interweaving that political alliances and ultimately hegemonies can be constructed. The complex of interweavings provides the ground upon which a writing project emerges.

The writing project, then, is co-extensive with the research project in so far as searching out the forms of inscription through which the psycho-social realities of people are carved, marked out, wounded. Around the cut, the bruise, the separation, as symptom or as treasure texts are woven, interwoven, laced, knotted, twisted to create a meaning for the lived experience. Between them is a tension. Surfaces vie one with the other. The forms of organisation of the one are not that of the other. But they feed off and feed into each other. The key themes arising from the project are the materials for the critique and radical thinking of the writing project. The themes and openings to the 'new' that result from the writing project pose questions to be addressed by the research project through which data is collected, processed and organised not through the application of routine procedures of categorisation but through what Gori (2011) calls 'the dignity of thinking'. Thinking disturbs the taken for granted, the routine, the unreflective. It is as essential for the 'new beginnings' of contemporary research as it was for Descartes project of questioning the basis upon which accepted the authorised knowledge, belief systems and practices of his time. It is thus the underlying principle of organisation.

Thinking, voices and the strategies of organisation

Thinking is organised around an attitude of questioning in order to identify something that may be found acceptable to provide grounds for 'knowledge', 'value,' 'belief', 'behaviour' and action. Such thinking although arising in the privacy of a consciousness has its grounds in an orientation towards others and otherness. The principle of thinking, then, necessarily implies questioning the organisation of the powers of individuals to create the conditions for a public sphere where thinking may be expressed. Such thinking cannot be expressed unless there are practices that enable the voices of all to participate freely and equally in the processes and practices of all forms of social organisation. Given that participation is always limited by the reach of a voice, and the conditions enabling or preventing its capacity to be heard within a social space then before a writing strategy can be developed these conditions affecting the reach of voice need to be mapped.

An assignment, thesis, report or publication adopting this approach employs the map to identify the prevailing and countervailing surface(s) of inscription as a ground for representing what is at stake for the different actors as a basis for critique, argumentation and action. At first sight for any researcher–writer there is a mass of data from the multiplicities of voices interviewed, or participated with in conversation or overheard in the course of being around in the various scenes of action that seems to escape all strategies of organisation. However, there is a structuring that the participants reveal in their orientations towards, against or away from each other. There are structuring boundaries between those who are valued as partners, potential allies or reviled as enemies. There are systematic 'inattentions' as well as the repetitions of glances towards particular objects of attention. How these are sensuously and conceptually sewn together – or sewn over in order to separate, repress and exclude – by actors as they depict their world(s) returns the writer to the principle of thinking and what Chapter 8 referred to as its tropological processes. These provide what may be called a first strategy for thinking in relation to the records of voices now made available as the 'database' resource for a writing project whether assignment, thesis, journal paper, news article, blog or book. The second strategy concerns how to employ the 'database' in the writing project. Both continuously interact until the project is declared 'finished'. In order to elaborate these strategies a first approximation will be made with Schutz's (1973) three 'postulates' for doing phenomenologically informed research.

- The postulate of logical consistency: The researcher must establish the highest degree of clarity of the conceptual framework and method applied, and these must follow the principles of formal logic.
- The postulate of subjective interpretation: The model must be grounded in the subjective meaning the action had for the 'actor.'
- The postulate of adequacy: There must be consistency between the researcher's constructs and typifications and those found in common-sense experience. The model must be recognizable and understood by the 'actors' within everyday life.

(Schutz 1973: 43–4; source: Fereday and Muir-Cochrane 2006: 3)

Rethinking the first postulate, each voice is interrogated for what counts as 'consistency' within the resources provided by records made in relation to each voice.

[Name]: I think also, um, I find that it's interesting because sometimes when I get community managers coming back and this site is screwing up (or, really not?) working for me. I'll say, what do you mean it's not working for you? I just can't get staff engaged. But are the community using it? Oh yeah, they're using it. And I'm like, well actually, in the broader scheme of things then actually it is working. You know ... it's imperative to get staff engaged but it's more important to make sure the community 'a' want and 'b' still like and 'b','c' getting use out of the site that was created for them. I think I would see it as more of a problem if we had staff engaged but the community are up in arms because they didn't want it in the first place, or it's not being used.

(unpublished transcript excerpt, interview by JFS 27 June 2007)

Firstly, what voice is this? It relates to the recorded voices of the team in the bank that has been undertaking the CSR programme to develop sports facilities in selected areas around the country. It is part of a continuing conversation between the researchers and the team that at the time of recording had extended over two years. Elements of the extract are not understandable without recourse to multiple other conversations. Consistency can be conceived in a multiplicity of ways. First, from the point of view of the Bank's team member, there is an implicit temporal consistency where what had been said – or contracted – at an earlier stage is still in force 'now'. Although there is some questioning of the effectiveness of the project by 'community managers', the process of thinking employed by the team member involves pointing to instances of use of the sports site that can legitimately come under a more generalised criterion – the 'broader scheme of things' – to form the judgement 'it is working?'. The logic of consistency may be explicated as: there is something, say 'x', that the community wanted; they still like 'x'; 'x' is an instance of use. Whether or not 'x' is being achieved, the community generally speaking is using the site for a variety of purposes that may or may not include x. Use has always been a key criterion for the success of the programme. Hence whether or not the specific desired 'x' is identifiable, there are other instances of use that are just as good. However, in this sequence of reasoning that attempts a temporal consistency, there is also a value consistency as implicit in the reference to 'use', that is, a use value that works in two spheres of action: the community and the bank. As explored earlier in Chapter 9, the overriding logic of the programme is its PR value, and use scores as a PR activity. In short, there are discoverable logics of consistency that in the context of Chapter 4 can be more fully elaborated in terms of the prevailing analytics being articulated through the voice that the bank's team member represents.

Identifying the voices in the database enables the writer to provide an account of how the processes of subjective interpretation – Schutz's second postulate – is being addressed. Voice, then, is subjectively articulated through the records. In the extract above, there are implicit other voices: the community managers, the community itself, customers of the bank. Placed in relation to all the other resources in the research database a fuller *dramatis personae* of voices can be educed, each with subjective interpretations of each other and of the actions being undertaken and the events produced. How they draw out the particulars that are important to them and place them under key categories of interpretation creates their own lines of distinction setting one voice apart from another. Each individual reveals then how he or she aligns his or her particular voice with a more general voice composed of those they see as his or her group, side, 'people like me' and so on. In the contestation between voices, a specific meaning of commonly occurring views expressed by particular actors is addressed/asserted. Subjective textualities are thus revealed through competing forms of organisation structured through the struggle(s) of each voice to make their meanings count. In order to get at these struggles and how they order social practices a principle of voice renders audible – and visible – what may have been ignored and put out of reach by the prevailing forms of subjective organisation.

Schutz's third postulate positions the researcher's voice in relation to the voices educed during the course of the research. It is conceived by Schutz as a second-order level of analysis undertaken at a theoretical level being mapped over the first order level of everyday life – in the context of Chapter 8 discussions, it has a metaphorical flavour. However, if voices are to be democratically organised, then the researcher's voice has no privilege, hence opening up the possibility of movement, of slippage. Yet who researches and who writes presents always a perspective, a framing, an agenda. The items to be done listed on an agenda implies, always, a politics, an action in that wider sense of Arendt's (1998) discussed in Chapter 4. In terms of writing for social justice, for democratic inclusion, the action in question is drawn from the ways in which each voice encountered in the course of the research in making accounts of and interpreting its action(s), provide the grounds for thinking about how to create forms of social organisation that recognise and value difference. If the frame is one where all voices are to be included in the sphere of debate, then the writing agenda, the list of things to do, involves representing the range of voices, the ways in which those voices are articulated in practice with the resources within their reach and the outcomes, the consequences, the events that occur as a result. In the research undertaken to explore the impacts of the bank's CSR programme

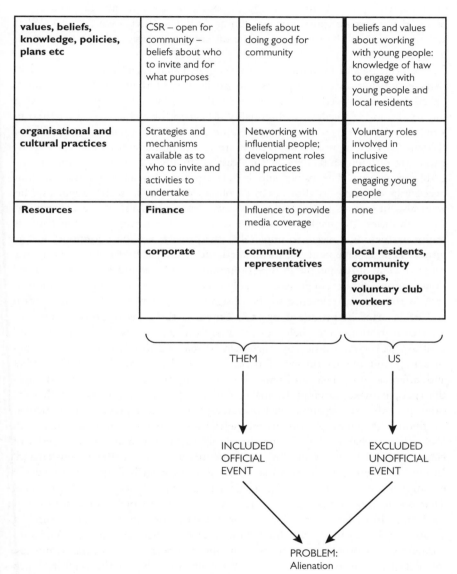

values, beliefs, knowledge, policies, plans etc	CSR – open for community – beliefs about who to invite and for what purposes	Beliefs about doing good for community	beliefs and values about working with young people: knowledge of haw to engage with young people and local residents
organisational and cultural practices	Strategies and mechanisms available as to who to invite and activities to undertake	Networking with influential people; development roles and practices	Voluntary roles involved in inclusive practices, engaging young people
Resources	Finance	Influence to provide media coverage	none
	corporate	community representatives	local residents, community groups, voluntary club workers

THEM   US

INCLUDED OFFICIAL EVENT   EXCLUDED UNOFFICIAL EVENT

PROBLEM: Alienation

Figure 3 CSR problem structure

on the lives of communities, the following schema described by figure 3 was constructed as a way of 'explaining' and 'theorising' the relationships between a given *dramatis personae* and the outcomes of their interactions.

This figure provides a way of exploring the range of strategies individuals may employ to pass from ideas – or more broadly their symbolic frames of thinking – to action. Acts of inscription then may be directed by the actors involved or impacted upon whether directly or indirectly towards all the dimensions required for making something happen according to their own agendas. What actually occurs will be the result of the differential powers that can be brought to bear.

The principles of thinking and of voice mean that each individual or collectivity expressing a view suspends the privileging of their knowledge, values, beliefs and ways of conceiving the 'real' above others thus aspiring to create the conditions of freedom with equality necessary for a voice to be counted in a debate, the processes of decision-making and the consequent undertaking of action. What the figure seeks to illustrate is the inequality of freedoms experienced by different members of the 'cast(s)' in the scene(s) of action of the CSR programme. The values and beliefs espoused by the bank staff are not necessarily the same as those of the voluntary or public sector agencies who were also in various ways involved as, say, 'representatives' of the community. As 'authorities' the bank and the agencies combine forces (with the bank as senior partner, as it were) to implement the project in a local community. The terms of the engagement are formulated and managed by the bank. From the point of view of the people in the community, the bank and the other involved organisations can be categorised broadly together as 'them' doing something to 'us'. With constant reference to the observations of actors, the documentation and other artefacts produced by their activities, the transcriptions or notes of their conversations, and their views drawn from interviews the similarities and contrasts as between different voices can be mapped in relation to their scenes of action and the legitimacy of their voices to be heard in ways that effect and affect action. That mapping, in following the contours of inscriptions that people make, attempt to make, fail to make as they engage with each other provides the organisational resource of the writing project. In particular, by finding the lines of connection, separation and repression, key headings focusing on what is at stake for the actors researched and for the points of view expressed by the range of voices identified can be textually constructed. In figure 3 there are two axes that correspond to what is frequently called the paradigmatic (vertical) and diachronic (horizontal) dimensions of language. That is, the choices that can be made from particular words (for example, hut as distinct from house as distinct from mansion; or run as distinct from jog as distinct from gallop) and how these selected words may be arranged into sequences of words or utterances as in the composing of phrases, sentences, instructions, conversations, speeches. What emerges then is the ways in which the selections made by particular individuals, groups, organisations reveal the lines of agreements, antagonisms and alliances that may be made between them in order to bring about action.

Take the following journalistic write-up of how ideas held by people become rationales to act or to prevent action:

> San Pedro, California – On January 12, a great blow was struck against freedom, if you subscribe to the philosophy of Ron Paul. The Ohio Civil Rights Commission voted 4–0 to uphold its earlier finding that a Cincinnati landlord, Jamie Hein, had discriminated against a ten-year-old biracial girl by posting a 'White Only' sign in June 2011, aimed at keeping her out of a swimming pool. According to Paul's worldview, this was a grave and terrible blow to the white landlord's liberty.
>
> The girl's white father, however, sees things a bit differently.
>
> 'My initial reaction to seeing the sign was of shock, disgust and outrage,' the girl's father, Michael Gunn, said in brief comments the day the final decision was announced. The family quickly moved away, in order to protect their daughter from exposure to such humiliating bigotry – but they also filed the lawsuit.
>
> According to Ron Paul's view of 'liberty', they were right to move, but wrong to sue. Both Ron Paul and his son, Rand, oppose the 1964 Civil Rights Act, because it outlaws private acts of discrimination. This is an 'infringement of liberty', they argue. And they're right: just like laws against murder, it infringes the liberty of bullies. And that's precisely what justice is: the triumph of right over might.
>
> The same logic also applies to the Civil War. It resulted in the abolition of slavery – infringing the liberty of hundreds of thousands of slaveholders. And Ron Paul thinks that was wrong, too.
>
> (Rosenberg 2012)

The key word is freedom. Two distinct contents are placed under it. The contestation that takes place sets up the structural dramatis personae that plays out in the courts, the media and everyday life. In the places of confrontation, there is a struggle to dominate and thus impose a meaning. A second key word is 'private', a term that marks the boundaries of occupation and defends a space from an outside. In the private space, there is no need to include another. The private individual has sovereign dominion to make acts of discrimination and organise the private space according to an analytics that inscribes that space with its key defining discriminations between one thing and another, one person and another, one act and another. It is a domain of pure private freedom, what Max Stirner (1971) might call the place of the 'ego and its own'. Since Ron Paul, at the time, was a republican fighting to be selected by his party to go head to head with Obama in the presidential elections, much was at stake not simply for the biracial girl but for what was to count as the limits of the private and the public. Identifying key boundaries between the discourses of adversaries in a public provides a mapping of the range of voices through which the powers of individuals are organised and managed.

In Rosenberg's article, rather than a stable analytics that can be applied algorithmically, as in computing, without the necessity of a thinking agent, there is here a question of thinking and a call to thinking framed around the organising analytic category: freedom. The writing makes clear what is at stake. Returning to the CSR programme of the bank and figure 3 it is placed within a capitalist and corporate logic whose analytics are inscribed deeply into the lives of people. These inscription strategies frame the choices that shape how the ideas, values, beliefs and decisions of individuals, groups and organisations are to pass into action. As a response to a given set of circumstances, the occurrence of an event, different individuals, groups and organisations have differential access to and ability to organise resources. It is this differential access and ability to organise that determines the success or otherwise of a course of action. Elite access has increased as the access of the vast majorities of people(s) has decreased. That is to say, elite dispositifs in Agamben's sense (see Chapter 1) prevail over the more fragmented and weakly connected dispositifs available, if at all, to the wider population(s). There is no natural order as such. Only the order that has been inscribed. For example, according to Hilgers (2012) the neo-liberal founders considered that market order did not arise naturally thus there needed to be 'a political programme able to facilitate the emergence of spontaneous market order' and institutions to ensure competition – a 'regulated de-regulation' (p. 81). That is to say, for competition to exist, there needed to be a level playing field:

> Competition requires that the state be properly positioned to correct the natural phenomena that hamper competition (e.g. the creation of monopolies, or price instability). The legitimacy of the state depends on economic growth; economic growth is determined by the ability of the state to shape a framework within which individuals are free to pursue their individual interests; this freedom in a world of competition should lead to the recreation and rebuilding of the state itself. Competition and maximisation become the organising principles of the state. The reengineering of the state appears clearly in neoliberal theory as a step necessary for triggering the modification of subjectivities and social relations, for making them correspond to the metaphysics of the spontaneous market order.
>
> (Hilgers 2012: 81–2)

Elites, of course, do not have an interest in any notion of competition that undermines their own privilege. As one of the masters of the market, the Bank's CSR programme can be re-read as a strategy – covert or otherwise – of employing sports as a way of managing their image by strengthening and shaping subjectivities and social relations amongst their actual and potential clientele. Through sports the value of competition, of talent and of reward for talent may be reinforced in a sphere of action – the level playing field of sports – that is displaced from the realities of corporate dominated markets. At a cultural level the impacts of neo-liberal financial practices that generated the profits from which a small percentage is allocated to community projects directed towards the very problems that market inequalities create. Hilgers (2011) reviewed three anthropological strategies for explaining the rise and global predominance of neo-liberalism. From these he distilled an approach that can be used as an organising research and writing framework that echoes the core themes already addressed in the chapters of this book:

> This repertoire comprises three broad principles with many internal variants: (1) The material and structural transformations produced by the mutations of contemporary capitalism give rise to representations and practices that generate new cultural forms directly linked to neo-liberalism. Beyond their idiosyncratic variations, these globalised mutations produce common traits that are transmitted by the classic means of socialisation: family, schooling, peer groups, and the professional sphere. (2) The impact of these cultural forms must be considered in the light of regulatory modes proper to neoliberal societies, which are being deciphered. For example, massive incarceration is one component necessary to the equilibrium of the neoliberal state. At the level of both deliberate choices and involuntary processes, the production of a specifically neoliberal state leads to the inflation of the prison population as part of the management of inequalities. (3) In a context characterised by uncertainty, insecure employment, and hyper responsibilisation, neoliberalism itself is flexible. Coming together in the technologies of subjectivity and subjection, the logics of flexibility, profitability, and maximisation raise competition to the rank of prime motor of the rationality of power and the rationality of subjects.
>
> (Hilgers 2011: 361)

Reading this alongside figure 3 the three principles are articulated in terms of the ways in which ideas (or thinking processes) pass into action through practices applied to resources in order to generate desired outcomes. Thus, the writing strategy is composed of three broad rhetorical strategies articulated through tropological processes (see Chapter 8) whereby particulars (free individuals) are transformed into parts under wholes (firms, consumers, markets, family, schools, peer groups, professions) or as 'non-parts' (prison populations, immigrants, enemies) excluded from the greater wholes (nation, society, world order, humanity). This has the appearance of providing an analytical closure that also generates a project of inquiry, explanation and theorisation. By analytical closure is not necessarily meant that all that can be said is both finite and already explicit but that the claims to be the ultimate view is a view that is capable of expanding infinitely and thus open to surprise and wonder at what is to be discovered. That is the claim of market capitalism allied to a neo-liberal interpretation of democracy (Fukuyama 1992). However, any organisation of writing must also think beyond the ends of writing, that is, as well as its goals and its purposes what must be thought is its limits and the beyond that enables writing to be inscribed. It is at this edge that a work of difference may be made (Schostak 2002: 102–9; Schostak and Schostak 2008: 73). It is also at this edge that a work of prohibition, of repression, of erasure may be drawn so that the visible, the real becomes an apparent ever shifting horizon without limits. This horizon is drawn by the letters of the law, of science, of morality, the little letters of science as Lacan called them that through their insistence on literality both cut and imprison us. They are the letters through which the fully human or artificial and abstract virtualised environments of modernity and postmodernity are designed and tools for organising behaviour and measuring performance are created as a condition for mastery. Weber (2001) called the world composed through such technical and bureaucratic rationality an 'iron cage', but it is also a face seen as if in a mirror (figure 2). Looking at our world humanly constructed we see ourselves looking back, peering through the grids created by the little letters of science, the information technologies of neo-liberal financial regimes, the legal frameworks of insistence to the letters of the law. There is an aesthetics of the mirror relationship between see-er and seen, seer and scene where artists, confidence tricksters and sorcerers alike never face a blank canvas because they work with a world already organized and structured through networks of visual clichés. It is a '"facialized" mirror object staring back, permeated by power relations that operate in conjunction with the mixed semiotic of the despotic-passional regime of signs'. And this 'same abstract machine of faciality converts the face into a structuring grid that interacts with signs without resembling them' (Bogue 2003: 158). The word 'facialization' evokes the process through which an anayltics is made familiar, transformed into a face, a something to be 'faced' that is both familiar and other. It operates an analytics over and against a lost realm of the 'undifferentiated' that may intrude into awareness like the lost object of Freudian psychoanalytics. The undifferentiated, the lost alternatives for seeing and interpreting that may have arisen through a free imagination formed by a critical and free reflection on experience become overwritten through the dominant abstract machineries that replace thinking. Recalling the discussion of Chapter 1, where Mauss (1979) wrote of body techniques and Billig (1995) of the flagging of bodies, Bogue writes of a machinic facialisation where:

> That same abstract machine similarly grids the body and landscape, not by making them resemble the face, but by establishing a corresponding complex network of corporeal gestures, postures, and attitudes and surrounding 'looks', atmospheres, spatial densities, orientations and vectoral regularities. And that complex network functions in conjunction with the face and linguistic signs as a disciplinary social machine.
>
> Bogue 2003: 158–9

In other words, the work of Dominion to stabilise, legitimise, secure its agenda, its framework, set the pervading analytics, reinforce its self-serving dispositifs, renew its rhetorics of evidence and explanation presents a formidable unity of a facialized world reflecting the familiarity of the seer in the seen as a force that counters the possibility and the credibility of thinking otherwise. In short: the world of writing is "facialized" by Power relations that depict the public as phantom and thereby of no account, by political strategies that operate a double speak, on the one hand following a path of single-mindedly reinforcing and consolidating neo-liberal values and practices, but, on the other hand, purporting to adhere to and honour democratic ideals and practices. In short, the struggle is between Power and powers, between the dictat of the Leviathan as Dominion over all and the multiple voices of democracy, and between the self-serving ego of a free market and the socially responsive egos directed towards each other through cooperation.

A writing project, then, faces the 'facialized' world of academic criteria, funding bodies, ethical committees, legal systems, publishing agendas and all the organisations that in various ways manage the agency of the 'public', the individuals sense of agency of the 'masses'. These compose the 'audience' for the writing project. Each has their own particular agenda and framework that may map closely on to the researchers' own agendas and frameworks but may possess areas of contention to various degrees. The place and the individuals being researched will add further dimensions of facialization. There are histories to consider: the story of the place (institution, office, centre, set of practices, operating systems, etc.) and the story of the individuals themselves in relation to the place. Questions of how each individual casts himself in relation to his role in the place and in relation to others are important considerations. The degree to which these histories are ingrained, fixed and perceived as essential to being and identity add further tensions to the writing project. These are some of the outer forces at play. Then there are questions of what is seen to be visible and of what is named and of how the world is cut up into manageable pieces. Here such inner forces at play would include the choice of analytics of the discourses deployed by the writer/ speaker and the dispositifs brought to bear upon the argument, the exposition, the inscription, and therefore the writing. How can this abstract machine of faciality, this disciplinary social machine be challenged? And how can a 'writing-otherwise' be organised?

Writing to dis-organise

The emergence of a critical public faces a serious struggle challenging such facialisation. It is a question, as Gori (2011) puts it, of the dignity of thinking. Thinking is human as opposed to machinic. Reduced to being functions of a system, people lose their dignity. Thinking always opens the possibility of another, of the otherness of experience as a ground for conversations, that is, in an old sense of the term, the action and manner of living with others.[1] Living together, as discussed already, can be organised either to support the free and equal agency of people or the management of agency for the interests of elites. Living together creates a space of choices and of action in that political sense of action employed by Arendt (1998). As a space for the work of powers to create mutually beneficial organisations it is also the place of the erosion of mutuality through the aggregation of powers into Power. It is a critical space occupied either by Power or by a radically dynamic space of living together where each voice within the incessant conversation(s) of voices is organised always towards other voices, and where thinking inscribes a space of aloneness, alone only in relation to the voices of others. Thinking opens out through questions that disaggregate Power; that dismantles, subverts, shakes the frames, disturbs the analytics, and slips out of the grip of the dispositifs. The critical operates through the differences voiced in the perpetual conversations of the public. The work of the critical is effective in the 'empty place of power' (Lefort 1988) when no one voice dominates. The writing project thus has two key foci: the analysis of Power and its dismantling to enable the effectiveness of the critical. In short, it is a writing to dis-organise Power.

If Power operates through controlling the range of voices taken into account in a public space, the analytics employed in framing what can or cannot be represented, and the deployment of dispositifs to shape, seduce, engineer, or coerce compliance then the work of the critical is to open up possibilities for alternative explanations, theorisations and action to create alternative forms of social organisation inclusive of the range of voices through which their agency in collective debate and decision-making is realised. But inclusive social organisation necessitates a continual, unfinishable dis-organisation to re-create an analytics of the real of people's powers to act, to create. It is like the artist whose

> goal of painting is to contour the clichés of facialization, to deterritorialize the face-landscape, and in so doing to render visible the invisible forces that play through bodies and the world.
>
> Bogue 2003: 159

The writer's goal is to enable other lines of articulation to materialise, ones that will open up the textual space to 'the metamorphic forces of becoming and sensation' (Bogue 2003: 160) by engaging in a writing that generates the 'metamorphic forces of what Lyotard calls the figural and Maldiney the systolic and diastolic rhythms of a spatializing space' (Bogue 2003: 159). This rhythmic textual spacing draws together or sunders, in an education of alternative possibilities, the public spaces that ground new forms of social organisation. It is both a filling and an emptying of space as voices make their claims, their demands,

---

1   see: http://www.etymonline.com/index.php?term=conversation

their seductions, their pleadings and formulate their visions through which 'the facialized universe [that] is one of stable forms and fixed shapes, rational coordinates and coherent narratives' can be unsettled, disturbed and dis-organised (Bogue 2003: 159). Making a difference and creating a critical public involves escaping from the practices through which prevailing forms of order are reproduced and reinforced, whether it is through the symptomatic reading of Balibar and Althusser, Riffaterrre's hypogram, Merleau-Ponty's inborn complex, Lacan's complex or Derrida's deconstruction. What is important is not that any particular approach is right, but that they are useful as ways of disturbing the fixity of the machinic algorithms of Dominion and allow glimpses of possible other ways of seeing.

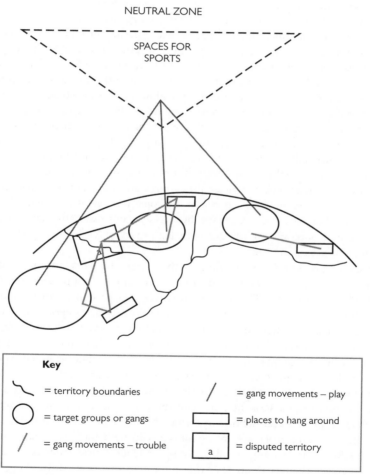

Figure 4 Mapping territories

The 'us' and 'them' of figure 3 above can be read as expressing opposed ways of seeing and applying opposed analytics through which the visible is named, constructed and communicated. Its face-landscape can be visualised in figure 4 above that maps a 'community' according to zones that are defined by gangs in relation to a bank defined sports facility as 'neutral zone'. The gangs are an alternative form of social organisation that is targeted by the bank and other community groups. The idea is to dis-organise the gangs through creating alternative narratives focused around sports. Where gangs would fight on disputed territories, they can be placed into 'mixed' sides in sports and thus create new relationships and identities that in turn create new ways of thinking about their lives, the areas in which they live and the identities that they can adopt. The textual project then can be organised into its parts that can be written down as a report on the success or otherwise of the programme. These 'parts' are visualised in figure 3 above in terms of an organisation of ideas, practices, procedures, mechanisms and resources that together produce either desirable or undesirable outcomes depending upon whether the evaluator adopts the position of 'us' or of 'them' or claims a position outside of the us–them axis to provide a research perspective that in representing both can show their processes of construction and thus opening the possibility of de-construction and transformation (see also figure 2). Similarly, figure 4 above offers a visualisation of 'parts' that are territorialised. Each figure can be read in relation to each other. There are the areas of the gangs that are organised and 'patrolled' according to ideas of ownership, domination, and what can or cannot be done. Each area may be a 'green zone' for one group but a 'red zone' for another (see Chapter 8). They have their own practices, procedures and mechanisms through which membership of a gang is managed and the roles and activities of gang members organised. They have their resources by which to enforce compliance and bring about desired outcomes. However their legitimacy extends only to the boundaries that they can enforce.

Recalling Chapter 8, the thinking of the gangs, the bank, the sports coaches and the community workers and other community groups and residents is managed tropologically. The specific instances and particulars of their lives are drawn under unifying metaphors, symbols and universal categories that explain, theorise and justify their actions. In the sense employed in this book, this is itself a textual project. Through the textual project associated with a particular group, the actions of one group become 'proof' for another group either of their good or their malign intentions, as each instance is gathered under a category of instances that are 'typical' of 'their' attitudes and behaviours towards 'us'. From the point of view of the bank and the community workers, the success of their textual project can defined in terms of information that purports to show that gang thinking processes are being replaced with those associated with the sports facility. It is a strategy to disorganise the tropological processes of the gang only to replace them with another that reinforces the forms of thinking that are beneficial to the bank, the community groups and the residents.

In each case, the textual project aims to construct and re-construct the place of power. The logic is that in a given territory the place of power has been filled first by the gang, it is then to be evacuated and re-filled by another agency that can generate a suitable degree of awe, whether the bank, or its substitutes as in the police, the youth workers, the community authorities. Critical to the process is the 'place of power', how this is filled, evacuated and what forms of organisation can be constructed, and what institutions and resources can be called upon to occupy the space where Power can be exercised. The dis-organisation of Power itself involves a quite different textual project, an un-writing (see Chapter 1) that begins and ends with the freedom and equality of the powers of individuals. As a countervailing force to Power, it requires the extreme writing necessary to democracy that is the theme to be elaborated in the next chapter.

Gesturing towards writing

An ethnography of how people weave the incompatible, the different, the 'heterogenous' into meaningful wholes provides an insight into the overdetermination of 'objects', of 'practices' of 'identities', of 'organisations' and all the composing elements of 'community', 'society' and 'People'. Writing is both a weaving and an unweaving. It explores the ways in which social realities, their sense of 'factness' are structured through strategies of constructing 'particulars' that are in turn drawn under 'classes' for use in forms of reasoning to support 'explanations' and 'interpretations' that underlie the development of motivations and reasons for action.

In cases studies of spaces constructed to serve the interests of groups, communities, organisations and social arrangements of all kinds, writing and its processes of unweaving can play with and explore the legitimacies of boundaries, their rigidity, their openness or resistance to redefinition and redrawing.

Chapter 12

End Games – extreme writing, writing the extreme

In the end it is a game of limits, an art of composing and a creative involvement in realising futures. Within the limits is what is acceptable. However, pushing the limits tests acceptability and creates opportunities. It is the space at the edge where there are opportunities for new legitimacies and for new lines to be drawn. It is a matter of creative mapping where, as in figure 4 (Chapter 11), map and territory are co-created, named and rendered as red or green zones (Chapter 8) according to an axis of friend and enemy. A map creates a picture in the mind (Lippmann 1922). But it is always a crude picture:

> A 'coastline', for example, is not a line, but an indeterminate dynamic zone in which natural processes have been overlaid with a succession of anthropogenic boundary practices territorial waters defined by the flight of a cannonball, the 12-mile limit, the Law of the Sea, and so forth (Carter 1999; Steinberg 2001). Although apparently linear, rivers are similarly indeterminate. It matters, for example, if a boundary follows a bank (if so how defined?), the centre of the watercourse, or the centre of any navigable channel within it (Wood 1992). There is, as this suggests, nothing remotely 'natural' about a boundary line despite its implied materiality (cf. Febvre in Burke 1973, 215).
>
> (Cameron 2011: 420)

Cameron goes on to explore the vacilation or sneakiness of lines and boundaries that over time can be politically reimagined. It is this space of reimagining in relation to 'indeterminate dynamic zones' of experience of the real where boundaries can be made to shift according to desire, demand, need, imagination that point to the powers of individuals to make their worlds rather than be in thrall to their worlds. The critical power of every voice is to reimagine the mapping of boundaries through which their lives are lived, organised, empowered, managed and constrained. However, for some reimagining the mapping of boundaries may threaten their interests and securities. Generally, the stability of analytic boundaries and of the framing of everyday life in terms of such totalising binaries as friend–enemy, good–bad, right–wrong, fair–unfair is what enables people to identify opportunities, ascertain agendas, engage with the available forms of social organisation, understand the rules of play, anticipate events, predict outcomes and work to obtain necessary resources in order to pursue their personal plans. Any change that disturbs this may on the one hand feel exciting as new possibilities open up but on the other can bring a sense of chaos and demands for order. It is here, in the space of the uncertain, that the powers of individuals can be asserted and the world differently inscribed with new forms. It is here that the forms of extreme writing are composable. On the one hand, it takes the form of managing agency by radically excluding voices; on the other it is by the radical inclusion of voices.

Strategies for the management of agency

If there is only one voice, a voice that assumes total command of all that can be surveyed, then there is never an alternative to that voice, only alternatives within its dominion. Everything else is nonsense, mad, illusion.

> If there is one science of nature (and Kant seems to have no doubt of it), if all phenomena and all objects are spread on one and the same plane, so as to produce an experience unique, continuous, and entirely on the surface (and such is the constant hypothesis of the Critique of Pure Reason), then there is only one kind of causality in the world, all phenomenal causality implies rigorous determination, and liberty must be sought for outside experience. But if there is not one science but several sciences of nature, if there is not one scientific determination but several scientific determinations of unequal rigor, then we must distinguish between different planes of experience; experience is not simply on the surface, it extends into the depths ; finally it is possible by insensible transitions, without any sharp break, without quitting the field of facts, to go from physical necessity to moral freedom.
>
> (Bergson cited by Lindsay 1911: 97–8)

Bergson thus offers a glimpse of an alternative to the dominion of empirical science over all matters. He writes of 'planes of experience', hence re-mapping the two dimensionality of the empirical as an n-dimensionality by making imaginatively visible other discoverable planes that connote a depth below a surface and imply the existence of multiple kinds of 'causalities'. In the terminology of Chapter 8 this implies alternative tropologies through which thinking about the world takes place. For example, recalling Obama's speech to AIPAC (Chapter 6), the rhetorical trope of the child was employed as a powerful symbolic process of inclusion and exclusion, seeing and not seeing, where attention was managed towards the interests of one group and by implication away from another. As the speech was directed towards AIPAC as a pro-Israel lobby and significant funder of American political parties, the tropological structure of the speech was created to inscribe itself into its organisational and resource structures. Massad's (2011) criticisms of the speech as discussed in Chapter 6 required a counter reading that drew upon the 'gaps', the 'lapses', the omissions where the children of the Palestinians were excluded from the concerns of the speech. In short, he had to read beyond its framing, passing the limits set by the key definitions of Obama's and AIPAC's concerns, to make visible the repressed texts of others. Such a reading becomes extreme in the sense of moving beyond the policed boundaries of the text.

In a writing project that has as its object a writing at and beyond the boundaries, de-composing the bounds is a necessary first step. From the data, these bounds can be drawn out, drawn together and drawn asunder to establish a tropology of the extremes. There are two critical boundaries that have been explored throughout the chapters, between the private and the public on the one hand and on the other, between Power and powers. Around the boundaries, protagonists line up their differences, their friends, their enemies, their agendas, their analytics and call upon the dispositifs through which their powers to manage the agency of people and exchanges between people are enhanced. From the point of view of Power, all writing that is not of Power is seen as either 'meaningless' or 'extreme' or both. However, Power is vulnerable to the organisation of the powers of the multitude, the masses, when they begin to transform from a 'phantom public' to an 'effective public'. In Lippmann's (1927) terms a phantom public is the name given to the mass that is capable of being herded, shaped, led by elites who are the real decision makers. In Laclau's (2005) terms, a public is an empty signifier that particular interest groups can fill with contents that preserve their interests. Filled with the meaning content of a 'phantom', the public is thus something that can be appealed to without ever giving it the dignity of decision-making. As a phantom, its opinions are to be planted by elites and then 'discovered' through opinion polls to provide proof that the public is on their side. However, like the coastline described by Cameron (2011: 420) above, the public – as the mass of humanity – is 'an indeterminate dynamic zone' overlain with inscriptions. As such, there is always the possibility for counter readings and writings as interpretations play across the multitudes of alternative viewpoints. There is then an erosion of the dominant interpretation, it is at this point that politicians are concerned to 'get their message across'. From their point of view, it is not that their message is wrong but that it is not getting across to the 'public'. Rather than listening to the 'public', the message is played louder and repeated faster and more frequently. What is being managed is how the 'public' is to be defined as a signifier of democratic 'agency' through which elected representatives of the public can act in their name.

This was the position of Andrew Lansley (Health Secretary in the UK coalition government elected May 2010) when his proposed changes to the National Health Service (NHS) met their limit of 'public' acceptability. On 2 June 2011, Hélène Mulholland reported his 'first remarks since the end of the government's listening exercise on the plans which was ordered by David Cameron' in The Guardian:

> Lansley – who has been under increasing pressure over the reform plans outlined in the health and social services bill – said he accepted the case for a rethink on certain elements 'if they help us improve care for patients'.
>
> (Mulholland, The Guardian, 2 June 2011)

Lansley at this point tried to keep to the policy text that itself can be read alongside a multiplicity of other texts – both preceding and contemporaneous – that composes a neo-liberal political project in order to counter a socialist or welfare project through which whatever was public is transformed into private ownership. The conflict is at the heart of modernity that seeks a settlement as between the individual and the social. In Hegelian terms: 'the social world is a home if and only if it makes possible for people to actualise themselves as individuals and as social members'(Hardimon 1944: 99).The notion of home and the way that it is inscribed in the lives of people is vital to an understanding of the political and of the construction of the phantom public that represents 'opinion'. In this formulation are three positions: the individual, the social and the home. How is each of these to be written in the end games through which a political future is written into the consciousness, the behaviours and the forms of organisation that can be directed to bring about agreed, dictated or legislated outcomes?

In Lansley's case, he is negotiating legislation that benefits a small group of individuals directly by creating or extending a health market and the possibility of ownership by private individuals – that includes the corporate 'person' as an 'individual' – of new business that had been the province of the public sector, that is, had been collectively owned. The appeal is to a public that is 'at home' with this. This 'public' is as much a member of the *dramatis personae* through which decisions and actions are fashioned as politicians like Lansley, the pressure groups that seek to influence him, the big donors and corporations that fund political parties, the media through which 'opinions' are fashioned and, of course, the 'voters'. Like a corporation, a public is a fictitious entity endowed with personality, legitimacy and agency and is thus able to act. However, a corporation unlike a public is a legal individual able to own property in its own right. Only the state may own property on behalf of a public – hence removing the public from direct ownership.

How the public acts and how the corporation acts is a matter of how powers are organised, legislated, written through the agency of the state. The state – whether dictatorship or democratic and all the degrees between as in figure 5 below – is underwritten by the public and managed by representatives of the public. The less the state owns and directs, the more is in private management and thus outside of the realm of public decision-making. The progressive deregulation of markets has been a key feature of policy since the 1980s – and the neo-liberal ideal is the total absence of a State and the absence of 'society'. The strategy is underwritten in the funding of political parties by corporations and by the wealthy. Figure 5 provides a crude analytic sketch of a 'multitude' being transformed through discourses into either a sense of there being only individuals or only subjects of a community and how each may in turn be transformed into a sense of 'home'. For those who stress individualism above all else, then home is the individual's home, made secure only through the individual's free use of powers to survive whether this is by some combination of talent, hard work, luck or ruthlessness. There is no recognition of 'society', if that means an equality of voice in the allocation of resources, goods and services across all people. Above all else, however, democracy is the recognition of the freedom and equality voice in these and all other social and cultural matters especially where there is difference and disagreement.

Democracy is diluted as soon as some voices count more than others, particularly when they claim to speak for others 'in their best interests', for the 'common good', in order to achieve and maintain 'consensus'. That consensus may be seen as the good to be created by the 'good society'. Rather than recognising disagreement in Rancière's (1999) sense as a positive and as the reality motivating innovations and the creative production of social goods, disagreement is a problem to be removed through consensus building around a notion of the 'fair' (e.g. Rawls 1971). Or perhaps, in Walzer-like (1985) terms, it is about resolving the issues of competition and difference by locating them and sealing them into different spheres of value. In such a view, it is perfectly appropriate in the economic sphere to amass fortunes and thus the billionaire

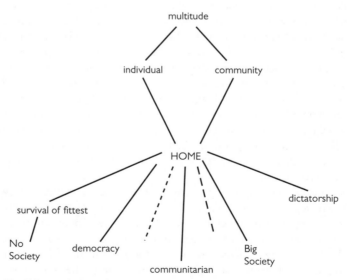

Figure 5 **Transformations of the multitude**

is justifiably of greater value than the pauper, just as in the religious sphere the saint is greater than the inconstant member of the flock. What is not appropriate is that, say, the wealth of the billionaire 'leaks' into the sphere of the political or some other sphere and influences decisions. Each sphere is to be equal and within each sphere there is freedom to compete and create inequalities, that is, where one individual is accorded more value than another due to talent, wisdom, beauty, hard work. This 'complex equality' (Walzer 1985) may be seen as one solution to containing competition while creating a community that goes beyond the individual spheres. Its difficulty is precisely in keeping the spheres from 'leaking' into each other. How can such boundaries be written if each individual evokes their freedom to inscribe them where they please? How can the contests between one individual's decisions as to the boundaries separating 'mine' from 'yours' and from 'ours' be settled?

The contest of boundary making could be resolved through drawing upon the pre-existing values, beliefs, practices of a given society. It is a broadly 'communitarian' position that the social should have precedence over those of the aggregated acts of atomistic individuals each freely shaping their destinies as in the 'free' market of neo-liberal economics. Chapter 1 discussed the extent to which the social is inscribed bodily and Chapter 4 discussed the directedness (intentionality) of the senses as the individual bodily reaches towards or away and takes the other into account or discount. It is precisely the inertia of the pre-inscribed social that is at stake in any major transformation. It is what can be counted upon by those with interests in a given status quo. It frames the resources to be commanded in the end games that are set in motion as protagonists vie to impose their vision, their will, their agenda. From a given viewpoint, a *dramatis personae* can be cast across the population, the multitude, the otherwise aggregate of individuals in order to define how public and private space is to be separated and internally organised. Thus, for example, the *dramatis personae* being cast through the perspective of neo-liberal political and economic interests is formed of subjectivities that privilege the spaces of private property over those of collectively open, public ownership; self interest over collective interest; competition over co-operation; markets over collective planning; and, individual profit over free and equal mutual benefit. The countervailing discourses targeted by neo-liberals are any that privilege the freedom and equality of all people to voice, discuss, decide and take action in relation to all collective activities. More specifically, they target all those discourses privileging the state, the government, society and the community over individual interests.

The end games are composed of such competing mutually destructive discourses through which no individuals can escape being cast as taking sides with their powers as living individuals being subjectively drawn out (educed) and schooled to adopt an analytics of the perceptible world in which they recognise their part in its realisation and enforcement to the exclusion of all others. This clash played out across Europe in the aftermath of the financial crisis as neo-liberal governments struggled to inscribe the necessity of austerity narratives in the minds, behaviours and laws of their citizens. In classical neo-liberal terms, the crisis provided the necessary shock that created opportunities for wealth accumulation as bankruptcy made assets available cheaply, rising unemployment and the resulting fears of job insecurity weakened resistance against de-regulating labour markets, and strengthened governmental power to reduce public spending in order to open the way for tax cuts so as to incentivise business.

End games play the public upon which the Power of the tangle of corporate, military and government mutually supportive relationships depends. If, as Lippmann (1927) argues, the public is a phantom, then it is played as an ideal representation that fills in for the absent reality. It is a chimera constructed through the formation of opinion across 'readerships', 'audiences', 'clients', 'voters'. By playing with opinions the public is shaped, its consent manufactured (Lippmann 1922) or engineered (Bernays 1947). It is the end game of propaganda where the only 'truth' is when people believe whatever is told to them. In terms of the textualised public of Chapter 7, propaganda seals off any possibility of another voice, another story, another history. It was the triumph of capitalism over socialism that the fall of the Berlin Wall symbolised for Fukuyama in 1989 (1992), who proclaimed the 'end of history'. According to this story, there was no longer a competitor for the place of global Power and thus dominion by Western values, economic neo-liberal philosophy and forms of political 'democracy' had been achieved. That argument received a major setback with the destruction of the Trade Center towers on 11 September 2001, adding weight to Huntington's (1993, 1996) counter-argument that history continued as the clash of civilisations. In 2008, when the financial crisis erupted with the crash of Lehman Brothers, it seemed again a fatal blow to the dominion of capitalist neo-liberal discourse and practice. Yet, Power across each country brought in 'austerity measures' that reduced the income, security and quality of life of millions, while the 1 per cent, and in particular the 1 per cent of the 1 per cent, increased their wealth. In Klein's (2007) terms, the crisis offered the necessary 'shock' for wealth to be stripped from the masses. In Europe the drama was nowhere more stark than in Greece, a position summed up by Greek politician Alex Tsipras in Helena Smith's *Guardian* article (2012). She saw Greece as:

> on the front line of a war that is engulfing Europe.
>
> A long bombardment of 'neoliberal shock' – draconian tax rises and remorseless spending cuts – has left the immense collateral damage. 'We have never been in such a bad place,' he says, sleeves rolled up, staring hard into the middle distance, from behind the desk that he shares in his small parliamentary office. 'After two and a half years of catastrophe Greeks are on their knees. The social state has collapsed, one in two youngsters is out of work, there are people leaving en masse, the climate psychologically is one of pessimism, mass suicides.'

The war, in Tsipras's view, is not between 'nations and peoples'. Rather, 'On the one side there are workers and a majority of people and on the other are global capitalists, bankers, profiteers on stock exchanges, the big funds.' Between them 'revolving door' strategies have been employed. This is a practice whereby corporations can offer high paid positions to politicians and where business people, media pundits and think tank 'experts' take up government positions and then move back to the private sector. Thus, for example, the students of the neo-conservative political philosophies of Leo Strauss and the economic theories of Hayek and Friedman worked their ways into positions of governmental and financial power (Norton 2004; Harvey 2005; Klein 2007). From such a position they were able to write their agendas into the social, cultural, work and everyday practices of people. It results in what Eisenhower (1961) first saw as the industrial military complex and what Beder (2010) called business-managed democracies. In short, they are 'democracies where the politics and cultural life of nations are managed in the interests of business'. Democratic practice requires that all people have a free and equal voice in their communal political affairs. Neo-liberal practice requires that governments should be minimal so as not to interfere with market operations. A parallelism is seen between democracy and the free market where the free vote in the one equals the free demand in the other. However, there is a difference. Where the vote is free and equal and effected unconditionally as essential to inscribing a political demand, market demand is qualified as 'effective demand', that is, a demand that is effective only when backed by money (or more generally as an exchange of 'equal' value). A demand not backed by money remains as a wish that cannot be realised, that is, impossible to inscribe in the real. It can be argued, too, that the apparatuses of government reduce the ability of people to exercise their will democratically, just as government taxation and control of public services 'distort' the operation of the market. So, for example, Beder referred to Rockerfeller's (1999) article in *Newsweek*, where he argued:

> that business people favour lessening the role of government but that this means that 'somebody has to take government's place, and business seems to me to be a logical entity to do it.' Rockefeller was founder and chairman of the Trilateral Commission, an elite group of business leaders and others from the US, Japan and Europe seeking to guide international affairs.

The critical issue is how the space left by government is to be filled: by church, military, monarchs, dictators or the 'people'? It is Lefort's (1988) notion of the empty space that emerges at the point when a dictatorial power falls. Democracy, in that sense, is a permanent revolution in that the place of power can never be permanently occupied if Power is not to emerge and have dominion. Although in Western democracies, the 'leader' and the party elected is subject to elections and thus people are able to change governments, Power remains written deeply into the mission statements, policies, mechanisms, and procedures of the key organisations of the economy, politics, legal, military, social and cultural domains of everyday life.

The 'revolving door' strategies of Power ensure a close association between media tycoons and politicians, financial corporations, legislatures, media and the public sector (see, for example, Reid 2010; Wachtel 2011; Gibbs 2012; Martin and Ellicott 2012). The closeness between corporations and governments were well illustrated during the Leveson Inquiry into the activities of Rupert Murdoch's News International empire, focusing upon phone hacking (for example, O'Carroll 2012). The historical depth of that closeness was clear when the Thatcher archives were released, which showed that Murdoch had a secret meeting with her 'weeks before his 1981 purchase of the Times newspapers' (Wallis 2012). Being able to purchase the *Times* was a critical amplification of his powers to reach, cover and manage the expression of public opinions, thus increasing his dominion over the textualised public. The Murdoch affair illustrates the closeness of relationship which together with the 'revolving door' strategy strategically places the levers of power always within reach of the powerful while ensuring they are out of reach of the masses. It is through unequally managing access to the technologies and combinations of technologies that a given individual's or group's or class's or community's reach is socially managed and by which the powers of individuals are combined and moulded into the necessary forms of social organisation to maintain Power. Being out of reach there are no direct mechanisms by which ordinary people may un-write or de-construct the connections to resources and the machineries of government sewn up by the elites composing Power. Yet as long as the place of power is subject to voting procedures involving a mass, there is always a minimal gap that can be opened up. And as long as the concept of democracy is associated with the principle of freedom, then individuals and collectivities will always have the potential of saying 'me too' and 'why not us?' when demanding rights to be written into democratic processes and laws. Therefore, whether for example in schools (Milne 2012) or in health (Hudson 2011), the UK neo-liberal strategy of crowding out the public through privatisation of public services is open to democratic challenge. The discourse has to be taken into account as soon as it is woven into the public discourses creating new variants to be engaged with in the textualised public that is textually woven through triangulations of voices. Thus for example, returning to Lansley's proposals for UK Health reform, he was forced to 'rethink' these in the light of persistent concerns. These were challenged by the health professions, in particular the British Medical Association, which considered a key measure to be 'completely unethical' and thus 'urged the government to remove plans to introduce performance-related bonuses because that could undermine patient trust' (Mulholland, The Guardian, 2 June 2011).

Nevertheless, a gap, however slender, that had been extended can always be retracted by a pretence at accommodation, by the manipulation of voices into subordinate positions re-opening the way for their suppression . Can Lansley's promise of:

We will never privatise our NHS. But if we chose to ignore the pressures on it, the health service will face a financial crisis within a matter of years that will threaten the very values we hold so dear – of a comprehensive health service, available to all, free at the point of use and based on need and not the ability to pay.

(Mulholland, The Guardian, 2 June 2011)

be trusted in the long run?

It is a question that marks out the disputed edge between the private and the public that in health marks the inscription of a dividing line between a conception of social responsibility that all owe to all on the one side and on the other a world of personal responsibility whose sole support is the wealth accumulated by the individual. For an American audience the equivalent occurred when Obama and Clinton tried to bring about health service reforms. Only, of course, the reform was in the opposite direction. Imre Karacs reported the 'summer of discontent' in the US over Obama's health care reforms in August 2009:

Town hall meetings, intended to drum up support for President Obama's controversial health reforms, are turning into violent battlegrounds between conservative voters said to be marshalled by sinister right-wing forces and trade unionists accused by opponents of resorting to thuggery.

The latest clash, on Thursday night in Tampa, Florida, pitted about 1,000 opponents of 'socialised health care' against several hundred Democratic supporters, mostly unionists. Some protesters managed to get inside the hall and began shouting 'tyranny, tyranny'; organisers locked out hundreds more chanting outside.

(Karacs, *Times* online, 8 August 2009)

To make a difference, to change something, to be innovative, all require knowing the limits of what is publicly acceptable and performable. At the boundaries, there is always the potential for conflict, unless written into the textualised public are the principles, the real mechanisms, procedures and cultural practices through which organisations create the conditions for the full range of voices to be heard, respected, and taken into account freely and equally in all decision-making about resources and courses of action. When they are not, then inscription strategies take the form of protest in all its forms from peaceful civil disobedience to violence as well as the responses to the various forms of protest by adherents of competing groups and State-controlled organisations. In these cases a given writing project may contribute to inscribing consent, or inscribing dissent. However, the most radical project is to erode the conditions under which sides become 'fatal' to each other. The writing project is most radical when it adopts the strategy of unpicking the intertextually composed nestings of inscriptions upon surfaces coded into multiplicities of other surfaces. It demands an imagination of seeing beyond the organised limits of surfaces, being at the extreme and going over the edge.

Playing the game of limits

Radical writing projects explore the extremes, test the limits, de-construct the taken for granted and work to transform the perceptual field into something where new possibilities for the powers of individuals to express themselves create new social, cultural, political economic realities. The perceptual 'real' is a play of backgrounds and foregrounds where objects of consciousness appear as 'out there' or 'in here' as individuals go about their daily lives. It is this play that is the object of challenge. The cultural, organisational and personal repertoires of patterns of attention to objects frame what is to be seen at a given time according to given agendas. Whether it is explored as the body techniques of Mauss (1973) or the 'flagging' of bodies (Billig 1995) or the facialisation of Bogue (2003) or the scientific revolutions of Kuhn (1970), the real is inscribed bodily and psychologically. Its signs map out the lines that separate this from that, point to over there as distinct from here and me from we, you, us and them. Rather than being the real, such a map of signs stand for a real. Thinking works upon a given real, composing perceived phenomena into objects of consciousness that can be manipulated in thought and materially as described in the tropological strategies of Chapter 8. The everyday repertoires for doing this are an object of research and a focus for challenge through radical writing.

Rather than a particular perspective calling game over, apparently watertight arguments can be challenged through the effects of a writing that keeps the place of power open to all voices thus creating an effective, not a phantom public. Although cast as phantoms to be constructed into whatever *dramatis personae* serves the prevailing needs of Power, each individual has the counter-vailing power of thought and imagination to cast themselves into alternative narratives. Rather than being corralled into a politics of the middle ground that excludes and custodialises those voices that challenge, people can construct their own public where disagreements rather than consents can be formulated and inscribed. Disagreements and dissents challenge the acceptability, stability and dominion of analytic categories, arguments, decisions and courses of action. Disagreements nibble at the edges of the consensual domains of the political 'middle ground', emptying it of Power.

> Overcoming barriers is about freedom. This is the point that is clearly so difficult to convey. The Pirates are not an internet party but a party interested in freedom. The internet can be seen as a metaphor for what that means today: freedom through equal rights, freedom through the expression of opinion, freedom through open access to education and knowledge. Freedom through the erosion of hierarchy and authority. And freedom through participation and pluralism.
>
> (Zeh 2012)

In the context of a war about who controls resources the representation of voices and perceivable worlds in the arenas of decision-making are critical. Between systems of representation, the war is articulated through the challenges, the clash, and strategies of domination employed by proponents of each system of representation where what is 'real' is to stand in place of the real and in the place of the real. It is most dangerous in the siren songs of the 'nation' through which individuals are subjectivised and friends and enemies produced. However, globalisation has challenged the boundaries in the flow of capital and information as it has reinforced them for the management, manipulation and policing of labour. The critical task, then, is whether writers can re-imagine, redraw and reinscribe to produce a new world for the hopes and practices of people – perhaps, as Gupta thinks it, a nonaligned world (1992).

To achieve deep nonalignment is a process that is as much aesthetic as political (Rancière 2004), educational and philosophical. Prior stabilities are unfrozen as dividing lines between categories are contested and systems of concepts lose their ties. The Cartesian method of doubt could be seen as a first try, Spinozan realignment as between powers and Power another. However conceived, the fluidity that is sensed from the adoption of such methodologies can be experienced either as a threat to the solidity of all that has been known and loved or as freedom to invent. This fluidity, then, is a challenge to the aesthetics and is a challenge to the political order of the real that covers over what Lyotard calls the 'other space' as an echo of Freud's other scene (Lydon 2001: 20–21). Or, indeed, this other space is the inter-view, the space between views (Schostak 2006), the unrepresentable 'space that is the ungrounded 'ground' of deconstruction (Gasché 1986). Aesthetically it is glimpsed in what Lyotard calls Klee's 'interworld' (Lydon 2001: 21), where there is no 'alternative kingdom', but rather a world uncovered through 'critical deformation' (Bogue 2003: 114–15).

In other words, there are two spaces that in Lyotard's terms involve 'a textual space of recognizable, coded entities, and a figural space of metamorphosing unconscious forces (Lyotard, 211)' (in Bogue 2003: 115). Thus, in Lyotard's opinion, for example, Klee's interworld is no alternative world scenario but a critical methodological stance towards the politics, the culture and the social practices of this world. It is 'an energetic space of forces' (Bogue 2003: 116). If this connects with Spinoza's view of the individual as an active being of powers, then to glimpse these powers is the individual's most fundamental political act, the groundless ground of the political. To see it involves what Lyotard calls a *dé-jeu*, an un-gaming, through which the normal patterns of the eye are thwarted (*déjoué*), through which a world is read (Hudek 2011: 54):

> The complexity of Lyotard's phrasing, with its words taken at face value (all their possible meanings layered one on top of the other) and neologisms ('dé-jeu') is indicative not only of the often perilous task that awaits any translator of Lyotard's writing, but also of the ambiguity Lyotard invests in the proper pronoun ('s'attendre' as 'waiting for each other/oneself ') and thus of the care he takes in foiling [déjouer] the grasp of the philosopher,

the historian, and the biographer-critic. This evasion is playful, no doubt, but also deadly serious: un-game, dé-jeu.

(Hudek 2011: 52)

This playfulness is disruptive, making new meanings by displacing and deferring expected meanings. It is the kind of meaning making or creating to be found in poetry, a poiesis (Kristeva, 1984) in its more general terms, that brings about disruptive displacement through pushing language to its limits through, for example, the art of combining normally unrelated words which gives rise to a space of a leaping across that effectively creates the conditions for new meaning threads to emerge and weave together to form alternative inscriptions. Such a poesis when it is turned to glimpsing, making audible and experienceable the invisible, the inaudible and the unfeelable is a tropology of the extreme.

Jill Schostak, for example, in an experiment with poesis, created in her doctorate 'a body of writing that celebrated the slippage of meaning in the English language' (Schostak, 2005: Vol I, i) that can be read as a tropology of the extreme. Strategies were designed to unsettle fixity of meaning such as trying to stop readers momentarily in their tracks, and to write in a style of undecidability, imperceptibility and indirectedness in order to a) invite the reader to actively engage in the reading/inscription process in order to uncover and reveal potential meanings for themselves, and b) that deliberately disturbs 'the balance between the expected and/or taken-for-granted and the unexpected and/or un-looked for' (Schostak, 2005: Vol I, i). However, the irony was (already and always) that the body of writing, of any writing, requires an agenda, a framework, a literature review that all tend to 'fix' meaning and disallow slippage of meaning. In other words, whilst writing in a style invoking imperceptibility and indirectedness that deliberately created undecidability, ironically there was no escaping there being 'purpose to how I write' (Schostak, 2005: Vol I,). Various writing strategies were adopted including designing 'a repertoire of 'tools' that paradoxically would slip into plurality and yet quietly signal, albeit in subtle ways, a slippage of meaning (Schostak, 2005: Vol I, ii). One such tool – irony – infused the thesis, sometimes explicitly, at other times implicitly. Irony, like other rhetorical tropes explored in Chapter 8, are the designer-tools that tropologically frame and shape thinking processes. However, these tools are double edged, double faced and thus place and displace the expected at the same time.

In a deliberate play with this doubleness the thesis is both a doctorate and not a doctorate as the fields of forces set into play in different spaces vie to establish, de-stabilise and thwart the 'good' order (policing) of levels and orders of meaning. Where a standard academic tropology designs thinking processes to move from particulars to generalities or universals in a strategy of shaping interpretations to develop arguments that validate explanations and generate understandings; a tropology of the extreme is a de-sign (Schostak and Schostak 2008: 253) that 'pushes', 'stretches', 'holes', 'steps beyond' the fixed categories, the hard boundaries that clearly and distinctly separate 'this' from 'that' and so the watertight logics that operate across analytical domains sink under their weight, spring leaks, crumble or liquify while also providing a glimpse of a something else that in Gasché's (1986) terms is the groundless ground. This in democratic politics, as in an aesthetics of a real or a radical project for action, is evoked through the powers of people as distinct individuals to associate one with another in creating their world(s) as a vocative practice. Each associated voice creates the conditions to formulate particular demands, complaints, debates and imaginative courses of action under a principle of freedom-with-equality that safeguards mutual benefits, is faithful to disagreements (Rancière 1999) and prevents authoritarian dominion. It is a work of voices rather than a machinic work of analytically constructed formulae cast over the flux, flow and endlessly re-composable powers of people to think, critique, imagine, associate, decide and act. It is a process of design and de-sign where design operates according to a presumed fixed or fixable relation between signs and the 'things' to be represented by signs and de-sign operates on design. Each slippage of meaning, each displacement of meaning, through the process of de-sign thus operates on the 'glue' and the 'thing' presumed to exist as a real that cannot be de-constructed. In the processes of de-construction writing at the extreme reveals the designed underpinnings of texts organised by an analytics that limits patterns of attention to the production of objects, subjects, explanations, interpretations and arguments according to the ground rules of a prevailing logic where particulars are 'discoverable' and combined according to prescribed rules under general categories to produce arguments, theories, visions, philosophies. The double evocation of design and de-sign is an anti-totalitarian game, a game without end.

It is seen in the most fundamental game of life, where, following Arendt (1998), the new-born child is the guarantee of a new viewpoint to be drawn into the world of the public. The voice of the child slips into, between and stands apart from the voices of all the others as a de-sign in the heart of the already designed world(s) of the living. The introduction of the powers of each newborn are a threat to the forces through which Power is already designed. Whether socialisation through schooling, disciplining through policing, manufacturing consent through the media, or creating the fear and anxiety that prevent disobedience by making people vulnerable and alone against authority, or through market forces, the newborn is to learn powerlessness. Yet, the powers of individuals to associate with each other are a constant threat to Power organised to manage people as a dispositif for the private accumulation of wealth into increasingly few hands. With the child these powers are gifted with the potential of a future different from that of the parents. If parents see in their children hope for a different future, then he countervailing forms of organisation need to be prefigured through new forms of education that generate the conditions for democratic practice (Moss and Fielding 2011), that is, a practice always alert to the inclusion of the voices of all to create effective publics for decision-making.

It is not that the powers of the child are a de-sign, but that the powers of all associated as an effective public provide a complex intertextuality as a resource always able to operate as in Schostak's thesis on already designed spaces as a space in which 'to uncover and reveal many details of the disguises and the secrets' that engendered and birthed some other experimental or traditional space of vested interest. If each individual is an address positioned within a system of addresses, whether house address or email address or IP address or more generally locatable and identifiable by dates of birth, bank accounts, social security and passport numbers amongst many other strategies of accounting, then address as a Power over individual powers achieves dominion. But in a game of limits address itself can be opened up through a *dé-jeu*, an ungaming, a thwarting through an extreme writing to inscribe alternative lines of force for powers to play with: 'I often 'annotate' and 'anatomise' the word through a strategic positioning of brackets round certain letters in order to create a variation of the self-same word ...'(Schostak 2005: Vol I, xii).

For example, the word 'address' was written as '[ad]dress' to invoke a slip between item of clothing and a range of devices for locating someone or something and thereby set going a space within which images of fashion and concepts of identity circle and dance around each other engendering alternative ways of thinking, seeing and doing to come to the surface and slip into being through acts and action that a reader might take (Schostak 2005: Vol I, xiii). It is not that the spellings of words are split up, but that that the binding of energies spelled by words are broken. It is when a new flow is released from its pathways thus opening textual repertoires to re-inscribe a delicate imbalance between keeping to an agenda, following a framework – having something to say, in other words – and yet saying it indirectly, to detach language from its prevailing codes so as to stop it producing a pre-given structuring of the world. In creating tensions between tropes and subjects of desire, figures suggestive of secrets, of mystique, emerge and take root as countervailing alternatives for thinking, speaking and acting as members of an effective public where in the conclusion to a debate is always the introduction to the next writing project.

Like and unlike the mystic writing pad of Freud (1925), one writing on the surface gives way to another, but the inscriptions on the wax beneath remain as resources for exploration. Unlike the pad, the multitude is no fixed or fixable entity, and no part of a system. As a no-part it is the ground of all possible writings without being committed to or commanded by any. To reach it requires an end game that drives de-construction to its limits, to the very letters and the materiality of letters, to the codes by which letters create sounds and associations with other letters to be the basis of meaningful signifiers. The multitude is generative of associations, loosing itself in its creativity to become something, to voice something. And that is why the end game is always a radical beginning.

Gesturing towards writing

An ethnography may be conceived to explore the unwriting of 'People' in processes of disassembly, of protest, of rejection and abjection. Such a writing can explore the fragilities of what is perceived as solid, unavoidable, and the unquestionable reality, denial of which is a sign of 'madness' or 'stupidity'. An ethnography of becoming other than People, other than Subject, other than Us, or We-the People defined by You-the-Enemy. It is to discover the conditions of possibility in the given forms of the social for people to become un(ad)dresssed, to become 'multitude'.

If then there are case studies, they are of how the composed and the aligned become decomposed and unaligned, creating new possibilities for social organisation that do not simply repeat with variation the hierarchical forms of address. This is to redefine action outside of the analytics through which the prevailing social forms are reproduced with variation to give the illusion of 'progress'. The extreme is written against the maps that order, provide the conditions of co-ordination, and drive the techniques of addressing individuals deep into every material, social, symbolic and psychological surface of their lives. Its objective is simple: to escape. And in escaping, its project is to write the countervailing forms of organisation through which people can effect a public voice, participating in the decisions and courses of action in the forms of organisation that sustain their communities, their families, their lives. It is a creative endeavour subversive of recipes.

Conclusion

For those who are engaged in freedom, there is only one research project and only one educational project. No matter the detailed focus of a project, if it does not contribute to the practice of freedom, it is of no value as research or as education. Writing is essentially about the practice of freedom. I cannot be free unless freedom is written across the world with each individual reading his or her freedom in the freedom of others. Such freedom is not bought by the accumulation of wealth but is destroyed by it as the few overwrite the many with their demands. At stake, equally for all, is the democratic voice. It is the universality of the demand for voice and the voicing of demands that is eroded by the counter creation of phantom publics in the service of accumulated wealth. A writing project, radical in intent, supports the prerequisites under which new publics can inscribe themselves within all the forms of social organisation through which societies are composed and continually composing the supports for their lives. To the extent that such conditions are inscribed in the everyday lives of people, in their practices of decision-making and the undertaking of courses of action is the measure of democracy. That democracy is eroded with every private organisation, every decision closed from view, every act undertaken without debate. The criteria of democracy are simple and straightforward: you either have a voice that carries into the decision-making that either critically, or routinely and intimately impacts upon your life, or you do not. This is as true at home, in school, at work, while shopping or when at play. The radical writing project begins here.

A demand cannot be formulated without naming its contents, framing the categories through which a good analysis can be formulated, and applying those categories to a mapping of the world in ways that enable the co-ordination of discourses, practices and actions to bring about outcomes. A demand will not lead to the defined outcomes unless there is a consistent dispositif available to underwrite it. Hence, the politics of the range(s) of decision makers able to call upon dispositifs is as much an object for radical research to deconstruct as it is a project for radical writing. Thus, a 'public' that raises its voice only to endorse leaders whose decision-making is private and self interested is fundamentally maladjusted to the multiplicity of interests, needs, demands, hopes, fears and pleasures of other individuals. To the extent that there is no means, no organisation and no opportunity to voice demands in a public arena for decision-making there is no public worthy of the name. The organisations and instruments of government and of management generally are thus maladjusted to the democratic demands of people (Schostak 1983, 2012).

Only if organisations are created under the democratic principle of freedom with equality will publics be consistently generated that are effective in formulating practices appropriate to the ever-changing demands of people. The lessons of the Arab Spring have been and will continue to be a significant reference for those who are intent on creating effective publics in the places occupied by tyranny or autocratic management, however nuanced through the machineries of representative government that currently occupy the place-of-power. At the fall of Mubarak, the military apparatus remained in the place-of-power. After the ruinous impact on Western economies by speculators, the financial system was saved and the wealth of elites increased at the expense of tax-paying publics. Despite protest, the apparatus of support and enforcement in each case remained. Whether the machineries of law, the lures of advertising and public relations, or the bruising of a police baton, the tearing of skin, muscle and organs by a sniper's bullet, or the shelling by tanks, the signifiers of Power are indelibly inscribed in minds, bodies and all that surrounds them.

There is an urgency, then, to the writing project that counters the work of Power to inscribe itself in all that a person is and does. It means knowing how to transcend – or transgress – deconstruct and defuse those otherwise binding texts in ways that can create or constitute new publics that have new conceptual tools and discourses of what is possible and through collective action, actualisable. The difficulties are exemplified in the hopes and realities of the Arab Spring that inspired not only protest across the Arab world but also kindled the 'Tahrir Squares' of Occupy Wall Street not only in the US but across the world or the Indignados of Spain and the Anonymous of internet direct action through hacking government and corporate computers. However, protest is not enough to write a new public and a new future.

Nesrine Malik writing in The Guardian on Monday 26 December 2011 described 'Life after the Arab Spring' with an article subtitled as 'Egypt's progress from dictatorship to democracy is messy but offers hope to the Arab world'. Malik views Egypt's contribution to the Arab spring as 'delivering a dose of reality, a promotion of a politically mature understanding that things will take time' and that the mere 'toppling of presidents' is not enough. The setbacks she then saw as 'not demoralising' but as 'refocusing' opportunities. Following the fall of Mubarak, the so-called 'second wave' of protests heralded in her view 'a different dynamic', something 'encouraging', that displayed 'a covetousness, a monitoring of the aftermath of the revolution, and a knowledge and determination to ensure that it is not aborted':

> Commentator Firas Al Atraqchi refers to it as 'a new social contract'. He states that 'events in Tahrir Square, to some extent in January/February

and more so in the past week, have forced the foundation of a new social contract along the lines of how nations were formed during the Greek city-state era' redefine the relationship between people and government, and the very meaning of citizenship in the country.

(Malik, The Guardian 26 December 2011)

It is this and more. The social contract is not so much about inscribing the relation between people and government but of transforming the notion of government itself as something not separate from the people. It is in the personal – or peer-to-peer – relations where people inscribe government into the place-of-power rendering it always empty of a single dominating voice, a leader who imposes dictatorship or a plutocracy that overpowers the voices of the many. The struggle is for a conception of government where people freely and equally inscribe their views and demands into a public arena that does not consolidate into a place occupied by one voice, symbolised by one leader or indeed a ruling plutocracy of voices. At the time of writing, rejecting any government but a civilian one, shows how Egyptians protestors and activists are no longer subject to and subjugated by 'political smoke and mirrors', but determined to hold on to the 'lively and robust political dynamic' that has emerged, writes Malik. But at the time of writing, the struggle to create and inscribe the counter texts in the place-of-power is national, international and global. It is both an end game and a game of ends as between a democratic public inscribing freedom with equality of voice in public and an authoritarian monopolisation of space into the private voice of the one or the few over the many. To many, the many, the autocratic, or plutocratic voice create categories of friends and enemies by inscribing interest, blame and hatred across the dividing lines of faith, ethnicity, nationality, even by generation (as when the 'baby boomers' of the post-war generation are blamed by the political classes for the economic woes experienced by the young) and gender to cut across and thereby de-fuse alternative dividing lines of social, political and economic class. As a multitude there are no dividing lines that are given and absolute. The fear felt by Power of the multitude is in its dynamism, its potential to form and reform, its capacity to refuse obedience and to demand alternatives. Its analytics of power is to divide the multitude into factions, as when in Bahrain – as Khalifa (2011) wrote – to deal with the protestors, the Crown Prince Salman bin Al Khalifa 'intervened', 'ordered the army out of the capital', and 'let the protestors gather in the hope of finding a political solution'. This 'failed', however. Checkpoints were quickly organized by 'security and military organizations', leaving 'the opposition' outmanoeuvred and unable to 'control the anger of the protestors'. Help was obtained from the Saudi government:

The Saudi Arabian troops started entering Bahrain on the same day the Crown Prince proposed seven principles to resolve the situation. By the time the opposition had accepted the principles, a state of emergency had been declared on 15 March 2011. Under this state of emergency people were abducted and killed, all independent media people and organizations were attacked, the main hospital was turned into a military garrison, and those who were being treated as a result of injuries during protests disappeared. Military courts started sentencing people to death, life imprisonment ... after short sessions. The country was forcibly divided by the authorities, Sunnis favoured over Shiites and a sectarian cleansing process started.

(Khalifa 2011)

An independent commission was set up to investigate the events of February 2011, which reported on 23 November 2011. Following the public release of its findings, the United Nations Secretary General Ban Ki-moon welcomed the findings and called upon the Bahraini government to implement the recommendations 'as a meaningful step in addressing serious allegations of human rights violations':

> He expressed hope that the report's issuance and implementation would help to create the conditions in Bahrain for 'all-inclusive dialogue, reconciliation and reforms that will meet the legitimate aspirations of the Bahraini people.'
> RTT Staff Writer, RTTNews 24 November 2011, at: http://www.rttnews. com/Content/PoliticalNews.aspx?Id=1768383&SM=1

The struggle is not just in terms of a people against a dictator, there are global interests at stake. At the level of principle it is a matter of human rights, but at the material level it is about Power and its exercise to manage the world order of Powers. Bahrain is host to a major US navy base and Saudi Arabia is seen as critical to maintaining the balance of Powers. Where in Libya the Western Powers intervened, in Syria they would not. Despite the deaths and the slaughter of people in Syria and the massacre in Houla in 2012 (http://www.bbc.co.uk/ news/world-18244738) and repeated 'strong condemnations' by Ban Ki-moon, the killings continued.

No matter where in the world, democratic struggles are 'internal' affairs when conceived in relation to Power with its transnational interests and emergent structures. This power and its forms of organisation are written deep down into the lives of people as they go about their daily affairs. It is only when they protest that the particular forms of local Power are manifested. Such protests may involve facing death as in the Middle East, or the confrontation between internal security forces and people may be more contained, even ritualised as in Western 'democracies'. In each case it is people against the global elites whose interests are at stake in any democratic action. When the IMF lends to a country, it does so on condition that it deregulates its financial and labour markets, that it reduces public spending and that it privatises publicly owned industries, utilities, banks and services. It writes its vision of the global market into national and local laws and behaviours. When military action is authorised in order to police the world order, there are the defence contracts, arms dealers, private militaries and (re)construction companies that stimulate home economies and open the way for private enterprise to 'develop' the resources of the state being 'defended'. As Adam Smith (1762: 290, 416) noted in his discussion of the 'police', one of its fundamental functions is to ensure the workings of the market. How that market is to work is written by the interests of the elites who manage the transnational and global corporations and institutions in ways that constitute Power. These interests are variously written into the national constitutions, the systems of laws, the corporate practices, the school curricula and the local institutions through which they are realised. Mapping these interrelations begins as much with the smallest incident or the most minute utterance as it does with the most spectacular event or crisis of national or global scale.

Against the pedagogies of Power is writing as an education of the powers of individuals to engage with each other and produce alternative realities. This is the most dangerous writing of all. It is what cannot be taught in the schools dominated by the strictures, the curricular demands and the inspections of government Power. Writing creates the conditions for sites of production and transformation by inscribing hopes, visions and demands into new forms of social organisation. Essential to this is the formation of the effective public where critical thinking with its dignity of creating the objects of its own thoughts and exploring their possibilities for realisation enters debate as a voice to be counted in the making of decisions and undertaking action. It is the idea of a public and the powers of a public to organise or indeed, dis-organise that motivates the writing agenda. What the 'public' for the writing project will become, provides a sense of the organising frame. Framing a synopsis of a writing project then involves identifying the current publics and the conditions under which future publics may emerge who will become the audience(s) that engage actively with the writing project in public spheres of debate, decision and action.

Writing creates the conditions under which voice circulates, making demands known, expressing hopes and authoring new forms of democratic organisation. In the end it is a choice as between adjusting ourselves to the strictures of maladjusted organisations that have as their purpose the construction of powerlessness or demanding the conditions to reform them, or creating democratic organisations as the vital tools for a global democracy. The time of writing is always with us, always necessary. It is not about creating a counter Big Power to battle with other Titans but of countering the conditions required by Big Power to rise up and dominate.

References

Agamben, G. (1998) *Homo sacer: sovereign power and bare life.* Stanford, CA: Stanford University Press.

Agamben, G. (2004) 'Friendship', *Contretemps* 5, December: 2–7; http://sydney.edu.au/contretemps/5december2004/agamben.pdf.

Agamben, G. (2005) *State of exception.* Chicago: University of Chicago Press.

Agamben, G. (2007) *Qu'est-ce qu'un dispositif?* Traduit de l'italien par Martin Rueffh. Paris: Rivage Poche, Petite Bibliothèque.

Agamben, G. (2009) 'What is an Apparatus?' in G. Agamben *What is an apparatus? And other essays*, trans. David Kishik and Stefan Pedatella. Stanford: Stanford University Press.

Al Jazeera (2011a) 'Egyptians rally for "civil state"', news report 13 August; http://www.aljazeera.com/news/middleeast/2011/08/2011812234438881704.html).

Al Jazeera (2011b) *Rage on Wall Street, Inside Story,* 4 October; http://www.aljazeera.com/programmes/insidestory/2011/10/201110472151800365.html. Downloaded 4 June 2012.

Al Jazeera (2011c) 'Deadly Cairo clashes over Coptic protest'; http://english.aljazeera.net/news/middleeast/2011/10/2011109155853144870.html. Downloaded 4 June 2012.

Al Jazeera (2011d) 'US university probes protest pepper spraying'. Americas, 21 November; http://www.aljazeera.com/news/americas/2011/11/201111205325523767.html. Downloaded 5 June 2012.

Althusser, L. and Balibar, E. (1970) *Reading capital*, trans. Ben Brewster. London: NLB; first published Paris: François Maspero, 1968.

Anderson, B. (1983) *Imagined communities: reflections on the origin and spread of nationalism.* London and New York: Verso.

Ardrey, R. (1961) *African genesis: a personal investigation into the animal origins and the nature of man.* New York: Macmillan.

Arendt, H. (1963) *Eichmann in Jerusalem: a report on the banality of evil.* London: Faber & Faber.

Arendt, H. (1978) *The life of the mind.* San Diego, New York, London: Harcourt.

Arendt, H. (1998) *The human condition*, introduction by Margaret Canovan. Chicago: University of Chicago Press, first published 1958.

Aries, P. (1973) *Centuries of childhood.* Harmondsworth, UK: Penguin.

Arrighi, G. (2007) *Adam Smith in Beijing: lineages of the twenty-first century.* London, New York: Verso.

Astor, M. (2011) 'Police officer laughs about beating Occupy Wall Street protesters', *International Business Times*, 6 October; http://www.ibtimes.com/articles/226438/20111006/occupy-wall-street-protest-police-officer-beating-baton-pepper-spray.htm. Downloaded 4 June 2012.

Badiou, A. (2005) *Being and event*, trans. Oliver Feltham. New York and London: Continuum.

Badiou, A. (2008) *The meaning of Sarkozy*, trans. David Fernbach. London, New York: Verso.

Balibar, E. (1994) ' "Rights of man" and "Rights of the citizen": the modern dialectic of equality and freedom', in Etienne Balibar, *Masses, classes, ideas: studies on politics and philosophy before and after Marx*. New York: Routledge. The original is: 'La proposition de l'égaliberté', in Les Conférences du Perroquet, n° 22, Paris, novembre 1989.

Balibar, E. (1998) *Spinoza and politics*, trans. Peter Snowdon. London, New York: Verso.

Barthes, R. (1977) *Image – music – text*, trans. Stephen Heath. London: Fontana.

Baudrillard, J. (1994) *Simulacra and simulation*, trans. Sheila Faria Glaser. Ann Arbor, MI: The University of Michigan Press.

Baum, S. (1992) 'Poverty, inequality, and the role of government: what would Adam Smith say?', *Eastern Economic Journal* 18 (2): 143–56.

BBC (2002) *Century of the self*, documentary, broadcast 29 April–2 May; http://www.bbc.co.uk/bbcfour/documentaries/features/century_of_the_self.shtml; transcript: http://hareloco.spaces.live.com/blog/cns!E7089CD7CF32AA20!239.entry.

Bauwens, M. (2012) 'Scope not scale', A Jazeera; http://www.aljazeera.com/indepth/opinion/2012/03/2012319125340857774.html.

BBC (2011) 'Cairo clashes leave 24 dead after Coptic church protest', 10 October; http://www.bbc.co.uk/news/world-middle-east-15235212. Downloaded 4 June 2012.

Beder, S. (2010) 'Business-managed democracy: the trade agenda', *Critical Social Policy* 30 (14): 496–518.

Bernays, E. L. (1928) *Propaganda*. New York: Horace Liveright.

Bernays, E. L. (1947) 'The engineering of consent'. *The Annals of the American Academy of Political and Social Science* vol. 250, March.

Billig, M. (1995) *Banal nationalism*. London, Thousand Oaks: Sage.

Boétie, de la, Étienne (1552) *The politics of obedience: the discourse of voluntary servitude*, http://tmh.floonet.net/articles/laboetie.html.

Bogue R. (2003) *Deleuze on music, paintings and the arts*. London: Routledge.

Bourdieu, P. (1977) *Outline of a theory of practice*. Cambridge: Cambridge University Press.

Brace, C. L. (1872) *The dangerous classes of New York, and twenty years' work among them*. New York: Wynkoop & Hallenbeck.

Butler, J., Laclau, E. and Zizek, S. (2000) *Contingency, hegemony, universality: contemporary dialogues on the left*. London, New York: Verso.

Cameron, A. (2011) 'Ground Zero: the semiotics of the boundary line', *Social Semiotics* 21 (3): 417–34.

Campbell, J. (1968) *The hero with a thousand faces*. Princeton, NJ: Princeton University Press.

Carman, T. (1999) 'The body in Husserl and Merleau-Ponty', *Philosophical Topics* 27 (2): 205–26.

Chantler K. (2007) 'Border crossings: nationhood, gender, culture and violence', *International Journal of Critical Psychology* 20: 138–66.

Charters of Freedom (undated) online archive: http://www.archives.gov/exhibits/charters/constitution_zoom_1.html. Downloaded 4 June 2012.

Cherkis, J. (2011) 'Occupy Wall Street mass arrest resembles infamous, costly police tactic, critics say,' *Huffington Post*, 4 October: http://www.huffingtonpost.com/2011/10/04/occupy-wall-street-mass-arrests_n_995047.html. Downloaded 4 June 2012.

Chomsky, N. (2011) 'Chomsky: 9/11 – was there an alternative?' Al Jazeera; http://english.aljazeera.net/indepth/opinion/2011/09/20119775453842191.html.

Cicourel, A. V. (1964) *Method and measurement in sociology*. New York: Free Press; London: Collier-Macmillan.

Claeys, G. (2000) 'The "survival of the fittest" and the origins of Social Darwinism', *Journal of the History of Ideas* 61 (2): 223–40.

Cohen, M. R. (1944) *A Preface to Logic*. New York: Dover.

Commisso, G. (2006) 'Identity and subjectivity in post-Fordism', *Ephemera* 6 (2): 163–92.

Connor, S. (2010) Chiasmus, keynote talk at Song, Stage and Screen conference, University of Winchester, 3–5 September.

Critchley, S. (2006) *Infinitely demanding: ethics of commitment, politics of resistance*. Verso.

Cunningham, H. (1998) Review essay: 'Histories of childhood', *American Historical Review* 103 (4): 1195–208.

Davies, L. (2011) 'Tunisian elections: polling day as it happens', *The Guardian*, Sunday 23 October; http://www.guardian.co.uk/world/middle-east-live/2011/oct/23/tunisian-elections-2011-arab-and-middle-east-protests.

de Mause, L. (ed.) (1975) *The history of childhood*. New York: The Psychohistory Press.

Dejours, C. (1998) *Souffrance en France: la banalisation de l'injustice social*. Edition augmenté d'une preface et d'une postface 2009. Paris: Éditions du Seuil.

Dejours, C. (2003) *L'évaluation du travail à l'épreuve du reel: critique des fondements de l'évaluation*. Une conference-débat organisée par le groupe Sciences en questions. Paris, INRA, 20 mars 2003. Paris: INRA Editions.

Deleuze G. (2001) *Francis Bacon: the logic of sensation*, trans. Daniel W. Smith. London: Continuum.

Deleuze, G. and Guattari, F. (1972) *Anti-Oedipus*, trans. Robert Hurley, Mark Seem and Helen R. Lane. London and New York: Continuum, 2004.

Delingpole, J. (2011) 'Goldman Sachs rules the world', *The Telegraph*, 16 November; http://blogs.telegraph.co.uk/news/jamesdelingpole/100118071/goldman-sachs-rules-the-world/. Downloaded 4 June 2012.

Derrida, J. (1998) *Monolinguism of the other*, trans. Patrick Mensah. Stanford: Stanford University Press.

Derrida J. (2005) *On touching – Jean-Luc Nancy*. Stanford: Stanford University Press.

Diken, B. and Laustsen, C. B. (2005) 'Becoming abject: rape as a weapon of war', *Body & Society* 11 (1): 111–28.

Dilthy, W. (1977) *Descriptive psychology and historical understanding*, trans. R. M. Zaner and K. L. Heiges, with an introduction by R. A. Makkreel. The Hague: Martinus Nijhof.

Diprose R. and Ferrell, R. (eds) (1991) *Cartographies: poststructuralism and the mapping of bodies and spaces*. St Leonards, NSW, Australia: Allen & Unwin.

Douglas, M. (1966) *Purity and danger: an analysis of the concepts of pollution and taboo*. London and Boston: ARK edition 1984.

Dreyfus, H. L. (1996) 'The current relevance of Merleau-Ponty's phenomenology of embodiment' in H. Haber and G. Weiss (eds), *Perspectives on embodiment*. New York and London: Routledge.

Duhem, P. (1954) *The aim and structure of physical theory*. Princeton: Princeton University Press, translation of second edition 1914; first published 1906 as *La theorie physique, son objet et sa structure*.

Duhigg, C. (2009) 'Stock traders find speed pays, in milliseconds', *The New York Times*; http://www.nytimes.com/2009/07/24/business/24trading.html. Downloaded 3 June 2012.

Durkheim, E. (1938) 'What is a social fact?' in J. Wender (Comp.), *The Intersections Collection* (pp. 8–18). Boston, MA: Pearson Custom Publishing.

Eisenhower, D. D. (1961) Farewell Address; http://www.americanrhetoric.com/speeches/dwightdeisenhowerfarewell.html. Downloaded 2 June 2012.

Elliott, J. (1991) *Action research for educational change*. Milton Keynes: Open University Press.

English.news.cn. (2011) 'Libya's NTC announces interim government' on English. xinhuanet.com; http://news.xinhuanet.com/english2010/world/2011-11/23/c_122320509.htm (23 November 2011). Downloaded 5 June 2012.

Fereday, J. and Muir-Cochrane, E. (2006) 'Demonstrating rigor using thematic analysis: a hybrid approach of inductive and deductive coding and theme development', *International Journal of Qualitative Methods* 5 (1): 1–11.

Feyerabend, P. (1975) *Against method*. London: NLB.

Fink, B. (1995) *The Lacanian subject: between language and jouissance*. Princeton, NJ: Princeton University Press.

Frank, M. (1999) 'Style in Philosophy: Part 1', *Metaphilosophy* 30 (3): 145–67.

Frankl, V. E. (1963) *Man's search for meaning*. London: Hodder & Stoughton.

Freeman, D. (1974) The evolutionary theories of Charles Darwin and Herbert Spencer', *Current Anthropology* 15 (3): 211–37.

Freud, S. (1925) 'A note on the "Mystic Writing Pad"; "Notiz fiber den 'Wunderblock'".' First published simultaneously in Int. Z.Psychoanal., 11 (1925), 1, and in Ges. Schr., 6, 415; reprinted Ges. W., 14, 3. Translation, reprinted from Int. 1. Psycho-Anal., 21 (1940), 469, by James Strachey.

Friedman, M. (1962) *Capitalism and freedom* (Preface, 1982 edition). London: University of Chicago Press.

Fukuyama, F. (1992) *The end of history and the last man*. New York: Free Press; second paperback edition with a new Afterword, Simon and Schuster, 2006.

Garfinkel, H. (1967) *Studies in ethnomethodology*. Prentice-Hall.

Gasché, R. (1986) *The tain of the mirror: Derrida and the philosophy of reflection*. Cambridge, London: Harvard University Press.

Gates Jr, H. L. (1985) 'Editor's introduction: writing "race" and the difference it makes', *Critical Inquiry* 12 (1), '"Race," Writing, and Difference' (Autumn,

1985), pp. 1–20, The University of Chicago Press: http://www.jstor.org/stable/1343459.

Gibbs, B. (2012) 'This revolving door risks undermining trust in government'. *The Independent*, 12 March; http://www.independent.co.uk/news/uk/politics/blair-gibbs-this-revolving-door-risks-undermining-trust-in-government-7561447.html.

Gödel, K. (1992) *On formally undecidable propositions of principia mathematica and related systems.* New York: Dover.

Goffman, E. (1970) *Strategic Interaction.* Oxford: Basil Blackwell.

Gori, R. (2011) *La dignité de penser.* Paris: Les Liens Qui Libère.

Gould, S. J. (1977) *Ever since Darwin: reflections in natural history.* New York: W. W. Norton & Company.

Grant, J. (2005) 'Children versus childhood: writing children into the historical record, or reflections on Paula Fass's Encyclopedia of children and childhood in history and society', Essay review, *History of Education Quarterly* 45 (3) (Fall): 468–90.

Gupta, A. (1992) 'The song of the nonaligned world: transnational identities and the reinscription of space in late capitalism', *Cultural Anthropology* 7 (1): 63–79.

Gupta, A. (2008) 'Globalisation and difference: cosmopolitanism before the nation-state', *Transforming Cultures* eJournal 3 (2); http://epress.lib.uts.edu.au/journals/index.php/TfC/article/viewArticle/921.

Hall, S. (1980) 'Popular–democratic vs. authoritarian–populism: two ways of "taking democracy seriously"', in A. Hunt (ed.), *Marxism and Democracy.* London: Lawrence and Wishart.

Hammersley, M. (ed.) (2007) *Educational research and evidence-based practice.* Los Angeles, London: Sage.

Hardimon, M. O. (1994) *Hegel's social philosophy: the project of reconciliation.* Cambridge: Cambridge University Press.

Hardt, M. and Negri, A. (2000) *Empire.* London: Harvard University Press.

Harris, M. (1968) *The rise of anthropological theory.* London: Routledge & Kegan Paul.

Harvey, D. (2003) *The new imperialism.* Oxford: Oxford University Press.

Harvey, D. (2005) *A brief history of neoliberalism,* Oxford: Oxford University Press.

Harvey, D. (2006) *Logos* 5.1 Winter; http://www.logosjournal.com/issue_5.1/harvey.htm.

Hayek, F. A. (1944) *The road to serfdom.* Chicago: University of Chicago Press.

Hawkins, M. (1997) *Social Darwinism in European and American thought 1860–1945: nature as model and nature as threat.* Cambridge: Cambridge University Press.

Hegel, G. W. E. (1979) *System of ethical life and first philosophy of spirit,* trans. and ed. H. S. Harris and T M. Knox. Albany: State University of New York Press.

Henley, J. (2011) 'The UK riots and language: "rioter", "protester" or "scum"', *The Guardian*, 10 August; http://www.guardian.co.uk/uk/2011/aug/10/uk-riots-language. Downloaded 3 June 2012.

Heydebrand, W. (1994) *Max Weber: sociological writings.* Continuum

Hilgers, M. (2011) *The three anthropological approaches to neoliberalism.* UNESCO ISSJ 202, Oxford: Blackwell.

Hilgers, M. (2012) 'The historicity of the neoliberal state', *Social Anthropology/Anthropologie Sociale* 20 (1): 80–94.

Hobbes, T. (1651) *Leviathan*, 1914 edition, London, Dent.

Hofstadter, R. (1955) *Social Darwinism in American thought*. George Braziller: New York.

Hook, D. (2003) 'Language and the flesh: psychoanalysis and the limits of discourse', London: LSE Research online: http://eprints.lse.ac.uk/958/1/LanguageandthefleshPDF.pdf

Huberman, J. (2003) *The Bush-haters handbook: a guide to the most appalling presidency of the past 100 years*. Nation Books.

Hudek, A. (2011) 'Seeing through discourse', Figure, *Parrhesia* 12: 52–6.

Hudson, B. (2011) 'NHS bill is "privatisation by stealth" of healthcare', *The Guardian* JoePublic Blog, 22 November; http://www.guardian.co.uk/society/joepublic/2011/nov/22/nhs-bill-privatisation-stealth. Downloaded 19 May 2012.

Hughes, T. (1976) 'Myth and education', in G. Fox et al. (eds) *Writers, critics and children*. London: Heinemann.

Hume, D. (1772) *An enquiry concerning human understanding*. Indianapolis: Hackett Pub. Co., 1993.

Humphries, S. (1981) *Hooligans or rebels? An oral history of working class childhood and youth 1889–1939*. Oxford: Basil Blackwell.

Huntington, S. P. (1993) 'The Clash of Civilizations', *Political Affairs*,

Huntington, S. P. (1996) *The clash of civilizations and the remaking of world order*. Simon & Schuster.

Husserl, E. (1970) *The crisis of European sciences and transcendental phenomenology*. Evanston, IL: Northwestern University Press, 1954.

Isaackson, W. (2008) 'Chain reaction: from Einstein to the atomic bomb', *Discover Magazine*, 18 March; http://discovermagazine.com/2008/mar/18-chain-reaction-from-einstein-to-the-atomic-bomb.

James, W. (1890) *The Principles of Psychology*, 2 vols. Dover Publications

Janson, J. (2009) 'Nine brutal disappointments for Obama fans', OpEdNews, 18 January; http://www.uruknet.de/?p=m51328. Downloaded 3 June 2012.

Kant, I. (1784) 'An answer to the question: what is enlightenment?' Online at: http://theliterarylink.com/kant.html.

Karacs, I. (2009) 'Right-wing protest over President Obama's health bill ends in violence', *Times* online, 8 August.

Kellner, H. (1981) The inflatable trope as narrative theory: structure or allegory? *Diacritics* 11 (1) (Spring): 14–28 : http://www.jstor.org/stable/464890.

Kellner, D. and Lewis, T. (2007) 'Liberal humanism and the European critical tradition', in W. Outhwaite and S. P. Turner (eds), *The SAGE handbook of social science methodology*; http://srmo.sagepub.com/view/the-sage-handbook-of-social-science-methodology/n22.xml; and http://gseis.ucla.edu/faculty/kellner/essays/libhumanism.pdf.

Kennedy, J. F. (1961) 'Ask not what your country can do for you' speech. Inaugural address by John F. Kennedy, 20 January 1961, online at: http://www.famousquotes.me.uk/speeches/John_F_Kennedy/5.htm. Downloaded 12 June 2012.

Khalifa R. 'The Arab spring in Bahrain: pearl democracy', *European Magazine*, 29 November 2011; http://theeuropean-magazine.com/432-khalifa-reem/433-the-arab-spring-in-bahrain.

Klein, N. (2007) *The shock doctrine: the rise of disaster capitalism*. New York: Metropolitan Books.

Klein, N. (2009) 'Climate debt: why rich countries should pay reparations to poor countries for the climate crisis', interview by Amy Goodman; http://mobile. zcommunications.org/climate-debt-why-rich-countries-should-pay-reparations-to-poor-countries-for-the-climate-crisis-by-naomi-klein.

Kristeva, J. (1982) *Powers of horror: an essay on abjection*, trans. Leon S. Roudiez. New York: Columbia University Press.

Kristeva, J. (1984) *Revolution in poetic language*, trans. Margaret Waller. New York: Columbia University Press.

Kropotkin, Prince P. A. (1904) *Mutual aid: a factor of evolution*. London: Heinemann.

Kuhn, T. (1970) *The structure of scientific revolutions* (2nd edition), vols. I and II, *Foundations of the unity of science*. Chicago: University of Chicago Press.

Labbett, B. (1988) 'Skilful neglect', in J. Schostak, *Breaking into the curriculum: the impact of information technology on schooling*. London and New York: Methuen.

Lacan, J. (1977) 'The function and field of speech and language in psychoanalysis', in J. Lacan, *Ecrits: a selection*, trans. A. Sheridan. London: Tavistock.

Laclau, E. (2005) *Populist Reason*. London: Verso.

Laclau, E. and Mouffe, C. (1985) *Hegemony and socialist strategy: towards a radical democratic politics*. London: Verso.

Laing, R. D. (1965) *The divided self*. Harmondsworth: Pelican.

Leach, E. R. (1965) 'Claude Lévi-Strauss: Anthropologist and Philosopher', *New Left Review* 34, November–December.

Lefort, C. (1988) *Democracy and political theory*. Oxford: Polity Press.

Leyva, R. (2009) 'No child left behind: a neoliberal repackaging of social Darwinism', *Journal for Critical Education Policy Studies* 7 (1): 356–81.

Lazenby, P. (2012) 'Remember Kinder Scout – give back Britain's common land', *The Guardian*, 30 April; http://www.guardian.co.uk/commentisfree/2012/apr/30/remember-kinder-scout-britain-common-land.

Lindsay, A. D. (1911) *The philosophy of Bergson*. New York: Hodder & Stoughton.

Lippmann, W. (1922) *Public Opinion*. New York: Harcourt Brace & Company.

Lippmann, W. (1927) *The Phantom Public*. New York: Macmillan; New Brunswick, NJ Transaction Publishers.

Lydon, M. (2001) 'Veduta on "Discourse, figure"', *Yale French Studies* 99: 10–26.

MacDonald, P. S. (2000) *Descartes and Husserl: the philosophical project of radical beginnings*. Albany, NY: State University of New York Press.

Mack, M. (2010) *Spinoza and the specters of modernity: the hidden enlightenment of diversity from Spinoza to Freud*. New York, London: Continuum.

Malik N. (2011) 'Life after the Arab spring: Egypt's progress from dictatorship to democracy is messy but offers hope to the Arab world', *The Guardian*, Monday 26 December; http://www.guardian.co.uk/world/2011/dec/26/arab-spring-egypt

Martin, M. and Ellicott, C. (2012) 'Revealed: Tories have held cosy meetings with Google every month since election', *Daily Mail*, 18 May; http://www.dailymail. co.uk/news/article-2146552/Tories-held-cosy-meetings-Google-month-election.html. Downloaded 20 May 2012.

Massad, J. (2011) 'Are Palestinian children less worthy?' Al Jazeera, Opinion, 30 May: http://english.aljazeera.net/indepth/opinion/2011/05/2011529115795 33291.html.

Mauss, M. (1973) 'Techniques of the body', *Economy and Society* 2 (1): 70–88.
Mauss, M. (1979) *Sociology and psychology: essays*, trans. Ben Brewster (originally published 1935). London: Routledge & Kegan Paul.
McCormick, J. P. (2011) 'Post-Enlightenment sources of political authority: biblical atheism, political theology and the Schmitt–Strauss exchange', *History of European Ideas* 37: 175–80.
McVeigh, K. (2011) 'Occupy Wall Street: "Pepper-spray" officer named in Bush protest claim', *The Guardian*, Tuesday 27 September; http://www.guardian.co.uk/world/2011/sep/27/occupy-wall-street-anthony-bologna. Downloaded 4 June 2012.
Mead, G. H. (1934) *Mind, self and society*. Chicago: University of Chicago Press.
Mearsheimer, J. J. (2011) 'Obama doomed to disappoint', Al Jazeera; http://www.aljazeera.com/indepth/opinion/2011/05/2011521165854325150.html. Downloaded 3 June 2012.
Mehta, N. (2011) 'High-frequency firms tripled trades amid rout, Wedbush says', Bloomberg, 12 August; http://www.bloomberg.com/news/2011-08-11/high-frequency-firms-tripled-trading-as-s-p-500-plunged-13-wedbush-says.html. Downloaded 3 June 2012.
Meltdown (2011) 'The men who crashed the world', Aljazeera Part 4; http://www.youtube.com/watch?v=osAYMnqZyZc. Downloaded 4 June 2012.
Merleau-Ponty M. (1962, 2003) *Phenomenology of perception*, trans. Colin Smith (originally published 1945. London: Routledge.
Miller, J-A. (2005) 'A critical reading of Jacques Lacan's Les complexes familiaux', trans. Thomas Svolos. *Lacanian International Review*, Summer; http://www.lacan.com/jamfam.htm.
Mills, C. W. (1940) 'Situated actions and vocabularies of motive', *American Sociological Review* V (December): 904–13.
Milne, S. (2012) 'Crony capitalism feeds the corporate plan for schools', *The Guardian*, 14 February; http://www.guardian.co.uk/commentisfree/2012/feb/14/crony-capitalism-corporate-schools. Downloaded 19 May 2012.
MMU Team (2007/8) 'Full Legacy Report to the Bank on the programme "Barclays Spaces for Sport", unpublished version. Published summary version: 'Barclays Spaces for Sports. Developing people and places through sport. The legacy highlights report, September 2007'. Published by Barclays Bank.
Moor, A. (2011) 'Obama's broken promises', Al Jazeera; http://www.aljazeera.com/indepth/opinion/2011/06/201161912635848326.html. Downloaded 3 June 2012.
Morris, D. (1967) *The naked ape*. New York: Dell Publishing Company.
Morris D. (2008) '"Body" in R. Diprose and J. Reynolds(eds), *Merleau-Ponty: Key Concepts*. Stocksfield, UK: Acumen.
Moss, P. and Fielding, M. (2011) *Radical democratic education and the common school*. London: Routledge.
Mouffe, C. (1993) *The return of the political*. London, New York: Verso.
Mouffe, C. (2005) *On the political*. London, New York: Routledge.
Mulholland, H. (2011a) 'NHS reform: changes need to be made to health bill admits Cameron', *The Guardian*, Tuesday 19 April; http://www.guardian.co.uk/politics/2011/apr/19/nhs-reform-changes-need-to-be-made-david-cameron?INTCMP=ILCNETTXT3487.

Mulholland, H. (2011b) 'Lansley to accept "significant changes" to NHS reforms', *The Guardian*, Thursday 2 June; http://www.guardian.co.uk/politics/2011/jun/02/lansley-ready-accept-changes-nhs-reforms.

Naiman, R. (2011) 'Hand in hand, the army and the people are one', *Huffington Post*, 30 January; http://www.huffingtonpost.com/robert-naiman/hand-in-hand-the-army-and_b_815856.html. Downloaded 3 June 2012.

Norton, A. (2004) *Leo Strauss and the politics of American empire*. New Haven and London: Yale University Press.

Obama, B. (2008a) 'Remarks in El Dorado, Kansas: "Reclaiming the American dream"', 29 January. The American Presidency Project; http://www.presidency.ucsb.edu/ws/index.php?pid=77030#axzz1wqC6hMC9. Downloaded 4 June 2012.

Obama, B. (2008b) 'Transcript: "This is your victory," says Obama', Politics.com election centre; http://edition.cnn.com/2008/POLITICS/11/04/obama.transcript/. Downloaded 4 June 2012.

O'Carroll, L. (2012) Rebekah Brooks: David Cameron signed off texts "LOL"', *The Guardian*, 11 May; http://www.guardian.co.uk/media/2012/may/11/rebekah-brooks-david-cameron-texts-lol. Downloaded 20 May 2012.

Pagin, P. (2000) 'Publicness and indeterminacy', in P. Kotatko and A. Orenstein (eds), *Knowledge, Language and Logic: Questions for Quine*. Boston Studies in the Philosophy of Science: Kluwer.

Pagin, P. (2001) 'Semantic triangulation', in P. Kotatko, P. Pagin and G. Segal (eds), *Interpreting Davidson*. Stanford: CSLI Publications.

Patrick, J. (1973) *A Glasgow gang observed*. London: Methuen.

Pearson, G. (1983) *Hooligan: a history of respectable fears*. London: Macmillan.

Pollock, L. (1983) *Forgotten children: parent–child relations from 1500–1900*. New York: Cambridge University Press.

Positive Futures (undated) online website; http://www.posfutures.org.uk/index.asp?m=794&t=About+us. Downloaded June 4, 2012.

Propp, V. (1968) *Morphology of the folktale*, trans. L. Scott, 2nd ed. revised by L. A. Wagner. Austin and London: University of Texas Press.

Pulido, M. (2010) '"An Entirely Different Kind of Synthesis": Reflections on Merleau-Ponty's Analysis of Space in the Phenomenology of Perception', *Aporia* 20 (1): 27–44.

Quinn, J. (2010) 'Goldman Sachs, Fabrice Tourre and the complex abacus of toxic mortgages', *The Telegraph*, 16 April; http://www.telegraph.co.uk/finance/newsbysector/banksandfinance/7599970/Goldman-Sachs-Fabrice-Tourre-and-the-complex-Abacus-of-toxic-mortgages.html. Downloaded June 4, 2012.

Rabaté, J.-M. (2002) *The Future of Theory*. Oxford: Blackwell Publishing.

Ragin, C. C. and Becker, H. S. (eds) (1992) *What is a Case? Exploring the foundations of social inquiry*. Cambridge: Cambridge University Press.

Rail, T. (2011) 'How the US media marginalises dissent', Al Jazeera, 4 August; http://english.aljazeera.net/indepth/opinion/2011/08/20118164314283633.html. Downloaded 3 June 2012.

Rancière, J. (1995) *La Mésentente: Politique et Philosophie*. Paris: Galilée.

Ranicière, J. (1999) *Disagreement*. Minneapolis: University of Minnesota Press.

Rancière, J. (2004) *The politics of aesthetics*, with an after word by Slavoj Zizek, trans. and intro. Gabriel Rockhill. London, New York: Continuum.

Rand, Ayn (1957, 1992) *Atlas shrugged* (35th anniversary ed.). New York: Dutton.

Ratcliffe, K. (2005) *Rhetorical listening: identification, gender, whiteness*. Southern Carbondale: Illinois University Press.

Rawls, R. (1971) *A theory of justice*. Cambridge, MA: Harvard University Press.

Readings, Bill (1991) *Introducing Lyotard: art and politics*. London: Routledge.

Reid, P. (2010) 'Goldman Sachs' revolving door', CBS News, 7 April; http://www.cbsnews.com/8301-31727_162-20001981-10391695.html. Downloaded 19 May 2012.

Reynolds, D. and Stringfield, S. (1996) 'Failure free schooling is ready for take off', *Times Education Supplement*, 19 January: 10.

Richmond, S. (2011) '3D printing: the technology that could re-shape the world', *The Daily Telegraph*, 23 August; http://www.telegraph.co.uk/technology/news/8666516/3D-printing-the-technology-that-could-re-shape-the-world.html).

Riffaterre, M. (1978) *Semiotics of poetry*. London: Methuen.

Riffaterre, M. (1990) *Fictional Truth*, foreword by Stephen G. Nichols. Baltimire, London: The Johns Hopkins University Press.

Riley, S. (2008) 'Identity, community and selfhood: understanding the self in relation to contemporary youth cultures, commissioned as part of the UK Department for Children, Schools and Families'. Beyond Current Horizons project, led by Futurelab; http://www.beyondcurrenthorizons.org.uk/identity-community-and-selfhood-understanding-the-self-in-relation-to-contemporary-youth-cultures/.

Rockefeller, D. (1999) 'New rules of the game: looking for new leadership', Newsweek 4, 1 February.

Rogers, B. (1990) *'You know the fair rule': strategies for making the hard job of discipline in school easier*. London: Longman. second edition 1998.

Rose-Redwood, R., Alderman, D. H. and Azaryahu, M. (2008), 'Collective memory and the politics of urban space', *GeoJournal* 73 (3): 161–4.

Rosen, N. (2011) 'Western media fraud in the Middle East', Al Jazeera, Opinion, 18 May; http://www.aljazeera.com/indepth/opinion/2011/05/201151882929682601.html. Downloaded June 4, 2012.

Rosenberg, P. (2011) 'Pepper spray nation', Al Jazeera, 26 November; http://www.aljazeera.com/indepth/opinion/2011/11/20111124103714508499.

Rosenberg, P. (2012) 'Ron Paul and the liberty of bullies', Al Jazeera, Opinion, 23 January; http://www.aljazeera.com/indepth/opinion/2012/01/201211810446786665.html. Downloaded June 5, 2012.

RTT Staff Writer (2011) 'UN chief presses Bahrain to implement findings of report on crackdown' in RTTNews, 24 November; http://www.rttnews.com/Content/PoliticalNews.aspx?Id=1768383&SM=1.

Rudduck, J. (revised by) (1983) 'The Humanities Curriculum Project, CARE, University of East Anglia', for the Schools Council/Nuffield Foundation.

Russell, J. (2006) 'Tony Blair's authoritarian populism is indefensible and dangerous', *The Guardian*, 14 April; http://www.guardian.co.uk/commentisfree/2006/apr/24/comment.labour. Downloaded 3 June 2012.

Samuels, W. J. and Medema, S. G. (2005) 'Freeing Smith from the "free market": on the misperception of Adam Smith on the economic role of government', *History of Political Economy* 37 (2): 219–26.

Saussure, F. de (2005) *Cours de linguistique générale*. Paris: Éditions Payot et Rivages; Éditions Payot et Rivages publication1916.

Schatzman, M. (1973) *Soul murder: persecution in the family*. London: Allen Lane.

Schmitt, C. (1985) *Political theology: four chapters on the concept of sovereignty*, trans. and with intro. by George Schwah; new foreword by Tracey B. Strong. Chicago: University of Chicago Press.

Schmitt, C. (1996) *The concept of the political*, trans., intro. and notes by George Schwab with Leo Strauss's notes on Schmitt's essay, trans. by J. Harvey Lomax, Foreword by Tracey B. Strong. Chicago and London: The University of Chicago Press.

Schostak, J. F. (1983) *Maladjusted schooling: deviance, social control and individuality in secondary schooling*. London, Philadelphia: Falmer. Republished 2012 London, New York: Routledge Library Editions.

Schostak, J. F. (1986) *Schooling the violent imagination*. London, New York: Routledge & Kegan Paul.

Schostak, J. F. (1993) *Dirty marks: the education of self, media and popular culture*. London: Pluto Press.

Schostak, J. F. (2002) *Understanding, designing and conducting qualitative research in education: framing the project*. Milton Keynes: Open University Press.

Schostak, J. F. (2006) *Interviewing and representation in qualitative research projects*. Milton Keynes: Open University Press.

Schostak, J. F. (2010) 'Qualitative research: participant observation', in E. Baker, B. McGaw and P. Peterson (eds), *International encyclopedia of education*, 3rd edition. Elsevier.

Schostak, J. F, and Schostak J. R. (2008) *Radical research: designing, developing and writing research to make a difference*. London: Routledge.

Schostak, J. F. and Schostak, J. R. (eds) (2010) *Researching violence, democracy and the rights of people*. London: Routledge.

Schostak J. R. (2005) '[Ad]dressing Methodologies: Tracing the Self In Significant Slips: Shadow Dancing', PhD thesis, UEA, Norwich; http://www.imaginatives-paces.net/thesis/contentsthesis.html.

Schutz, A. (1964) 'The stranger: an essay in social psychology' in *Collected papers volume II: studies in social theory*. The Hague: Martinus Nijhoff.

Schutz, A. (1973) *Collected papers volume I: the problem of social reality*, A. Broderson (ed.). The Hague: Martinus Nijhoff.

Schutz, A. (1976) *The phenomenology of the social world*, trans. G. Walsh and F. Lehnert. London: Heinemann.

Schwartz, N. D. and Story, L. (2010) 'Surge of computer selling after apparent glitch sends stocks plunging', *The New York Times*; http://www.nytimes.com/2010/05/07/business/economy/07trade.html. Downloaded 3 June 2012.

Schwenger, P. (2001) 'Words and the murder of the thing', *Critical Inquiry* 28 (1): 99–113.

Semetsky, I. (2006) 'Semanalysis in the age of abjection', ASSA 17; http://www.chass.utoronto.ca/french/as-sa/ASSA-No17/Article5en.html.

Shelden, R. G. (2001) *Controlling the dangerous classes: a critical introduction to the history of criminal justice*. Boston: Allyn & Bacon, 2nd ed. 2008.

Simmel, G. (2004) *The philosophy of money*, Routledge Classics edition 2011, with a foreword by Charles Lemert. London and New York: Routledge.

Simons, H. (ed.) (1981) 'Towards a science of the singular', occasional publication, CARE, University of East Anglia, Norwich.

Slevin, T. (2008) 'The wound and the First World War: "Cartesian" surgeries to embodied being in psychoanalysis, electrification and skin grafting', *Body & Society* 14 (2): 39–61; http://bod.sagepub.com/content/14/2/39.

Smith, A. (1762) *Glasgow edition of the works and correspondence vol. 5: lectures on jurisprudence.* Liberty Fund.

Smith, A. (1776, 1961) *The wealth of nations: an inquiry into the nature and causes of the wealth of nations*: representative selections; ed. and intro. Bruce Mazlish. Indianapolis; Bobbs-Merrill.

Smith, H. (2012) Alexis Tsipras interview: 'Greece is in danger of a humanitarian crisis', *The Guardian*, 21 May; http://www.guardian.co.uk/world/2012/may/21/alexis-tsiparas-greece-interview-syriza. Downloaded 5 June 2012.

Spinoza, B. de (2004) *A theologico-political treatise, and a political treatise.* Dover Philosophical Classics.

Stevenson, F. W. (2005) 'Lyotard's future: figure, event, "space shivering"' in *Concentric: Literary and Cultural Studies* 31 (2) (July): 171–99.

Stirner, M. (1971) *The ego and his own*, ed. and intro. John Carroll. London: Cape.

Stratton, A. (2011) 'Cameron and Milliband to face off over riots as cross-party unity crumbles', *The Guardian*, 15 August; http://www.guardian.co.uk/uk/2011/aug/15/cameron-miliband-riots-unity-crumbles.

Strauss, L. (1988) *What is political philosophy? and other studies.* Chicago and London: The University of Chicago Press, originally published 1959 by The Free Press.

Swift, J. (1729) *A modest proposal*, online version: http://art-bin.com/art/omodest. html. Dowloaded 4 June 2012.

Taylor, F. W. (1911) *The principles of scientific management.* New York: Dover Publications; London: Constable.

Thorndike, E. L. (1904) *Theory of mental and social measurements.* New York: Science Press.

Tiger, L. and Fox, R. (1971) *The Imperial Animal.* New Brunswick, NJ: Transaction Publishers.

Torres, C. (2008) 'No child left behind: a brainchild of neoliberalism and American politics', *New Politics* 10 (2): 1–12.

Tragesser, R. S. (1977) *Phenomenology and Logic.* Ithaca and London: Cornell University Press.

Trammell, L. (2005) 'Measuring and fixing, filling and drilling: the ExxonMobil agenda for education', in Deron R. Boyles (ed.), *Schools or markets? commercialism, privatization, and school–business partnerships.* London: Lawrence Erlbaum Associates.

Travis, A. and Williams, Z. (2012) 'Revealed: government plans for police privatisation', *The Guardian*, 2 March; http://www.guardian.co.uk/uk/2012/mar/02/police-privatisation-security-firms-crime.

Tribe, K. (1999) 'Adam Smith: critical theorist?', *Journal of Economic Literature* XXXVII: 609–32.

Tye, L. (1998) *The father of spin: Edward L. Bernays and the birth of public relations.* New York: Crown Publishers; published as An Owl Book 2002, Henry Hold and Co.

Vandenberghe, F. (2001) Review, *European Journal of Social Theory* 4 (2): 237–40.

Wachtel, K. (2011) 'The Revolving Door: 29 People Who Went From Wall Street To Washington To Wall Street', Business Insider, 31 July; http://www.businessinsider.com/wall-street-washington-revolving-door-2011-4 ; dowloaded May 19, 2012

Wallerstein, I. (2003) *The decline of American power: the U.S. in a chaotic world*. New York, London: The New Press.

Wallis, H. (2012) 'Achived papers reveal Thatcher secrets', BBC News, 17 March; http://www.bbc.co.uk/news/uk-17366040. Downloaded 20 May 2012.

Walzer M. (1985) *Spheres of justice: a defence of pluralism and equality*. Oxford: Blackwell.

Ward, S. B. (1924) 'IV – The Crowd and the Herd', *Mind* XXXIII, 131: 275–88.

Weber, M. (2001) *The protestant ethic and the spirit of capitalism*. London and New York: Routledge; first published 1930, Allen and Unwin.

Weber S. (1987) 'Ambivalence: the humanities and the study of literature' in S. Weber, *Institution and Interpretation*. Minneapolis: University of Minnesota Press.

Welsh, T. (2007) 'Primal experience in Merleau-Ponty's philosophy and psychology', *Radical Psychology* 6 (1).

Whittaker, M. and Savage, L. (2011) 'Missing out: why ordinary workers are experiencing growth without gain', Commission on Living Standards, Resolution Foundation; http://www.resolutionfoundation.org/media/media/downloads/Missing_Out.pdf.

WHO (2008) report from the committee on the Social Determinants of Health.

Wikipedia (2012) 'Analytics'; http://en.wikipedia.org/wiki/Analytics. Dowloaded 3 June 2012.

Williams, R. (1961) *The Long Revolution*. Chatto & Windus.

Wolf, Z. B. (2011) Secretary of State Hillary Clinton: Al Jazeera is 'Real News', U.S. Losing 'Information War', ABC News, Political Punch, 2 March; http://abcnews.go.com/blogs/politics/2011/03/sec-of-state-hillary-clinton-al-jazeera-is-real-news-us-losing-information-war/. Downloaded 4 June 2012.

Zeh J. (2012) 'Pirates fit the political gap', *The Guardian*, Saturday 19 May: 46; http://www.guardian.co.uk/commentisfree/2012/may/18/germany-pirate-party-political-gap. Downloaded 19 May 2012.

Zizek, S. (2011) 'Slavoj Zizek: capitalism with Asian values', Al Jazeera, 13 November; http://www.aljazeera.com/programmes/talktojazeera/2011/10/2011102813360731764.html. Downloaded 4 June 2012.

Index